THE COMPLETE BLOODY HISTORY of BRITAIN

JOHN FARMAN

THE COMPLETE BLOODY HISTORY of BRITAIN

TED SMART

A TED SMART Publication 1999

5 7 9 10 8 6 4

Copyright © John Farman 1995

John Farman has asserted his right under the Copyright, Designs and
Patents Act, 1988 to be identified as the author and illustrator of this work

This edition first published 1995 by
The Bodley Head Children's Books
Random House, 20 Vauxhall Bridge Road, London SW1V 2SA

Originally published as individual editions:

The Very Bloody History of Britain
First published in the UK by Piccadilly Press 1990
Reissued by The Bodley Head Children's Books 1994

The Very Bloody History of Britain: 1945 to now
First published in the UK 1994

Random House UK Limited Reg. No. 954009

A CIP catalogue record for this book is available from the British Library

Printed and bound in Great Britain by
Mackays of Chatham PLC, Chatham, Kent

Contents

The Very Bloody History of Britain

The Very Bloody History of Britain 1945 to now

The Very Bloody History of Britain

WITHOUT THE BORING BITS!

Introduction

My old teacher 'Basher' Bowker was largely responsible for a disinterest in history that had served me well, right through into adulthood. His dreary lessons seemed, in retrospect, to be an interrogation the like of which hasn't been seen since the Spanish Inquisition. His presentation was so desperately dull, that all I seemed to have been left with was an unparalleled knowledge of paper-dart making and the refined craft of desk-top carving. He used dates as a hunter uses traps. One false move – and the evening would be spent copying out, in my neatest joined-up writing, a mindless repetition of what he said I should have written earlier.

By the time I took my O-level (which I failed magnificently) I could only recite, parrot-fashion, everything one wasn't ever going to be asked about the Industrial Revolution (see boring revolutions) in the eighteenth century, or the Corn Laws of the nineteenth: nothing else! It was a bit like owning a rather dreary jigsaw made drearier by having over half the bits missing, or a bike with no pedals.

Before setting out on this mighty work I knew considerably less British history than the average man in the street (and we all know how thick he is). The further I got

into it, however, the more I realised just what I'd been missing. Our ancestors turn out to be the most fascinating, bloodthirsty, disreputable bunch that you would ever be lucky enough to come across.

Everything you are about to read I've either been told by experts, or read in other books. As everyone's view of history is different, I've steered right down the middle. As it is my book I've chosen the best stories.

I'd like this account of history to be enjoyed. If by some fluke you manage to learn something, don't blame me!

Chapter 1:

Where Do I Come From?

No two people agree about where the first people to live in Britain came from. Mr Patel down the road, was fairly sure they came from India (well he would, wouldn't he), while my chum Seamus Murphy seems to remember being told in the Goat and Shamrock that they came from County Wexford. Although it's common knowledge you could once walk to France, there is no record of England ever being

joined to Ireland. Most confident of all was my old schoolmate Winston who '*knows* they came from Africa'. After asking real experts I've found out Winston's probably right, but I'd never hear the end of it if I told him. Since we now all appear to be immigrants there's probably no such thing as a proper Englishman.

Native Britons
Anyway, wherever we came from, our ancestors were a pretty scruffy, lazy lot spending most of their time hanging around waiting

for history to begin. They only ate what stumbled right in front of them and, unlike their posh relatives in the south of France and Spain, didn't even get round to trying to cheer up their caves by painting those daft-looking animals on their walls. Mind you, there are some amongst us, mentioning no names, who believe they did the caves a favour!

However, when really at a loose end, they did do strange things with huge stones; stacking them in circles or lines like those at Stonehenge or Avebury, probably for no better reason than to drive everyone crazy centuries later trying to work out why they did it.

Long after you couldn't even paddle to France, but long before the Channel was chock-full of strange greasy people swimming backwards and forwards for no apparent reason, the first tourists started turning up. These swarthy continentals didn't have to go through Customs. No ships, no ports – therefore no Customs. They didn't even have to state how long they intended staying. All they had to do was slay anyone who challenged them and set up home wherever they pleased.

This began in 4000 years BC, give or take a century. In those days they always said BC after the date. 'B' stood for 'before' and 'C' stood for 'Christ'. God knows how they knew he was coming.

Simply the fact that they turned up in boats of some kind proves that the new visitors had more marbles than the poor old native Britons, which wasn't difficult. They proceeded to invent clothes, wheels, refrigerators (only joking) and very sharp iron spears which made stabbing our poor forefathers (and foremothers) much quicker and easier.

Meanwhile (and these dates always seem to cause fights among historians)

1,400,000 BC – An unknown apeman lit the first fire.

500,000 BC – First 'upright' man made a sort of tool out of a bit of flint.

25,000 BC – Someone dropped a bit of meat in the fire and discovered it tasted better.

20,000 BC – Wheel invented but proved pretty useless until someone invented another one.

10,000 BC – Weapons used for killing animals and each other.

8600 BC – Someone planted a seed and discovered he could eat what it grew into.

8400 BC – First domesticated dog in North America. Sorry, I don't know his name.

5000 BC – Sea filled up between Britain and Europe (hooray).

2500 BC – Skis invented in Norway. No package holidays till much later however.

1500 BC – Bronze Age hit Britain.

1400 BC – Pharaoh Amenophis got his first engineer to build a water clock. Shadow clocks had been OK, but weren't much use if you'd wanted to check if it was bedtime.

600 BC – Welshman invented the first proper boat – a coracle. It was made from skin stretched over a wooden frame. Amazingly, they've only just stopped using them!

Chapter 2:

The Cunning Celts

Once the new visitors began to settle in, life went quite smoothly until England was invaded properly for the first time by the Celts. They came here in 650 BC from central Europe apparently looking for tin – please don't ask me why! The Celts were tall, blond and blue-eyed and so got all the best girls right away. This, of course, annoyed the poor Britons even more, but there was not much they

could do about it as they only had sticks and fists to fight with. The Celts set up home in the south of England around Surrey and Kent – the stockbroker belt – building flash wooden forts which the poor boneheaded locals could only mill around in awe and envy.

Now England wasn't too bad a place to live for the next few hundred years (providing you were tall, blue-eyed and blond). Then in 55 BC the late great Julius Caesar – star of stage and screen – arrived with a couple of legions from Rome, Italy. The refined Romans were repelled, in more ways than one by the crude Celts, who by this time had turned blue (from woad). They did, however, come back a year later with a much bigger, better-equipped army – and guess what – were repelled again.

55 BC – The Romans

You couldn't get away from the fact, however, that the Romans were much sharper than the Celts – hence the term 'a Roman knows'. They therefore decided that they'd infiltrate peacefully rather than invade; which was just a sneaky Italian trick. How the Celts didn't notice the daftly-dressed Roman soldiers I'll never know.

The first ruler of southern England was a chap called Rex. Under his rule, these smart Italians made money by turning the poor natives into slaves and swapping them for eastern luxuries – probably cheap scent and Turkish Delight.

AD 43 Boadicea

This gradual infiltration took longer than expected and the Romans became rather impatient. Emperor Claudius (of 'I' fame) sent another lot of legions to conquer us properly – which they did – properly! The only real trouble they encountered was a strange

17

woman warrior from somewhere near Norwich. Her name was Boadicea and, from the only available picture I've seen, she seemed to travel everywhere in a very snazzy horse-drawn cart with blades sticking out of the wheels. This must have made parking in London rather tricky, which is probably why she burnt it to the ground. She went on to kill 70,000 Romans but, when they started getting the better of things, poisoned herself. (Some people are such bad losers!)

SPOT THE ROMAN!

Chapter 3:

When In Britain Do As the Romans Do

If you can't beat a Roman, join him. Gradually the hostile Brits came round to the Roman way of thinking. The smart ones even managed to make a few lire and live Hollywood-style, in centrally heated villas covered in naff mosaics. The unsmart ones stayed in their hovels, being only serfs and slaves. Let's face it, we can't all be chiefs or there'd be no Indians! Soon everybody knew their place. Christianity was made the imperial religion and the first two centuries (whew! AD at last) were to be among the most prosperous and peaceful in England's history.

The Scottish Highlands were a no-go area because the Picts and the Scots were far too rough and beastly. The Romans, who only knew how to build dead-straight roads, soon gave up on mountainous Wales. Mind you, I expect they soon changed their tune when they discovered gold in the hills.

Furthermore, they ignored Devon and Cornwall not only because they were terribly barren and remote, but also because beaches and cream teas hadn't been invented yet.

They therefore stuck to ruling England. Hadrian, the new Supremo in Rome, decided around AD 130 to build a socking great wall, once described as 'the rampart of sods', right across the north of England. The theory behind it was obvious. If those ghastly Picts and Scots wouldn't let 'em in, then the Romans wouldn't let 'em out!

AD 350 – Mini-Romes
So for the next couple of centuries all the new 'associate citizens' of the Roman Empire had a fairly grief-free time. Anyone who was anyone, except the serfs and slaves, intermarried and started talking Latin. Mini-Romes like Bath (hence bath) and Verulamium (hence St Albans) became dead-posh centres of culture and high life. Best of all, there wasn't some hairy yobbo hammering on your door threatening to rape and pillage you every five minutes.

Back in Rome, it seems that life had become one continuous party. When they weren't having orgies (which sound rather fun), or making movies like 'Ben Hur' or 'Spartacus', they'd idle away their hours converting Christians – to lion food. Unfortunately, they were having such a brilliant time that they carelessly

neglected the rest of their Empire, which soon started to decline and fall. I wonder if that would make a title for a book?

Meanwhile

55 BC – Romans brought heated bathrooms, glass windows, swimming pools, temples, aqueducts, proper writing, chariot races, kids' dolls and good wine.

4 BC – Christ is born. I know! You don't have to tell me. How can he have been born four years before himself? Apparently an almighty cock-up was made in the sixth century when calculating the calendar and it was too late to do anything about it.

Chapter 4:

A Horrible Hole In Hadrian's Wall

Build a wall and before long everyone will want to be on the other side of it (see East Berlin). The Picts and the Scots were no exception. In AD 367, when the Romans were at their wits' end

EARLY SCOTTISH DOG

trying to keep the horrid hordes at bay, the McScoundrels broke through and were extremely unpleasant to everyone they ran into.

AD 400 – Angles, Saxons and Jutes

If, at the time, you managed to escape with your life (and your wife) from the Picts and Scots, you could bet your last goat you'd meet a bunch of Saxon pirates coming the other way. They'd just waded ashore with their mates, the Angles and Jutes, from Denmark and Germany. What is it with those Germans? If you thought the Scots were uncouth this crowd had no couth whatsoever. They were tearing up and down the Roman roads ravaging and ravishing everything that hadn't been ravaged and ravished by the first lot! The Romans, fed up with horde-hindering, packed their bags and high-tailed it back to Rome in AD 407.

The poor old Celts, who'd become somewhat refined (Roman style), could hardly believe what was happening. Many had turned to Christianity, which was all the rage after the Roman Emperor Constantine had given it the thumbs up. Seeing that there was no point hanging around, they packed up and rushed off to Wales and the Cornish peninsula where they all opened tea 'shoppes'. So

21

you have this incredible scenario: one minute all the nice guys are in the middle surrounded by hooligans, and then, before you can say King Arthur, it's all about face. The remaining heathen peasants never took baths or went in for culture. All they did manage to keep from the Roman occupation were the roads and the pheasants (another Roman first).

AD 500 – The Irish

Believe it or not, the Irish, at this time, were the good boys of Britain – having not invented Guinness yet. Being mostly monks and saints they appeared to spend all their time praying and illuminating manuscripts (what went wrong?).

THE FIRST BAD IRISH THOUGHT.

AD 500 – King Arthur

When King Arthur was invented, as he well might have been, in the beginning of the fifth century, he became the champion of all those Christians who'd run away. He was an odd king, by all accounts, spending most of his time chatting round round tables, with his tinned cronies (see armour). He had a magic sword called Excalibur which, having spent ages trying to pull from a rock, he proceeded to chuck into a lake. He was never able to be away on battle business for long because his wife, Guinevere, who apparently was a great looker, spent too much time at night with knights. Hence the famous line – 'Once a knight is enough'.

HAVE YOU MISSED ME DEAREST?

AD 520 – More Royals

Even the Saxons eventually ran out of people to fight with and the natives, having forgotten Rome and Christianity, were quite happy to settle down to peace and quiet as if nothing had ever happened (history please note!). They did have a big thing about kings, however, and divided England up into seven – yes, seven – kingdoms. These were Kent, Sussex, Essex, Wessex (south), Northumbria, East Anglia and Mercia (midlands). Imagine having seven Royal families to support!

Meanwhile

AD 407 – The Romans took all the great stuff in the last 'Meanwhile' back home to Italy.

Chapter 5:

Here Come The Vikings

In AD 597 a monk called Mr Augustine (he wasn't a saint yet) was sent by Pope Gregory to convert these nice new Anglo Saxons to Christianity again. With a little help from his 'monky' friends it took just half a century. This brought us into a sort of ecclesiastical common market with Europe and everybody got educated again. Hallelujah!

England settled down and there followed a couple of boring centuries during which farming was in, and fighting was out. Egbert of Wessex became head king and everything seemed jolly peaceful until . . .

Vikings and Danes

Towards the middle of the eighth century, what had been the odd raid at the seaside, turned into a full-blown invasion by the dreaded Vikings and Danes. These guys were even taller, blonder and

tougher than the last lot. They came in huge pointy boats with dragons' heads on the fronts (sorry prows), wearing daft tin hats with horns on. They managed to make mincemeat of the natives who'd forgotten how to fight. The Vikings from Norway started in the north of Scotland and worked down; while the Danes from Denmark hit the east and went west.

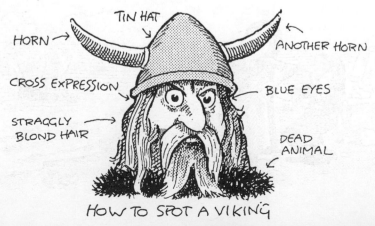

HOW TO SPOT A VIKING

AD 870 – Alfred

The Danes were eventually stopped by the great Alfred the Great who was then King of Wessex. He persuaded them to stay where they were, letting them have all the towns ending in 'by' – ie Rugby and Derby. The rest jumped back in their boats and shot over to northern France, calling the bit where they stopped, Normandy. Our Alfred was a great scholar and taught his people to speak like this:

Swa claene hio waes oðfaellenu on Andlekynne ðaette swþiðe feawe waeron behionan Humbre þe hiora ðenunga cuðan understandan on Englisc.

This means 'So clean was it fallen away in England that very few were there on this side of the Humber who could understand their service books in English'.

They didn't really learn to talk properly (like what we do), for another three hundred years or so.

AD 975 – Conquered Again

Alfred died in 900 leaving a fairly peaceful land (and a few dodgy cakes). This quiet life was only to be mucked up by King Ethelred the Unready some years later when he foolishly massacred a whole load of Danes which really annoyed them. This brought about another invasion in 1016 by a very cross Sweyn Forkbeard who captured England and sent Ethelred – who still wasn't ready – packing. His son, Canute, became King of England and big white chief of the whole Scandinavian Empire. When poor Ethelred died,

Canute really got his rather damp feet under the table by marrying Ethelred's widow, who was obviously no fool. His feet became damp (and he became legendary) following an incident on the beach one day. His grovelling courtiers reckoned their boss would only have to say the word and the tide would stop advancing. Canute, rather sceptically, tried it but got drenched. He was, by all accounts, a bit grumpy and prone to severe barbarity and crime. Gradually, however, it seems he cheered up and became rather nice and even a bit popular.

1041 – Edward
Unfortunately this particular Empire collapsed shortly after, so Ethelred's boy, Edward the Confessor, got England back which was a real stroke of luck. I must confess, however, that Edward was a bit of a wimp, so all the real ruling was done by Harold, Earl of Wessex, who was head of the anti-Norman party (poor Norman!). When Harold was made king it really annoyed Edward's French cousin, Monsieur William Conqueror (head Norman), who decided to get an army together to invade England yet again.

By the Way
The Vikings managed to work themselves into such a fury (now thought to be drug induced) that they roared, howled, slashed, and even bit anything in their path. The people who managed to escape from these invincible furry madmen, described them as 'berserk' which in Norse-talk means 'clad in bearskin'.

Meanwhile
AD 500 – Stirrups invented, taking pressure off certain parts of the anatomy.
AD 550 – St David converted the wicked Welsh to Christianity.
AD 563 – St Columba did the same for the Picts.
AD 890 – Horseshoes invented (four), to stop horses wearing their legs down to their knees.
AD 891 – Alfred the Great started writing a history of England. It's not fair, he only had a few centuries to swot up!

AD 950 – Padded horsecollars saved a lot of horses (and probably a few serfs) from choking to death when pulling heavy loads.

AD 1000 – Everybody thought that the day of judgement was due and that the world was going to end. Bet they felt stupid in 1001!

Chapter 6:

Halfway House

1066 was probably the most important date in history. Harold, England's heroic King (how can you have a hero called Harold?), was at his London home confidently awaiting a call summoning him to repel cousin Will (the Norman) who was expected

SORRY! NOT INVENTED YET

any day. Unfortunately, Harold was called away at the last minute on more pressing invasion business up north. It was those blessed Norwegians again. Just as he got there, and had shooed them off, he got the message that William was bringing his greedy garçons ashore on the south coast. If it had been nowadays he could have hopped in his Limo, belted down the M1 and been there before they could say 'allo allo'. Rushing back southwards, however, he could only round up 7,000 men who, by the time they arrived, were so knackered that they were carved up mercilessly. Poor Harold got something in his eye for his trouble and it was probably an arrow. Anyway it was enough to kill him, so unfortunately it's, 'Bye-bye, Harold'.

1087 – William the Conqueror

So it was another fine mess the Brits had gotten themselves into. The Normans had little trouble sorting out anyone who got in their way, including Hereward the Wake, possibly the son of Lady Godiva (famous nude mother), who was soon put back to sleep. William was crowned and suddenly everyone was French.

NUDE MUM

NUDE HORSE

All this features in the very first embroidered cartoon strip called the Bayeux Tapestry which was very long and very, very unfunny. Will's first major headache was how to sort out what he'd just conquered. He commissioned this whacking great book, known as the DOMESDAY BOOK which listed everyone in the country, rich and poor, and everything they owned down to the last chicken (and egg). This was to prove a real boon when working out how much tax he could sting everyone for. Lawyers and civil servants hadn't been discovered (along with many other useless inventions).

The Feudal System

William created the feudal system which was, almost, very clever. The deal was that the king snatched all the property from the Anglo-Saxon earls, and divvied it up amongst his barons who were called tenants-in-chief. In return for this they would drum him up

an army. They in turn sub-let their land to the Norman knights, called sub-tenants, who would do the actual fighting (those barons weren't daft). Under them were the poor old Saxon serfs and villeins. These poor so-and-so's were given measly strips of land, about the size of your average back garden, which they were allowed to farm for about ten minutes a week. They, of course, had to give rent, food, their pretty daughters and the rest of their time, farming the boss's land. AND they were supposed to tug their forelocks in gratitude. If anyone objected, William had a neat solution. He sent a bunch of his merry men round to burn down the village and kill all the animals. Problem solved!

Law and Order

The tenants-in-chief had their own courts as there was very little common law in the country. The king was represented by a sheriff (usually from Nottingham) who was in charge of every shire. Even so, there were quite a lot of outlaws and hoods (see Robin) who robbed the poor to pay the rich. Is that right?

What this meant, when you got down to the nitty gritty, was that all rank and power depended on what you owned. Some things never change! On the other hand it could be said that William now owned the whole shooting match and had rented England out.

By 1135 the English knew their place and were just beginning to speak Le Francais bon. Most people now reckon that the Norman Conquest wasn't such a bad thing, otherwise we could well be Scandinavian by now – driving around in Volvos, eating open sandwiches and beating ourselves with twigs (no thanks!). Anyway the now-nice Normans built lots of brill churches and castles and gradually the country began to run OK again.

By the Way

William has been recorded as one of the strongest men in history being able to jump on his horse wearing full armour. I notice his poor old horse doesn't get a mention.

Here's another little story. William died in 1087 when his horse threw him: the stupid steed trod on a hot ember from a town his master had just razed (or lowered) to the ground. Old William was so fat that when they tried to squeeze him into his sarcophagus (a stone coffin) it burst open and so did he! The smell was so horrid that everyone fled the church in Caen, Franch (urggh). In 1562 vandals broke into his magnificent tomb and stole all of him except a thigh bone which was given another burial eighty years later. Even that got nicked by looters during the French Revolution, so his tomb now stands empty. Nobody seems to know what happened to the horse.

Chapter 7:

Brotherly Love! – 1087

When William died, his son Rufus – who was really William II – took over England while his elder son Robert, got Normandy. Rufus was so named because when he blew his top – which was often – he'd go bright red. Rufus was apparently a bit of a naughty boy. He grew his hair long, got drunk, went out with boys, and generally found being king much more fun than anyone previously. He reigned for thirteen years, always under threat from his jealous brother. It was just as Robert was about to attack in 1100, spurred on by his rich, bossy wife, that Rufus fell off his horse (with an arrow in his back) while hunting and died. It obviously ran

in the family. Most people felt the 'accident' was a judgement from God and so weren't the least bit surprised when the tower of Winchester Cathedral collapsed on his tomb a year later.

1100 – Henry I

Suspiciously, Rufus's younger brother, Henry, happened to be in the forest the day he died. You don't have to be very bright to put two and two together and conclude that he might have had something to do with it. Henry I, therefore, inherited the throne, a big sparkly hat and a brand new enemy. When Robert did attack, Henry managed to smooth-talk his way out of it and gave his brother a pension of £2000 a year to stay away. Then Henry had  second thoughts, and, being a crafty beggar, kept giving his brother a hard time. He eventually nobbled brother Bob and deposited him in his dingy dungeons for twenty-eight years until he died, aged eighty. (Charming!)

Chapter 8:

Chaos! – 1135

This bit of history goes crazy.

Henry I was king for thirty years and married to a Matilda, as was his father. When he died in 1135, from an over indulgence in lampreys (little eels), he left only one legitimate heir (and twenty who weren't!). Her name was also Matilda and, although only recently a widow, her dad made her marry fourteen-year-old Geoffrey Plantagenet Fulk (what a mouthful) of Anjou. The deal was that, when she eventually became queen, it would expand the family empire.

Henry's nephew, Stephen, had other ideas and told a huge fib. He informed everyone that Uncle Henry had told him, on his deathbed, that he wanted Stephen to be king. When safely under the crown, just to confuse everybody, he married another Matilda. Perhaps the name Matilda was the twelfth century equivalent of Tracey. Anyway, there was a huge argument, followed by a civil war in which everyone pinched each other's castles and Matildas.

1135 – Civil War

Geoffrey died, and his son Henry – another one – took over the fight (confused yet?). He – that's still the other one – then married Eleanor of Aquitaine, the ex-wife of Louis VII of France, who was so cross he joined forces with Stephen. If anyone's still keeping up with this, please let me know!

To cut a long story short, Henry and Stephen did a deal. In 1153, at the Treaty of Westminster, it was agreed that Stephen should stay king for the rest of his life and then Henry could have a go which sounded rather fair if you ask me. This turned out to be brilliant for Henry, because Stephen keeled over a year later. None of the Matildas were ever heard of again until centuries later in Australia, of all places, where one was believed to have invented the waltz!

1154 – Henry II

So Henry II copped the lot. All of England and most of the left hand bit of France. Best of all, nobody wanted to fight him for it. The first thing he did was to demolish all Stephen's unlicenced castles. Hands up who knows what a castle licence looks like? Then, instead of using the feudal nobility (the barons) to keep down the English, as William the Conqueror had done, he used the English to keep down the feudal nobility (neat eh!). He then got rid of all the sheriffs and set up a proper legal system with judges and juries. This replaced trial by combat. Shame, really – I always thought it sounded rather a laugh (and quicker!). In fact, the whole system of trial and punishment at this time is worthy of a closer look.

HAVE YOU GOT A LICENCE FOR THIS LOT MATE?

Crime and Punishment

One of the best ways of finding out whether a chap was guilty of a crime, was to try him by fire. The accused was made to carry a piece of red-hot iron for three paces whereupon his hand was bound up (nice of them!). If, when it was undone three days later, there were no blisters, he was innocent, but if he had blisters he was punished and even killed. It might have been a smart idea to put the bandage on the other hand.

SEE – I, TOLD YOU I DIDN'T DO IT !

Cheats and thieves were put in the stocks, which allowed all the villagers to laugh and throw rotten food at them. (Football hooligans? I wonder.) Furthermore, bakers who sold stale bread were carted around the town on a sledge with loaves tied to their necks, while fishmongers who sold bad goods would have rotting fish tied round theirs. I think a word to our local trading standards officers might give them some new ideas.

Bad priests would have to ride through the town facing their horse's backside wearing a paper crown (the priest – silly) and, even better, nagging wives would be fitted with a Scold's Bridle, which had a piece of metal to hold their wagging tongues down. I wonder if they had one for door-to-door salesmen?

Ears and hands were lopped off and noses slit at the drop of a hat, but torture for fun, as such, was forbidden.

Henry II was also to become (in)famous for invading Ireland and martyring his archbishop and best friend, Thomas Becket, who'd been throwing his weight around. He was a great and energetic king, however, galloping from one end of his empire to the other, appearing to be everywhere at once. Apart from having a few rebellious sons, everything went like clockwork (yet to be invented) until his demise in 1189.

By the Way
Poor Thomas wasn't to rest easy in his grave. 350 years after his death that naughty old Henry VIII (see Henry VIII), determined to have yet another go at him, had him dug up. The poor old saint's skeleton was brought before England's Star Chamber and accused of 'usurping papal authority'. After a formal trial, which must have looked a touch weird, his bones – strangely unable to defend themselves – were convicted of high treason and publicly burned. Things never seem to go right for some people.

JUST ANSWER THE QUESTION

Chapter 9

Nice Richard And Horrible John

The first son, Richard the Lionheart, was handsome, kind, brave, clever, romantic, popular, and King of England and a big bit of France.

The second son, John, was ugly, cruel, cowardly, clever (also), unromantic, unpopular and only got Ireland.

The other two brothers carelessly died!

1189 – Richard the Lionheart

Strangely enough England liked Richard, but Richard didn't seem to like England. He preferred to spend all his time on his Christian Crusade (basically attacking when you think you're in the right) against the mighty Saladin who was head of the Muslims – otherwise known as infidels – in the Holy Land. It was while he was away that he got a call telling him that brother John was revolting. He got the first ship home, but was shipwrecked near Aquileia and had to walk the rest of the way. While strolling gaily (which some say he was) through Germany he was arrested and thrown into gaol. The greedy Krauts asked the English for £3,000,000 to get him back. While his fans were trying to raise the cash he was kept in a secret place. After a year his favourite minstrel Blondel – 'how

favourite?' I hear you ask – toured Europe strumming the boss's favourite tune outside every castle. The Germans must have thought he was barmy. One day Richard joined in the chorus and was found. He eventually came home, sorted out his bad brother and then, barely having time to unpack, rushed back to La Belle France to try to win back some of the lands lost while in prison. He didn't do badly apart from being killed in 1199. It was a bolt from a crossbow, which curiously enough he'd introduced into France, that finished him. There's gratitude for you! The path was now clear for the dreadful John.

1199 – King John

Now John really was someone you wouldn't let marry your daughter. A really nasty piece of work, grabbing cash from all his poor downtrodden subjects so that he could live in luxury and defend his French possessions. Come to think of it, I thought that was what Royalty was all about. He was always bad at battles (they didn't call him 'Softsword' for nothing) and lost most of them. He murdered Arthur his young nephew in 1203 because he had a better claim to the throne, and got into such trouble that, in the war that followed, he lost nearly all of what remained of his French dominions. He was always watching his back, as he was convinced all his men were trying to kill him. You can't really blame him, however, because they were!

His favourite hobby was extorting money from his subjects, which hacked off the public more than anything else. Then, just to put the tin lid on it, he upset the Church and was excommunicated (not allowed to talk to God). This didn't worry John too much – not being much of a churchgoer – but he did, out of spite, grab all the Church's possessions.

A bunch of barons, fed up with the fine mess John was getting the country into, rebelled and captured London (can you imagine?) and made him stick his seal on the Magna Carta in 1215. This famous document not only pointed out what a cock-up he and his ancestors had made of ruling, but also greatly reduced his enormous power. Sealing was one thing, but as he was a fully paid up creep, getting him to change his ways was a different matter.

In the end the rebels invited Prince Louis of France to come and sit on our throne (what cheek!), which he tried for five minutes in 1216. A long civil war followed, but John died that very year.

By the Way
John's enemies nearly killed themselves laughing when:

1. John had to watch most of his baggage train, with all his precious jewels, disappear under quicksands in the Wash. This

certainly disproves the old saying – everything comes out in the wash!

2. King John, famous for his disgusting feeding habits, literally ate himself to death in 1216.

Meanwhile
1100 – Knives and forks were brought back from the Crusades (who says Saladin's lot were barbarians?).

1120 – The Chinese invented playing cards.

1130 – Court of the Exchequer formed. A huge checked tablecloth was laid out, and coins were placed in the squares to help the court count incoming revenue.

1140 – Spices and pepper used in Britain for the first time.

1180 – Glass windows were used instead of brick ones! I bet that improved the view.

1180 – First windmills seen in Europe.

1185 – Oxford University began.

1209 – Just like the Boat Race – Cambridge came second.

1214 – Bacon invented – Roger Bacon. He was a great scientist, predicting automobiles, ocean liners and aeroplanes; so clever, in fact, that his monk mates called him a heretic and eventually threw him into jail.

Chapter 10:

Hooray For Henry – 1216

John's nine-year-old son, Henry III, was to turn out better at battles than his dad. When he was crowned he left virtually all the country-running to a council (which grew up into the first Parliament). When he came of age he started throwing his weight around and upset everyone by giving all the best jobs to his wife Eleanor's foreign relatives.

He got even more stick when he gave his son Edmund the island of Sicily. Lucky little beggar, the most I ever got was a train set! Henry had just been given it by the Pope. The snag was that the Pope had 'forgotten' to tell Henry that Emperor Frederick's son, Manfred, was actually living there, and that he'd have to conquer it. This turned out to be a touch expensive (conquering usually is) and a daft thing to do. Eventually, Parliament said enough's enough and took the government out of Henry's hands.

This caused a bit of a civil war in which a chap called Simon de Montfort, who was quite a rebel, managed to take over the country. He came to a sticky end when Henry's other boy, Edward, defeated and dismembered him at the Battle of Evesham (a very bad way of losing your arms and legs).

1272 – Edward Plantagenet

Edward became King (and the I) in 1272. He was very aggressive but strangely popular with the general public. With their help he checked the power of the barons and Parliament. The Church was also getting a trifle big for its ecclesiastical boots. A terrible nationalism – thinking your country's the best – swept through this green and pleasant land, resulting in most of the foreigners and all of the Jews being kicked out (sound familiar?).

Edward then turned on the Welsh who had always been a bit stroppy. He hunted down Llewelyn, the head Celt, killed him and left loads of soldier-filled castles to keep them quiet. Llewelyn has since become a cult hero with today's Welsh nationalists.

1305 – The Scots

He tried the same thing with Scotland, and managed to hang, draw, and quarter their leader William Wallace – a good way of being in four places at the same time. He also stole their Stone of Scone (or

was it Scone of Stone?) on which all their kings had been crowned. Keep it quiet, but if you peek under the throne in Westminster Abbey tomorrow, you'll see the English have still got it (tee hee!). Anyway, in spite of all this, he couldn't quite beat them and, in the end, Robert the Bruce, their best ever fighter, was made King of Scotland.

Robert looked round for allies and soon became best chums with France. Can you imagine a Scotsman with a French accent? (Mon McDieu!) In 1307 Edward died, aged sixty-eight, at Carlisle, still trying to catch Bruce the Robert who kept running away and hiding.

During his reign Edward managed to upset the 'Model Parliament' by continually jacking up the wool tax – so fleecing the farmers – to pay for all his battles with the French and the Scots. Parliament cleverly tacked a bit on the Magna Carta which basically said that he had to ask them first if he wanted to do anything (spoilsports!).

Apart from little squabbles like this, however, the thirteenth (1200–1300) had been a jolly good century – much more fun than in Norman times.

Meanwhile

1233 – Coal mined in England.

1250 – Goose quills discovered to be good for writing (and quite good for geese).

1250 – Westminster Abbey, thought to be out of date, pulled down and rebuilt in Early English style.

1250s – English spoken as a main language.

Sumer is icumen in
Lhude sing cuccu!
Groweth sed, and bloweth med,
And springeth the wude nu –
Sing cuccu!

Well! It's almost English.

1290 – Spectacles invented.

1290 – Mechanical clock invented, but no one seems to know by whom.

Chapter 11:

Out Out Damn Scot!

Edward I's son called 'II' was a bit of a good-for-nothing I'm afraid. He spent most of his time squandering the poor's hard-earned cash with his two best chums (also good-for-nothings) Piers Gaveston and Hugh Despenser – I wonder what he dispensed? When his father died, England's relations with Wales, Ireland, Scotland and France couldn't have been worse. Unfortunately, young 'II' was behind the door when tact was handed out, and all he managed to do was make things worse still. On top of all this the English barons were getting nastier and nastier. They murdered poor Piers, dispensed with Hugh and grabbed the government. If this wasn't enough Robert the Bruce the Robert, bored with being attacked, started raiding the north of England. He even managed to personally give Henry de Bohn (our top knight), a neat centre parting with his axe at the battle of Bannockburn in 1314.

1322 – Edward Beats the Barons

Honestly, it really was no fun being king in those days. Any plan poor Edward had for Britain to be one big happy family went right down the pan, and he was becoming extremely grumpy. Suddenly he snapped, and, after a short sharp battle with the barons, took all the power back. There was no peace for poor Eddie, however, as the next year things got even worse!

Finally in 1327 everyone possible had a go at him, forcing him to abdicate – which means give up being king (most people would have been quite glad).

If that wasn't bad enough his wife (the queen) and her boyfriend backed by a bunch of bad barons imprisoned Edward in a disused well and then did him in! It never reigns but it pours!!!

43

1327 – Edward III

Time for another Edward again. This time the unlucky fellow was only fifteen, and became a father and the III in the same year (more fool him). Like his old man, he was really good at spending the country's hard-earned cash fighting anyone and everyone. Another irritating habit was his slaughtering of any subjects who complained, which they didn't like one bit. He did, however, run one of the poshest courts ever, with all his friends and relatives dressed up in hitherto unseen finery (a bit like in 'Come Dancing' – urgh). Tournaments, jousting and feasting were all the rage and the court's revels were the gossip of home and abroad.

But history also has a nasty habit of repeating itself, and soon his friends became restless and started plotting against him – a national pastime.

1337 – 100 Years War

Edward's main claim to fame, however, was starting the biggest and best war ever, which went on for a hundred years and was called, (surprisingly), the Hundred Years War. Again, how did they know it would last that long? Three guesses who it was against? You're right – our old mates, the French. Strangely enough it was popular with nearly everyone – except those who never came back – and Parliament even gave Edward tons of money to spend on ships, soldiers and swords, etc. The trouble was, it was only a loan and they soon wanted it back. Poor Edward, as always, was flat broke, so paying back the odd million quid was out of the question. He was, therefore, the first king (and last) to go bankrupt.

The first twenty years of the war went splendidly and our brave lads, led by the King and his son, the Black Prince (so called

because of his groovy black armour), went through the French like a knife through butter – or should I say beurre. At the Battle of Crécy the score was England 15,000, France 100. Unfortunately, while they were all away having a 'bon' time killing the Frogs (and being killed), something rather unpleasant happened back home. Half the English died!!!!

1348 – The Black Death

It seems impossible. About 2,000,000 of our ancestors snuffed it. They had all caught a fascinating foreign disease from a group of travelling fleas who'd caught it from a group of travelling rats. It was called the Black Death because:

1. It turned you black.
2. It killed you!

This plague is now regarded as just about the most infectious ever known and very few people have ever recovered from it.

Having half the population six feet under was hugely inconvenient. For a start, there was hardly a spare man able to go to France – to get killed, and furthermore there were very few left to cultivate the land. They didn't starve as, fortunately, there was practically no one around to eat anything anyway.

Nevertheless, the few natives that were left were getting restless. The war was costing a bomb and the Church was running riot, with monks and friars doing a load of naughty things that monks and friars weren't supposed to do (use your imagination!). Also there was a heavy traffic in indulgences or pardons. A pardon was a piece of paper that absolved the purchaser from all guilt from his (or her) indiscretions in the eyes of God. They were also a neat way for the Pope – at this time there were two! – to make

YOU ARE NOW FORGIVEN

The Pope

pocketfuls of cash. Instead of the normal confession that a Catholic gets free in church today, the crafty old Popes were flogging them throughout the world like raffle tickets.

Meanwhile

1291	– Saladin and the Saracens captured Acre. Final whistle blows at the Crusades.
1314	– The first St Paul's Cathedral finished.
1315,16,20,21	– Terrible harvests caused famine and disease.
1328	– Sawmill invented.

1337 – First weather forecast by William Merlee of Oxford. I bet it was wrong.

1340–1400 – Geoff Chaucer wrote books like *The Canterbury Tales.*

I THINK ITS GOING TO RAIN.

Chapter 12:

The Peasants Are Revolting

By 1377 the picture had changed quite a bit in England. France had captured the Isle of Wight – shock! horror! The Black Prince was dead (from overfighting). His poor old dad, Edward, who'd gone slightly round the bend, was being practically spoon-fed by one Alice Perrers – who sounds far too down-market to be a king's mistress. She was also having the odd spoonful herself having requisitioned all of his dead wife Philippa's priceless jewellery. The Black Prince's brother, John of Gaunt (where's Gaunt?), was virtually running the country and as soon as dukes were invented, he became the Duke of Lancaster – the first of a famous dynasty. (Burt Lancaster?)

By the time poor old loony Edward died, England had lost nearly all of France except Calais. This was no great loss, as in those days you couldn't even nip across the old Channel for a few bottles of the old duty free vino. Strangely enough, historians record Edward as being rather a good king. Mind you, they didn't have to live with him!

1377 – Richard II

Little Richard (II) the Black Prince's ten-year-old lad was the next king. They sound a bit like rock stars don't they? After being crowned, he carried on 'the Expensive War' heavily advised by his uncle John of Lancaster – or was it Duke of Gaunt?

In order to raise funds he charged the first poll tax – but certainly not the last! Every male over sixteen had to pay one shilling (5p). This probably sounds fairly reasonable to you, but if you consider that your average sulky serf earned a penny (½p) a day you'll understand how miffed they all were. It was not unusual for the collectors to be burned alive or have their heads cut off. You might think this a little excessive, but we won't take a vote on it.

1381 – Wat Tyler

Suddenly the erstwhile pleasant peasants were really revolting. They were led by a certain Wat Tyler from Kent. Nobody seems to know what Wat did in Kent, but he brought them all to London anyway where they pillaged and burned everything they came across – a bit like Cup Final night these days. The King promised them everything they asked for, but it seems he had his fingers crossed because when the main crowd had dispersed, the mayor stabbed Wat for his cheek (Wat cheek!) and his friends were all hanged – for theirs!

Richard II married Anne (a REAL Bohemian) but they were to have no children – maybe the fact that he preferred men might have had something to do with it.

Things didn't run smoothly, however, and soon poor Richard was getting real stick from a posh gang called the Lords Appellant led by his cousin Henry and his uncle Gloucester. This suave bunch packed into Parliament one day and forced it to exile or execute all Richard's friends. Richard didn't think this was a terribly nice thing for your family to do, so nine years later, after much planning, he and his mates piled back into Parliament and turned the tables. They murdered his uncle (by suffocation) and exiled his cousin Henry. When John of Gaunt died, Richard snatched all the vast estates that made up the Duchy of Lancaster.

Henry IV

Rather unfairly Richard's supporters thought he'd gone too far and backed John of Gaunt's son Henry (the one in exile), who came back with his own army to get his dead dad's Duchy back. Poor

Richard was then de-throned and chucked into the tower where he was – you've guessed it – murdered. There followed the famous line from Henry on his way to be made king:

'In the name of Fadir Son and Holy Ghost, I Henry of Lancaster chalenge this Rewme of Ingland and the Corone.'

This might be much better English, but it's still a hoot if you say it out loud!

After the crowning ceremony Henry and his friends sat down to the following meal:

FIRST COURSE

Brawn in pepper and spice sauce – Royal pudding – Boar's head – Fat chicken – Herons – Pheasants (not peasants) – Cygnets (small swans) – Date and prune custard (yuk!) – Sturgeon and pike.

SECOND COURSE

Venison in boiled wheat and milk – Jelly – Stuffed sucking pig – Peacocks – Roast bitterns – Glazed chicken – Cranes (birds silly!) – Roast venison – Rabbits – Fruit tarts – Cold brawn – Date pudding.

ANY KETCHUP?

THIRD COURSE

Beef in wine and almond sauce – Preserved quinces – Roast egrets (little herons) – Curlews. Pine nuts in honey and ginger – Partridges – Quails – Snipe – Tiny birds – Rissoles glazed with egg yolks – Rabbits (again!) – Sliced brawn – Iced eggs – Fritters – Cheesecakes – Small rolls.

I bet you'd rather have a Big Mac, large fries and a chocolate shake!

By the Way
The first thing Henry did on being crowned was to have poor Richard embalmed and put on display in full royal kit. He was finally laid to rest in Westminster Abbey where they thoughtfully left a hole in the side of the tomb so that passers-by could touch the ex-king's head. One day, years later in 1776, a naughty schoolboy nicked his jawbone and took it home to his mum and dad (at least he didn't give it to the dog!).

TEACHING AN OLD DOG NEW TRICKS

Chapter 13:

Punch-up With The Percys

Although Henry had become IV in 1399 he wasn't taken that seriously because:
1. He'd got there by force and
2. Wasn't really next in line.
He was, therefore, bossed about by Parliament and, worse, the

Church, (which was keeping warm burning heretics – mostly called Lollards). As usual, there were punch-ups all over the shop; the most serious being that with the Percys from Northumberland, led by Lord Percy who, strange as it may seem, had put Henry on the throne in the first place (fickle? – not half!). The Percys joined up with the stroppy Scots and wild Welsh again but were beaten hollow at Shrewsbury. Percy's son Henry Hotspur – who sounds like a northern comedian – was severely killed.

It appears that Henry IV lived on the back of his horse (sorry, we don't know its name), tearing up and down Olde England fighting everyone. He did make it up with the French, however, and stopped attacking them for a few minutes. England became quite peaceful, and shortly afterwards he died – probably of boredom.

1413 – Henry V

In 1413 his son Hal became Henry V. Now Hal had been a bit of a lad in part I of his life (see Shakespeare), knocking around with some very dodgy ladies and a fat old drunk called Falstaff. When he was 'kinged', however, he got his act together and, having developed quite a taste for that old Lollard burning himself, executed his old mate Falstaff for good measure. When he heard that the King of France had gone barmy he thought it might be quite a giggle to go a-conquering. Watch out you Frogs!

He turned out to be rather good at this and, to cut a long story short (and loads of soldiers), he really knocked the stuffing out of them, particularly at Agincourt. So well, in fact, that he married the daughter of mad Charles VI (known as Charles the Silly) of France and became Regent (nearly king) of all France. Just as all was going well, Henry caught something rather unpleasant at Vincennes and died aged thirty-five. In the same year, the now completely wacko Charles VI of France, suffered the same fate.

By the Way

It might be of interest to note that the English soldiers won principally because of the superiority of the longbow over the crossbow, owing to their ability to reload much faster. Two fingers were used to draw a longbow string back so even without the actual bow the Frogs still got the message. The famous two finger gesture which means 'Please go forth and multiply', can be directly traced to Agincourt.

"Go Forth and Multiply"

Chapter 14:

King Of The Cradle – 1422

Henry VI became the first sovereign to wear nappies. At nine months old he became king of both England and France and had to wear two crowns. No problem, you might think. Well yes, it could have been all right had it not been for a rather strange French woman called Joan of Arc (where's Arc?). Now she really

was a fruitcake. She wore men's clothes and heard strange voices telling her to fight the English who she called the 'Goddams' (Goddam whats?).

She turned out to be rather good at war and actually kept the Brits at bay, helping 'hommes' like Dunois – known, rather rudely, as the bastard of Orleans. She was eventually captured by the Burgundians who were on our side. They, rather ungraciously, sold her to the English. We, even more ungraciously, set fire to her and threw her ashes into the River Seine (a fine way to treat a lady). Her spirit lived on, however, and the French won back the whole lot again apart from — wait for it – Calais, which I suppose served us right. Mind you, if you've ever been to Calais you'd know why the French didn't want it. As for Joan, however, everything turned out all right in the end. Twenty years after her execution she was

retried (unfortunately she couldn't be there) by Pope Calixtus III and found not guilty. In 1920 she was made a saint. So you see, all things come to those who wait!

1455 – War of the Roses

As young Henry got older it became fairly obvious that he had a screw loose like his grandad. Luckily, his wife Margaret was quite a tough cookie so that when the next war arrived she did the business for him. This came in 1455 and seemed to be about whether red roses were nicer than white ones. Margaret and the Lancastrians (the famous band) seemed to like red ones and the Duke of York and the Earl of Warwick favoured white.

1461 – Edward IV

Poor Henry the Daft got collared by the whites and the Duke of York got captured and murdered by the reds. The new Duke of

York got crowned Edward IV in 1461. The last huge battle occurred at Towton (No! not Toytown) where the Yorkists beat the Lancastrians good and proper. Henry, who was now out-to-lunch brainwise, ended up in the Bloody Tower (bloody shame) and was – you've got it, now – murdered.

As most of the noblemen who'd controlled Parliament had either been killed or executed, Edward got all their cash – King's perk! This caused no end of strife and his friend Warwick, who'd helped make him king, teamed up with Margaret (remember her? the tough one), and fought the new king at Barnet in a fog which seems

a rather strange place to do battle. Warwick fell off his horse, and because his armour was so heavy, couldn't move. He was badly killed and the battle was lost. Queen Margaret, her son and hubby six feet under, sloped off to France where she died in poverty. Edward, being the true heir to Richard II, became the new flavour of the month. He had a high old time in London; so much so that he died in 1483 from sloth and over indulgence. Sounds all right to me!

1483 – Edward V

His elder son Edward V was only twelve years old and was 'protected' by his wicked uncle Gloucester who had ideas of his own. Gloucester claimed that the king and his brother were illegitimate and had them smothered in the Tower (see bad places to spend a night). Their skeletons were found in an old wooden box many years later, and only positively identified in 1933.

Some modern historians now say old Gloucester didn't do it and that he probably wasn't such a bad bloke at all.

1483 – Richard III

He became the infamous Richard III, a horrid chap who managed to cut the heads off just about everyone. He was universally hated especially by Henry (Lord of the Lancasters) who fought him at Bosworth. Richard, who jauntily sported his crown into battle got the worst of it and at one point offered his kingdom for a horse. As

deals go, I don't think that's bad. Unfortunately, they didn't carry a spare and Richard was slain. His body was subjected to 'many indignities' (the mind boggles) and Henry picked up the crown, shoved it on his head, and became the VII, the first Tudor, in 1485.

1485 – Henry VII

When he married Edward IV's daughter Elizabeth, the Yorks and the Lancasters were united and it was generally agreed that red roses weren't any better than white ones. The War of the Roses was officially called a draw.

By the Way

Richard's naked body was taken to Leicester where it was displayed for two days at Greyfriars (no Billy Bunter jokes please!). When Greyfriars was dissolved they rather ignominiously chucked his body into the river.

Meanwhile

1376 – John Wycliff and the Lollards denounced the Pope and demanded reforms.

1378 – Two Popes at Rome and Avignon had a huge tiff and stopped talking.

1400 – Middle English gave birth to modern English.

1415 – Oil colours introduced into painting.

1430 – 'Mad Marjorie' a huge cast iron gun scared everyone.

1440 – Gutenberg, a German inventor printed from the first movable type.

1465 – First printed music. Sorry, don't know what the tune was.

1477 – Our boy Caxton printed *Canterbury Tales*.

Chapter 15:

Watch Out, There's A Henry About

Everyone then agreed to end the Middle Ages along with serfs, villeins and the feudal system. In fact, dukes also nearly ended because there was only one left. The invention of gunpowder made armour and castles useless and, as the king was the only one who could afford lots of cannons, it made rebelling a bit iffy.

Everyone at this time was rushing round the world (chaps like Chris Columbus), discovering new countries. I think they always

had, but the invention of maps and compasses meant they could at last get back to tell someone. The English started to get much cleverer owing to a rediscovery of Greek literature. Funny, the Greeks seem to have lost it! William Caxton discovered the book (but don't ask where), and most people read it. At this time there were 4,000,000 people living here quite peacefully as Henry had done away with private armies – and still (much more to the point) he had the best weapons. Also he had pots of his own money so didn't have to tax everyone as much.

His smartest move was to marry his daughter to the son of James II (King of Scotland) and his son Arthur to Catherine of Aragon, whose dad was King of Spain. When young Arthur died in 1502, Catherine was passed on to his younger brother Henry. I dread to think what the Women's Movement would have had to say about that.

Henry VII still had a bit of aggro from the remaining Yorkies, but generally left the country rich and peaceful when he died in 1509.

1509 – Henry VIII
The world famous Henry VIII became king at eighteen. He was an athlete, poet, musician, patron of the arts (and all round clever

Dick). He wasn't a bit like his dad and soon started giving the French a hard time again but with little success. Henry spent most of his money on a huge navy, greatly encouraged by Thomas Wolsey, Archbishop of York, Cardinal and Chancellor who had almost as much cash as the king.

1509 – Wife No. 1

Now, as you remember Henry was married to his dead brother's wife – or should that be ex-wife – Catherine the Spanish girl. The trouble was, he thought she was knocking on a bit, especially as all their five children were daughters and four of them unfortunately dead. As he fancied a son (and a housemaid called Anne), he decided to claim that the marriage was invalid – nice one, Henry – and got Wolsey to ask the Pope to let him off. The Pope, who was under the King of Spain's thumb, refused. Henry, therefore, cheekily told him where to get off and made himself head of the Church. Two outstanding heads of Church and State, Bishop Fisher and Sir Thomas More, wouldn't go along with it so Henry

promptly had their heads off. Thomas's poor head was apparently parboiled, stuck on a pole, and exhibited on London Bridge. His daughter bribed the bridge-keeper to knock it down and she, being a good catch, nicked it and took it home. Years later, when dead herself, she was buried with it.

1532 – Wife No. 2

Henry married Anne Boleyn and later charged Wolsey with extremely high treason which is a fine way to treat your mates!

He then appointed Thomas Cromwell to replace Wolsey and together they 'dissolved' all the monasteries (probably in Holy Water) and took all the Church's assets, as at that time the Church owned about a quarter of the country. The Pope went do-lally and excommunicated him, but Henry just laughed and said 'Go forth and multiply'! This became the beginning of the Reformation which was the biggest shake-down the Church had ever seen. Anyone who didn't agree with Henry was called a heretic and promptly burned. Most people tended to like it!

Anne, unfortunately, gave him yet another daughter (Elizabeth) in 1533. This really put Henry's back up, but not as much as her flirting with the courtiers. When he found out, he chopped not only her head off, but all her supposed lovers' (plural) heads too. It's interesting to note that Anne was a bit of a freak, having an extra finger on one hand, and – even more weird – three breasts. If the

adultery and incest (with her brother) charges hadn't stuck, Henry planned to have her charged as a witch, using her deformities as evidence. It really wasn't Anne's year, for after being executed her heart was stolen and secretly hidden. It was found again in 1836 and buried under the church organ in Thetford, Suffolk. The current vicar's favourite song is reported to be 'You Gotta Have Heart'.

1536 – Wife No. 3

Next up was Jane Seymour who – good news – bore him a son, but – bad news – died in 1537 doing so. Tudor surgery, unfortunately, wasn't up to much.

He then tried to marry his sister's baby granddaughter, Mary (one day Queen of Scots), but the Scottish nobles wouldn't have it (quite right too!).

1540 – Wife No. 4

Now it was the turn of Anne of Cleves, 'The Flemish Mare'. Although she was remarkably ugly, it was generally reckoned to be politically a good idea. The marriage wasn't consummated (ask your parents) and he soon divorced her. He obviously wasn't too fond of horses (Flemish Mare?). Poor Cromwell got the chop because the marriage had been his idea. That's what happens if you do your friend a favour.

HOW'S BUSINESS?

1540 – Wife No. 5

Henry then tried another maid-in-waiting, Catherine Howard, but she was a bit too bright for him so, true to form, he chopped her head off (an occupational hazard).

1543 – Wife No. 6

I bet Katherine Parr, Henry's last wife, was nervous on the wedding day. By this time Henry was in a terrible physical state and some of his afflictions were too disgusting to relate (which, believe me, is pretty disgusting) so Katherine outlived him. He died in 1547 aged fifty-six leaving a country, though broke from constant wars, more confident than ever before.

Meanwhile

1473–1543 – Copernicus reckoned that we were all going round the sun (and round the bend).

1489   — Symbols + and − came into use.
1494   — Whisky distilled in Scotland.
1498   — The Chinese discovered the toothbrush and had the best smiles.
1500   — Martin Luther, famous Protestant reformer, was one of the first people to have had a candle-lit Christmas Tree in his front room.
1503   — Noses blown all over Britain owing to the popularity of the handkerchief. I suppose that up to that time they must have used their sleeves.
1503   — Leonardo da Vinci painted his grumpy girlfriend Mona (Lisa).
1508   — Pope told Michelangelo to give the Sistine Chapel ceiling a coat of paint.
1517   — Coffee came to Europe.
1520   — Chocolate followed (at last).
1521   — Martin Luther (not King) condemned as a heretic and excommunicated.
1522   — Magellan set off across the world and proved it was round by coming back to the same place.
1533   — First lunatic asylums (but by no means the first loonies).
1547   — Terrible Ivan (The Terrible) crowned tsar of Russia.

Chapter 16:

Are You Ready, Eddie? – 1547

All this bonhomie and prosperity fell to bits in the next decade owing to the constant argy-bargy between the Catholics and the Protestants.

61

Poor little Edward VI (Henry's lad) became king aged nine and didn't know what to do for the best. He was helped by his uncle Somerset, a staunch Protestant, along with Thomas Cranmer (even stauncher). The economy took a nose dive until the Treasury was as empty as a politician's promise. Unemployment was rife and the country became totally cheesed off. Sounds a little familiar, doesn't it?

When the Duke of Northumberland took over from Somerset, he realised that the only cash left belonged to the Protestant Church which was now flavour of the month. He stripped the churches of all their good bits and left them with just a chalice and a bell (very big of him!).

Funnily enough, although he wasn't too struck on God, he made everyone else go to church. If they didn't, he fined or imprisoned them. Attendances improved miraculously (Church of England take note). When Northumberland spotted that the adolescent king was permanently looking a little peaky, and possibly not long for this world, he made his son Dudley marry Lady Jane Grey, a cousin of old Henry VII (the one with all the cannons). He sneakily bullied Edward into leaving her everything, including the crown, in his will. The first bit he got right, as the king snuffed it in 1553, but the rest of the plan was screwed up.

1553 – Lady Jane Grey

Lady Jane only managed to hang onto the crown for nine days before she and poor Dudley were found some rooms in the Tower. The British, fed up to the back teeth with Protestant rule, had said no way, as they were greedy, corrupt, and couldn't run a booze-up

in a brewery. They wanted Mary, daughter of Catherine of Aragon (first Mrs of Henry VIII), and got their way.

1553 – Mary Tudor

Mary Tudor turned out to be exactly what they didn't want. She was stroppy, inflexible and about as much fun as a wet Sunday. She thought God had sent for her to bring England back to Catholicism – here we go again. She married King Philip of Spain (free holidays?) and so brought England back (protestanting) under the Pope. Just to make things neat and tidy, she executed Lady Jane and her new hubby. I bet Dudley cursed his dad. After all, the marriage was his daft idea.

I MITRE GUESSED THIS WOULD HAPPEN

Then she set about barbecuing the Protestants at Smithfield – later, rather appropriately, a meat market. First she sent to the stake (or maybe steak) all the bishops, followed by anyone she could get her flames on. It was reliably reported that as Latimer, Bishop of Oxford, was waiting for his turn, he said these famous words, 'We shall this day light such a candle by God's grace in England as, I trust, shall never be put out'. Unfortunately, they lit him instead (and didn't put him out!). It seems there was a daily fry up for nearly a year. You couldn't do it now because they don't allow bonfires in central London.

So England became a province of Spain (olé) which made all us English-hombres muchos mad. They even made us join in their bloody war with France and guess what? We lost Calais. Mary was disgraced and died of extreme grumpiness in 1558 aged forty-two. England, to show its respect, had a huge, drunken party to celebrate.

Chapter 17:

Good Queen Bess — 1558

Elizabeth was the daughter of Anne Boleyn (see headless mums) and reckoned by the Catholics to be illegitimate. She was twenty-five when 'queened' and a rather plain, skinny sort, with bright red hair like her dad's. Her looks weren't improved by the use of a form of white, lead-based make-up which, although

fashionable, had a rather unfortunate habit of eating into one's face. It's worth noting, that in those days people never washed or changed their underclothes, so they often carried a cloved apple to disguise the pong (how pleasant). Elizabeth tried to compensate for her rather offputting personal features by wearing 'over the top' clothes the like of which had never been seen before.

Unfortunately, she had inherited a right mess. England was skint, divided, weak and surrounded by a bunch of extremely unpleasant enemies. To cap that, half the country thought Mary Queen of Scots should rule even though Scotland was now French. Lizzie, luckily, was as bright as a button and fortunately didn't give a damn which religion God wanted her subjects to be. She'd really

BON Mᶜ JOUR

had enough of the Catholics, however, so promptly told the Pope and the Spanish where to go, and set about making everyone in England friends and Protestants again.

She then helped Scotland give the French 'le grande elbow' in 1559. The Frogs were so dejected, having a civil war of their own, that they were to be as good as gold for years.

1568 – Spanish Trouble

Spain was a different matter. They threatened us with Armadas (nasty gangs of warships) every five minutes. Elizabeth was a gutsy lady, however, and didn't scare easily. She and her advisors set about getting the country back on its feet, inventing apprenticeships, relief for the poor (what a relief), and work for the unemployed. There was an enormous expansion in trade and manufacture and by 1568 England was back on its feet (Elizabeth II and Thatcher 1st take note!).

This was the year that Francis Drake aged twenty-eight set off for the New World with his chum, Sir John Hawkins, a second-hand slave salesman. Also this year, Mary (ex-Queen of Scots), was chased out of Scotland for marrying the guy that blew her husband up. In the rush to England she forgot her baby who then had to be King of Scotland (James VI).

Elizabeth was strangely unsympathetic and kept her virtually imprisoned. Of course it just could have had something to do with the Spanish constantly plotting to get Mary on the English throne. Never quite sure of just what they were cooking up she eventually cut Mary's head off in 1587 which seemed to do the trick nicely. The famous drink Bloody Mary was aptly named after her.

1588 – Spanish Armada

As you can imagine, her execution rather annoyed the Spanish who decided to invade us at last. Drake, who'd been having a ball robbing and plundering the Spanish merchant ships, became top hero when he snuck into Cadiz harbour and burnt most of Philip of

Spain's parked invasion fleet. When the Armada finally pitched up in English waters their huge lumbering galleons were outwitted by our nippy little ones. Add to that a teriffic storm which destroyed half their ships, and you can guess the result. The final score was one small ship to them and seventy-two great big 'uns to us. The 'Invincible' Armada returned to Spain with its sails between its legs.

The Elizabethans

While all this was going on, everyone was having a high old time in England. The Elizabethan Age had arrived. Elizabeth had a boyfriend called Essex (not David) and Shakespeare, the new hit writer, had his head well down, furiously scribbling plays. The

OUT DAMN SPOT.

English were reckoned to be the best musicians in Europe, even without a Eurovision Song Contest, and most certainly the most contented nation (those were the days). At last, thanks to Elizabeth, we were united under a common law, a common bible, a Book of Common Prayer, a common literature and a common language. (It all sounds far too common for my liking.)

Lizzie's other favourite was Sir Walter Raleigh who became famous for:

1. Introducing the potato to the Irish (they became instant friends).

2. Living in the Tower of London for twelve years without being murdered.
3. Showing the Queen how to walk on water without getting her feet wet (Jesus please note).
4. Bringing tobacco to England (it's all his fault).
5. Not finding the golden city of Eldorado.
6. Being executed in 1618.
7. Having his head kept in a leather bag (red) by his wife for twenty-nine years.

Good Queen Bess died in 1603, still a virgin, having rather stupidly cut off the boyfriend's head.

Chapter 18:

Two Kings For The Price Of One – 1603

James was the I of England and the VI of Scotland. He was the poor little perisher left as a baby by Mary his mummy when she had to leave in rather a hurry. He came down to London aged thirty-seven and was the first ever king of all the four countries of the British Isles. He was, overall, a peaceful sort of chap which suited the England that Elizabeth had left behind. There were hardly any murders, no feuds, no bandits and only a little war with Spain. James sorted the latter out fairly quickly and everything looked to be going OK, apart from – surprise, surprise – religion. At this time there were three denominations in England. The Anglicans (invented by Lizzie), The Roman Catholics, and the Puritans (hard-line Protestants). These last were a strange bunch who thought that anything that approached looking like fun was wicked (and quite right too!). They hated theatre, dancing, ornamentation and smiling.

1605 – Guy Fawkes

These three were always arguing. It became so heated that one day a guy called Guido Fawkes (a Catholic) accidentally invented Bonfire night by nearly blowing up the Anglican Parliament. Just imagine how much more famous (and popular) he'd have been if he'd actually got away with it. (Come back Guido, all is forgiven).

1610 – Distant Lands

James personally hated the Puritans and finally lost his rag and told

them that if they didn't conform to the Anglican church they could jolly well get lost. They took the hint and set out in a boat called the *Mayflower* to try to find Virginia. They got a bit lost, but did find America. Rather cheekily, they named the bit that they eventually landed on, New England (which it still is).

1613 – Funny Goings-On

James, although a bit clever, was thought to be coarse, scruffy, gross, and very cocky. He preferred the 'company' of men to women and proved it by making his special boyfriend, Buckingham, the first ever non-Royal duke. His whole court was a bit suspect

(nudge nudge, wink wink), and at one point in 1619 his former Lord Chamberlain, Lord Treasurer, Secretary of State and Captain of the Gentlemen Pensioners (sounds like a geriatric cricket team), were all banged up in the Tower. They were accused of various sexual or financial offences, which I'd prefer not to go into.

Britain at this time was the last of the European countries to rush overseas to set up colonies and trading stations in far distant lands. This was probably because our boats were a bit clapped out

following the Spanish war and James had been too tight with his cash to patch them up. Our first proper colony, however, was in Virginia and our first proper trading outfit was called the East India Company.

When James I finally called it a day in 1625 he left huge debts, an unsavoury court and a nice new war with Spain.

By the Way

Guy Fawkes had ten accomplices. When the Gunpowder Plot was discovered Guy was caught (and horribly executed) while the others escaped to a 'safe' house in Staffordshire. They arrived soaked to the skin and decided to dry their socks by the fire. While chucking on an extra log, a stray spark ignited the gunpowder they were still carrying. Several were maimed and blinded, and the blast attracted the attention of pursuing soldiers who promptly massacred the rest.

Meanwhile

1562 – Milled coins introduced. It appears some naughty chaps had been amassing gold and silver by clipping bits off the coins.

1565 – First graphite pencils.

1589 – Sir John Harington installed the first proper water closet (lavatory). Bet he was popular with his chums.

1596 – Galileo invented the thermometer – and found out he had a temperature!

1600 – Dutch opticians invented the telescope.

1611 – King James allowed each colonist in Jamestown, Virginia, to be given gardens to grow hemp as a fibre source. It was known, even then, that the top leaves of the hemp plant, when dried, produce hashish or cannabis – an intoxicating drug.

1619 – William Harvey discovered blood – and how it goes round us.

1624 – A crazy Dutchman, Cornelius Drebble, stretched some greased leather round a wooden frame and when it didn't float realised he'd discovered the submarine.

Chapter 19:

What! A Charlie? – 1625

Charles I (crowned in 1625) couldn't have been less like his dad if he'd tried. A right little runt (5ft 4ins) who was prudish, shy, shifty and st-stammering. If his father never really understood the English, Charlie never really understood anyone at all. He believed that if he set a good example, the world would follow. How wrong could he be. For a start, he went and married the horribly haughty Henrietta (the king of France's daughter) whom his faithful subjects soon learned to loathe. Then, with the help of his chief advisor, the Duke of Buckingham, handsome ex-boyfriend of his ex-dad, Charles managed to intensify the Spanish war.

1625 – War With Spain

He asked Parliament for money to fight with and they told him to get lost. Weedy Charles tried to do it on the cheap without them, but soon got into a right mess. He begged them again, and again they told him to go away – but probably not that politely. He then tried to borrow money off his friends. Cheekier still, he forced

people to feed his troops for free, throwing them into jail if they refused. Parliament eventually gave in and told him that if he was a good boy and behaved himself, they'd give him the cash. He blew it all though, and was forced, finally, to crawl to the Spanish king and make peace (what a Charlie!).

1629 – Trouble With Parliament

Charles was one of those kings who thought he was next in line to God, which meant nobody had the right to question him. This really peeved the patient Parliament. In the end things came to the crunch over – three guesses – religion again. Parliament passed a resolution against the Catholic faith which Charles, having Catholic sympathies, took rather badly. He sent them all packing and ran the country alone for eleven years. If you're wondering what happened to the beautiful Buckingham, he was assassinated by 'a ten-penny knife' owned by an obscure lieutenant, cross at not being promoted.

1635 – Civil War Looms

Charles was still strapped for cash so he taxed the wealthy landowners heavily, and, for reasons best known to himself, anyone who lived by or near the sea (the Ship Tax). Then he stuck his nose into Scottish religion, which miffed them so much they invaded England (so far – so good, Charlie!). Very few of his soldiers could be bothered to fight so he called a Parliament again in 1640 to

force them. Parliament refused and executed his two best advisers for luck, the whizz kid Earl of Strafford and William Laud, which again made Charles mad. He took what was left of his army to arrest them all in London, but they all hid. The whole country took sides and whoopee! we have a proper civil war (nice one, Charles!).

The Sides

The Roundheads	vs	The Cavaliers
Parliament		The King
The Commons		Catholics
The Puritans		The High Churchmen
Industrial areas		Most Lords
Navy and Ports		Old Gentry
London		The North and West
The East and South		Oxford

Although the Cavaliers – another word for swaggerers – initially had the most muscle, the Roundheads – so called because of their

73

short haircuts – soon caught up and overtook. Parliament had much better access to funds by taxing everyone like crazy. They did a sneaky deal with Scotland, promising them that they'd let England become Presbyterian (National Church of Scotland) if they helped fight the king. What really decided the whole shooting match was one man, a Puritan called Oliver Cromwell, MP for Cambridge.

1640 – Witches
It was also the time of the famous witch-hunts. Anything that went wrong in the countryside – bad crops, hens not laying, wives becoming ugly, etc. was blamed on witches. Any single old woman who had a broom and/or a cat was suspected of witchcraft. A nasty piece of work called Matthew Hopkins toured Merrie England for three years from 1644, killing old women willy-nilly. His best test involved throwing the poor old souls into any convenient pond. If they sank they were innocent and if they floated it meant Satan was helping them so they were guilty and promptly burned. It was heads

you lose, tails you lose. Hopkins became so good at witch-spotting (sure beats train-spotting) that, in the end, people wondered if Satan wasn't on his side and hanged him as well for good measure.

1642 – Oliver Cromwell
Cromwell started out drilling volunteers for the Parliamentary party, but soon emerged as one of their top men. In 1644 a

combination of Roundheads, Scots and Cromwell's new cavalry beat the pants off the Cavaliers or Royalists at Marston Moor. This gained him loads of Brownie points and Parliament was so chuffed that they asked Cromwell to build a flash new elite army of professional soldiers. It was called the New Model Army and the men were paid the unheard of sum of 10p a day. These guys were mostly 'Independents' as they hated the Anglicans and the Presbyterians. Though damn tough, they were a right bunch of

SCUSE ME - COULD I SEE YOUR HAIRCUT.

goody-goodies (though you wouldn't have dared tell them), trained not to drink, swear, rape or pillage. When it came to fighting, however, they were fab and beat the undisciplined Cavaliers wherever they came up against them.

Charles, seeing he was getting the worst of it, scarpered up to Scotland in 1646 thinking he'd get well looked after as his old man was once their king. No such luck. The Scots, never ones to miss the chance of filling their sporrans, promptly flogged him to Parliament — For Sale, one King!

Cromwell, who was by then Parliament's blue-eyed boy, was given £2,500 a year commission for fixing the deal. Lots of the Royalist soldiers, stuck without a leader and no wages, sloped home to their wives.

Roundheads
Things weren't too clever with the Roundheads either. Parliament was continually harassing them, and worse, sacking their no-longer-

needed army without paying them. Cromwell was well brassed off, so he seized poor Charles and offered him a generous deal.

As a result of Cromwell's actions civil war broke out between Cromwell's rough, tough army and a weird combination of the English Presbyterians, the surly Scots and what was left of the Royalists. In 1648 Cromwell's heavies beat them hollow at the Battle of Preston. Ollie then high-tailed it down to London and gave all the Presbyterians in Parliament the boot.

1648 – The Rump

This left just sixty Independents rather daftly called 'the Rump'. Cromwell then did his naughtiest thing ever. He tried the king for high treason and then in 1649, at a huge public ceremony, neatly severed his head (a rather disloyal thing to do to your king).

He nothing common did or mean
Upon that memorable scene . . .
But bow'd his comely head
Down as upon a bed.
   Andrew Marvell (Ode to Cromwell)

Very noble I'm sure, but it looks as if poor old Charlie didn't have much choice.

Not many folk know that when Charles's coffin was rediscovered in 1813, the Royal surgeon, Sir Henry Halford, did an autopsy on the body and nicked poor Charles's fourth vertebra. For years he used to horrify his mates by using it as a salt holder at dinner parties. Queen Victoria, never one to like a joke, ordered him to put it back in the coffin.

Meanwhile, although Charles had never been exactly a fave rave, the Brits didn't take too well to someone chopping their king's head off. In those days, however, if you'd had enough of the government (and we all know how that feels), you couldn't just moan about your leaders in the local take-away. Telling tales on people was a national sport, and public execution a great day out for all the family, providing it wasn't your turn. Part of the army eventually mutinied, followed by the navy. This situation intrigued 'abroad', who were always waiting on the sidelines for any opportunity to attack us.

Chapter 20:

Look Out, Charles – 1650

Meanwhile up at Scone (remember? We've still got their stone!) the Scots were crowning Charles's son, Charles II, who'd been in Holland hiding in the Hague. Cromwell was solving his problems as only he knew how. He shot the mutineers, invaded and massacred the revolting Irish and only then turned his attention to Scotland and their brand new king. It took a few bloody battles to show the Royalist Scots who was boss. Charles, who'd apparently spent much of his time hiding up a tree (funny lot, kings!), rather wisely went on a prolonged holiday to France in 1651 and I bet he didn't send any postcards.

EARLY SANDCASTLE

Cromwell kindly gave his soldiers, who'd all got nasty colds and flu, a nice rest. He then built up the navy and thumbed his nose at all our foreign enemies who'd missed their chance to get us while our trousers were down, so to speak. It wasn't long before we ruled the seas again and Cromwell's tough-guy sailor boys got back some of our colonies he'd lost by blowing away the king.

1653 – King Oliver?

Oliver obviously wasn't someone who was easy to get on with, and before long he fell out with his Rump, which sounds rather painful. He fired the lot of them and so, for the first time, England was ruled by a military dictatorship.

Some slimy creeps kept begging him to become king, but Oliver didn't fancy it much and who blames him. Instead of being King Olly I he called himself the 'Lord Protector of a United Commonwealth of England, Scotland, Ireland and the Colonies' (what a mouthful).

By the Way

Cromwell died of natural causes, believe it or not, aged sixty. Just before he was buried, his brain was weighed and found to be an incredible 82.25 ounces (the average man's weighs 49 ounces).

Some time later, when definitely wormbait, he was dug up (pooh!) with all his fellow king killers and strung up at Tyburn. As a special treat, Cromwell's head was displayed on a pole outside Westminster Abbey which jolly well served him right – not, I suspect, that he cared. It remained there for twenty-four years until

1685 when a strong wind blew it off. It was found by a captain of the guard who took it home and hid it up his chimney. Years later it turned up at a freak show and was valued at sixty guineas. An actor, Samuel Russell, had been paying his rent by charging the punters half a crown a look. After changing hands several more times it ended up on display in Bond Street. The syndicate which had bought it for £230 all died mysteriously and it fell into the hands of a Doctor Wilkinson. The Wilkinson family kept it in a wooden box, wrapped in red and black silk, for years and years until eventually giving it to Sydney Sussex College in 1960 where it was buried secretly.

Chapter 21:

Come Back, Charlie – 1660

After a bit more light anarchy, someone called up Charles II, probably on a French beach, and told him it was all right to come home. This he did forthwith and arrived by 'Hovership' at Dover in May 1660, aged thirty, now more French than English and probably sporting a beret.

The British went crazy and had a high old time. Life under Cromwell had not been exactly a barrel of laughs. Everyone was really looking forward to being quite the opposite of a Puritan or Quaker (same sort of thing). Britain was by now, despite everything, ever so rich and important and all those frightful foreigners had become quite scared of us (not like now – eh!).

Good-Time Charlie

Charles, I'm afraid, only came back to have a good time. Although witty, carefree, and a good laugh (if you were his pal), he was also totally selfish and unscrupulous and dead ugly. He wasn't, strangely enough, that keen on continuing to give the Catholics a hard time and set about making friends. He married a rather prim and proper Portuguese princess called Catherine of Braganza but, being a lecherous young chappie, spent most of his time with his many mistresses and millions of illegitimate kids. One of his famous girlfriends was a certain Nell Gwynne, an orange salesperson, famed for the size and quality of her – oranges!

Plague Again

It was during his reign that Britain had a nasty dose of the plague again. In London alone, 700,000 poor devils died. It wasn't really surprising because London was a filthy place with garbage piled in the streets and lots of people sleeping rough (so what's changed?). If it was suspected that anyone in your house was feeling a little poorly, your neighbours would paint a nice red cross on your door and then nail it shut with you and your family inside. The drag was, if it wasn't the plague, then you'd damn well starve to death instead.

If anyone did manage to escape the city to stay with relatives in the country, the simple rural folk weren't that sympathetic. They'd either murder you or cut off any village suspected of having the plague until you, and everyone else, perished.

Top of the Pops that year was a little song that went:

A ring, a ring of roses (the red spots on your body)
A pocket full of posies (thought to keep the infection away)
Atishoo! Atishoo! (the first symptom)
We all fall down (speaks for itself!)

1666 – The Great Fire

Just as the Londoners were getting over this lot, a daft baker in Pudding Lane accidentally set fire to his shop (he should have used his loaf) and started the Great Fire of London. You could say it never rains but it pours, but unfortunately it had been a real scorcher of a summer and they hadn't seen a spot – apart from red ones – for ages. As the houses were all made of wood, the inferno swept through the streets like 'the Roadrunner' and in the seven days that it lasted, 10,000 houses and eighty churches were destroyed. Fortunately, only six people were killed, but that could have been because the plague took the rest the year before.

1668 – Puritan Bashing!

Meanwhile Charles's first Parliament was really giving a lot of stick to the remaining Puritans. They weren't allowed to hold high office (serves 'em right) and if they met for religious reasons or showed their faces in the towns, they were promptly thrown into jail or transported to the colonies, which, all things considered, sounds like the safest place to have been.

Not only was there another big conflagration a year later but, to put the tin lid on it, the daring Dutch, with more than a little Dutch courage, sailed right up the Thames and set fire to our brill fleet. Charles's most faithful servant, the Earl of Clarendon, somehow got the blame for all this lot (someone's always the scapegoat) and was himself fired from running the government. Charles, meanwhile, had a real ace up his sleeve. He did a brilliantly tricky secret deal with Louis XIV of France. Believe it or not, he promised old Louis that in return for £1,200,000 a year cash in hand, he would help fight the Dutch (revenge is sweet) and also try to make England Catholic again. Parliament went barmy when it found out, and told him – NO WAY! They made Charles sign a Test Act excluding any Catholic from high office. It was a bit embarrassing, because this meant that his brother, the heir to the throne, James – Duke of York, was also excluded as he was a Catholic too.

1678 – Titus Oates

A real rascal called Titus Oates (I wonder if he was a Quaker?) reckoned he'd heard of a Catholic plot to top the king and put James on the throne. As usual, no-one checked the story and panic set in. Lots of poor, innocent Catholics were executed just

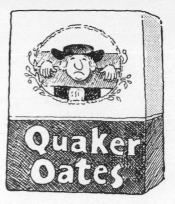

on Oates's say so. A new Parliament passed an act to prevent James ever being king. The supporters of the act were called Whigs, and those who didn't – Tories (sounds familiar).

1681 – Which King Next?

Civil war loomed again, but Charles being always ahead of the game, managed to keep all the balls in the air by ruling without Parliament. Remember, he was still getting a great pay-off from France. The joke was, that it was France which was becoming number one threat, not Holland as before. The trouble with the Whigs was that although they couldn't bear the idea of James on the throne, they couldn't make up their minds who they did want. It was a toss up between Monmouth, known rather unkindly as the 'Royal Bastard' or Mary, James's Protestant daughter.

This terrible, but admittedly, peaceful indecision allowed the Tories to become much stronger and they eventually hounded many of the leading Whigs to death. Soon there were none left in Parliament. James, meanwhile, was going crazy in Scotland taking it out on the Presbyterians in the vilest manner.

In the end Charles II totally won the day and died happy in 1685. He left a country ruled by Tories who believed the king knew best, the Church knew second best and all the localities knew third best.

Chapter 22:

Hanging Around In 1685

If England had thought that James II was just what they'd always been looking for – he wasn't. Despite telling them all he was a good guy, in his heart of hearts he was a real fanatic. He'd had an unconventional royal childhood eventually running away to France, dressed as a girl (no comment), to serve with the French army. When he became king the English Protestants were terrified, as French Protestants were turning up on our shores telling gruesome stories of what was happening to their mates being persecuted by Louis XIV, James's old chum. Their fears weren't helped by James keeping a huge menacing army on the outskirts of London.

1685 – Monmouth Turns Up

Things got off to an exciting start when his old rival for the throne, Monmouth, arrived in Lyme Regis with a weedy little army that was knocked into the middle of the next week by James's bully boys. This was the very last proper battle in England (apart from last year's F.A. cup tie).

Monmouth's execution was a particularly messy affair, as it took five chops (ouch!). Just as they were about to bury the two bits some bright spark realised that there wasn't a proper portrait of the ex-Duke. As he was the illegitimate son of Charles II they thought they'd better get one done. They therefore sewed his head back on his body, put him back in his clothes, sat him in a chair and, Bob's your uncle – one picture! If you don't believe me, the portrait's still hanging in the National Portrait Gallery, London.

1686 – Judge Jeffreys

One of James's employees, a nice chap called Judge Jeffreys, thought of an original way to decorate the streets. His job had been to try Monmouth's rebels on 'the Bloody Western Circuit'. To say he was strict was a bit of an understatement. He deported 800 rebels to the West Indies and Barbados not, I hasten to add, for the good of their health and the 300 left were dangled along the sides

of the roads as an example to others. (They must have got the message, wouldn't you?) Neither the Whigs nor the Tories were too pleased by James's cruelty but with his army of 30,000 professional soldiers behind him it was tough bananas!

Although James was always trying to get his mates the Catholics into the best jobs, he was tolerated because Parliament knew that when he died, his Protestant daughter, Mary, would take over. Everyone was gobsmacked therefore, when James's second Mrs – Mary Beatrice, really put the cat (or brat) amongst the pigeons (or Anglicans) by having a blasted boy (and not a bastard boy) after ten years of baby-free marriage.

1688 – William and Mary

Suddenly for once, everyone agreed and decided to ask William of Orange – James's nephew (and daughter Mary's hubby) – to come and have a nice friendly chat to try and talk James out of making Britain's future, Catholic (fat chance).

What actually happened was rather bizarre. William arrived with 500 ships and 14,000 'friendly' troops who came ashore at Brixham in 1688 and turned right towards London. James led his huge army towards them but started having terrible nosebleeds which tended to hold up the marching. He became increasingly peculiar and seemed to be going round the bend. Many of his officers and commanders thought 'blow this for a game of soldiers' and slipped away. James completely lost his bottle and ran back to London, soon to be caught up by a rather puzzled William. Had James not been a bit do-lally he could still have saved the situation. But no – not him. He just ran away with his son, only a nipper, to France where Louis XIV was really pleased to have them, as he was looking for any excuse to attack England. As James was leaving he dropped the Great Seal of England, the symbol of authority, into the Thames hoping it could hinder the running of the country. This didn't hinder anything, however (and the seal was probably happier anyway). From that moment he was considered to have jacked in the throne.

The Whigs and Tories seemed rather relieved and let Mr and Mrs Orange be their king and queen. So ended what came to be known as the Bloodless Revolution.

Chapter 23:

Oranges Are Good For You – 1689

William and Mary were crowned in 1689 and the British, who always liked a change, were delighted. William had been a sort of King of Holland and had become a bit of a hero shooing off the French who'd been trying to invade. He did this, rather cleverly, by opening all the dykes and flooding most of Holland apart from

Amsterdam – where he lived. This soaked the French and sent them swimming home. Fine, if all you want to rule is a lake, but I think his action defines the term 'cutting off your nose to spite your face'!

This Bloodless or Glorious Revolution, was important because it was the first time that Parliament had decided who should succeed to the throne. This, of course, suddenly made it jolly important, and although the Crown had to approve its measures, Parliament gained a power that it was never again to lose.

Another first, was the right to worship however and whoever you wanted without the fear of having your head parted from your body.

1689 – England United

It should be said that although England was feeling united, there were only 5,000,000 of us and 20,000,000 of those blasted French. Louis still reckoned James was our king, though I fail to see what business it was of his, and was prepared, at the drop of a crown, to fight to put him on the throne again.

Strangely enough Scotland, for once, supported England – apart from some horrible Highlanders who were promptly 'killied' at Killiecrankie. There wasn't a welcome either from the MacDonald clan of Glencoe who took far too long making up their minds whose side they were on. They were unfortunately made into Big Macs by the English, who just couldn't wait.

1690 – The Irish

The Irish, always ones to be difficult, decided to support James and invited King Louis over to form a Catholic army to fight the English. They decided first to besiege and then rout the remaining Protestants in Londonderry (a bit like the IRA are trying to do now). 'Orange Billy', as he was known, called up his old Dutch mates, who still thought the French were creeps, and an Anglo-Dutch Army met the O'Frogs on the banks of the Boyne in 1690. Although short, pock marked, weedy, asthmatic and anaemic, William stayed in the saddle for nineteen hours. His army crushed the French who, probably fed up with the dreadful Irish cuisine (potatoes and more potatoes), went home. The poor old Irish Catholics lost everything including the right to be educated (no Irish jokes – please!).

1690 – War with France No. 1

A Frenchman, like an elephant, never forgets, and we were soon at proper war with France. Wars were now evolving into something different, however, as soldiers from whichever side were beginning to dislike being killed in great numbers. Sieges were much more fun. All you had to do was sit around some city or encampment, smoking, drinking and waving your weapons around every now and again, while the ones inside did the same. The winner was the side that didn't get bored first. This is a simplification of course, but you get the idea.

Anyway that was how this particular war with the French was 'fought' so it tended to drag out for ages without a full-time score. When at last William decided to pull his finger out and fight properly, he got a result, beating Louis' lads 'game, set and match' at La Hogue in 1697.

This long war had been financed by the brand new Bank of England who raised cash by issuing shares to anyone who wanted to invest in it at 8% interest. This created the first  National Debt which I believe we're still paying back (maybe because we keep borrowing from it!). Another great first was William's idea. He discovered it was much easier to fight a war if you have a group of guys from only one party. They were called a Cabinet and met in secret which they still do.

1700 – War with France No. 2

Those damn French never learn and the eighteenth century opened with another war brewing. This time things looked a little more tricky. Louis XIV's grandson had taken over as King of Spain in 1700 which gave France control of the Spanish Empire and James II's young son, James III (still in France) was recognised (if only by the Frogs) as King of England when his dad died in 1702.

Much worse than this, our much loved Queen Mary died trying out an exciting new disease called smallpox. 'Orange Billy', not to be outdone, died a few years later making a mountain out of a molehill when his clumsy horse tripped over one.

Meanwhile
1630 – First public advertising was seen in France. (Perrier? Neau!).

1635 – First tobacco sold in France was on a doctor's prescription. Trust the French to get things round the wrong way.

1637 – The first umbrella kept a Frenchman dry.

1642 – Income and property tax introduced in England.

1650 – World population reached 500 million.

1652 – Tea first drunk in Britain. When it was sold to the public, eight years' later, priests and writers were outraged claiming the strange brown drink was dangerous to health, morals and public order (which of course it is).

1662 – The Royal Society for Improving Natural Knowledge was started by Christopher Wren (the church chap), John Evelyn (the writer chap), Robert Boyle (the scientist chap) and Isaac Newton (the apple chap). The age of science was on the starting blocks and superstition was on the way out.

1666 – At last! The first Cheddar cheese.

1666 – Stradivari made best violin ever seen (or heard).

1667 – French army chucked the first hand grenades.

1675 – Paris became the centre of European culture.

1680 – The last Dodo die-died!

1698 – Tax on beards in Russia (only on men).

Chapter 24:

Great Britain vs France – The Final

Mary's sister, Anne, was catapulted into power in 1702 aged thirty-eight. Although dull and lethargic herself she was ace at employing chaps who weren't. Best of all was a young soldier called John Churchill (watch out for that name). His official title was Duke of Marlborough. This name should have carried a French government health warning as he was determined to shut the pesky French up for good. He thought sieges were a bit soppy and decided to have a proper fight. So started the war of the Spanish Succession. Britain's main plan was to help put an Austrian prince on the throne of Spain instead of a French one. It seems like the Spanish princes didn't get a look in.

1704 – War with France No. 3

Marlborough and his army apparently marched straight up the Rhine to the Danube (bet they had wet socks) and joined our mates the Austrians. At the battle of Blenheim, this terrible team crushed the combined French and Bavarian army. This was the beginning of the end for Louis who asked nicely if he could make a pact with us (creep). The Tories in England were all for it, but it was just sour grapes because their opponents, the Whigs, were making cash out of the war. Marlborough pressed on and took Gibralta which pleased Anne so much she built, paid for and gave him Blenheim Palace, a socking great house north of Oxford.

THERE'S NO JACUZZI!

'See, Sir, here's the grand approach,
This way is for his Grace's coach . . .
The Council chamber's for debate,
And all the rest are rooms of state.'
'Thanks, Sir,' I cried, ''tis very fine,
But where d'ye sleep and where d'ye dine?
I find by all you have been telling,
That 'tis a house but not a dwelling.'

Pope . . . (not THE Pope)

1707 – Great Britain

Meanwhile, back at the war, Marlborough drove the French out of the Netherlands and the good old Austrians chased them out of Italy. Louis begged for peace but the Whigs, who were having a ball, made an act of Union with Scotland instead, and in 1707 we became GREAT Britain for the first time. Someone called Jack designed a rather gaudy flag and rather cockily named it after himself.

Crazed with success, the British went on to capture Minorca (big deal!), Nova Scotia in Canada and Newfoundland – which, by then, had been 'found' for a couple of hundred years. By this time poor Louis was positively grovelling for a treaty (yeah – he would, wouldn't he?).

1713 – Treaty of Utrecht

The Tories were by this time much more powerful than the Whigs, who were tottering. Being spoilsports they decided to call Marlborough in from abroad. Great Britain then signed the Treaty of Utrecht with France, and Britain and Austria divvied up the spoils. The Tories then set about destroying the Whig party, even though it seems their party was well and truly over.

Anne was absolutely whacked out having given birth to 15 children all of which unfortunately died. History says she died in

1714 of lethargy (having 15 kids can hardly be called lethargic!), leaving no heirs.

By the Way

Britannia, that funny woman we used to see on the back of old pennies, often confuses people. There she is, looking like a Roman, sitting in what looks like an amphibious wheelchair and draped in the Union Jack – which can't have existed. Don't worry, she's a fictional character representing Britain as a woman.

She first appeared on a golden Roman coin in AD 161 (without the flag), and later in 1665 on a copper coin (what a come-down). The model for Britannia was Frances Stuart, Duchess of Richmond – as if you didn't know.

Chapter 25:

German George 1714

In the last 700 years England had been ruled by Danish, Norman, French, Welsh, Scottish and Dutch sovereigns. The new Great British were still surprised, however, when an old, fat, non-English speaking German showed up to be their king. George I, a Hanoverian, arrived in London in 1714 having tidily imprisoned his wife, Sophia, for life. He'd spent much of his early life devoted to 'vine, vimmin and song' and didn't stop when he got here. He was terribly unpopular so we'll say no more about him, save he ruled for thirteen years and died in 1727.

DANK FÜR IHRE EINLADUNG!

1715 – Old Pretender

Soon after he arrived there was a Jacobite rebellion known as the '15, mostly supported by all the Scots uptight with England's newish Union with Scotland. They wanted James Francis Edward, Chevalier de St George, Prince of Wales (hope you've got all that) to be James III of England. He was known as the Old Pretender presumably because he had spent most of his life in France pretending to be a king. His rebellion only lasted six weeks, after which he sailed home feeling rather stupid. The trouble was that most people were far more interested in trying to make an honest (or dishonest) buck or two gambling on trade with the tropics, than in worrying who was king.

1720 – South Sea Bubble

The most famous outfit was the South Sea Company which everyone invested in. Unfortunately it grew out of all proportion through speculation until the 'Bubble' burst and everyone lost not only their shirts, but their trousers as well.

The first proper Prime Minister was then invented and called Sir Robert Walpole. His job was to clear up the mess and keep the country on an even keel under Whig rule.

Chapter 26:

George's Boy George

If George I was not much to write home about, his son Prince George was no better. His dad thought he was a rude little oik and chucked him out of the court (sounds a bit like some of our tennis players). The bolshy young prince promptly set up his own court round the corner, and became a real thorn in his father's side. Being totally ignorant in science, literature and reasonable personal habits, history would probably have preferred to forget about him. His reign, however, was to be chock-full of new exciting things albeit no thanks to him.

1727 – George II
Old George, his dad, died suddenly in 1727 on holiday in Holland, and the prince was crowned before the old man was cold. As well as

all his other shortcomings, he was a cocky devil by all accounts and although on the short side would strut and pose when given half a chance. He was no wimp, however, and it should be noted that he was the last British sovereign to lead an army in battle.

1739 – Another War
Walpole was forced into a nice little war with Spain which soon got out of hand to such an extent that we were soon mixing it with just about everyone. Walpole soon discovered that although OK as a domestic Prime Minister he was not much cop at wars. He was swiftly replaced by a chap named Henry Pelham, who, with his fearfully corrupt brother, the Duke of Newcastle, managed to

string the war out for eight years, settling nothing. All it did manage to achieve was a unique opportunity for another Jacobite rebellion called the '45.

1745 – The Great Pretender
This took place when another Stuart pretender to our throne, Prince Charlie, (known rather 'camply' as Bonnie) landed in Scotland with seven of his mates to stir up the heavy Highlanders again (as they'd all had a nice rest). Being a good looking, smooth talker, Charles soon had them all behind him and promptly took Edinburgh. They then went on to pan the English under general 'Johnnie' Cope at Prestonpans in 1745. Fortunately the English had their hands full with away matches so The Bonnie Prince thought the time was ripe to have a go down south again. All he needed was a little help from his old friends the French and a few thousand English volunteers that he'd been counting on from over the border. He waited and waited, but no one showed. Charlie, fed up with hanging around, set off south with 6,500 men. They got within 125 miles of London when they heard that loads of English soldiers had just arrived from Europe where they'd been defending Austria against France (busy business, soldiering!). Rather red-faced, they tiptoed back to Scotland with their sporrans between their legs.

1746 – Culloden
They thwarted the now-attacking English back at Falkirk but carelessly lost Edinburgh. The grand final was held at Culloden Moor in 1746. The English were led by William, Duke of Cumberland (later known as 'the Butcher'), who was the son of George II. It was a jolly fierce, nasty battle and, when the full-time whistle blew, there were a thousand dead Highlanders on the pitch. 'The Butcher' and his not-very-merry men rounded up the prisoners, survivors and injured and mercilessly 'kill-ted' them. The government in London then passed some neat laws to finish Highland clan life forever (what a McShame!). In gratitude the English named a flower 'the Sweet William' in the Duke's honour.

The Scots, rather ungraciously, renamed the Stinkwort weed 'Stinking Billy' as their mark of deep respect.

1748 – Redcoats

Charles, it seems, then made several movies in which he starred as the romantic fugitive, dodging round the highlands, seducing pretty maidens and avoiding the English patrols. These were called 'Redcoats' owing to their red coats. Centuries later, they appeared again – still as Redcoats – working in Butlin's holiday (or should I say prison) camps.

The Bonnie Prince caught the next French ship to Europe, where he ended up in Rome. He died forty years later – a hopeless drunk. When his brother gave up the ghost in 1807 the Stuarts had finally had it as far as the throne was concerned.

By the Way
George II was one of the loudest snorers in history (Abraham Lincoln was second).

By the Way (again)
All the weeping willows in England come from a Turkish basket of figs sent to Lady Suffolk in the early eighteenth century. Her chum, Alexander Pope, obviously not too struck on figs, planted a bit of the basket instead (that's poets for you) and this grew into the first weeping willow to be seen in this country.

Meanwhile
1705 – Halley predicted the return (in 1758) of his famous comet. The flaming thing keeps coming back.

1709 – Cristofori invented a piano, and probably could only play 'Chopsticks'.

1718 – Puckle patented the machine-gun enabling one to kill more people quicker.

1731 – 10 Downing Street built to put Prime Ministers in.

1752 – Benjamin Franklin invented the lightning conductor (no bus jokes please).

1754 – The Earl of Sandwich, a compulsive gambler, hated leaving the card table to get a meal. Instead he had a servant bring him some meat between two bits of bread and inadvertently invented – the ham roll!

IT'LL NEVER CATCH ON.

Chapter 27

Meanwhile, Back In The Old Country – 1750

It's surprising to realise that the population was still only around 5,200,000. It wasn't that people didn't know how to make babies – with no birth control (rubber hadn't been invented), it was quite the opposite. Britain was such an unhealthy place, that if you reached forty you'd done pretty well. Infant mortality was horrendous and many of their poor mums died in or around childbirth as well. Added to this, no one knew that disease was associated with dirt and, oh boy were they dirty! All drinking and washing water came from the rivers (Perrier – where were you) and, having no lavs, guess what they threw in the rivers?

Beautiful Britain
Rubbish, if not eaten by our little furry friends, was left to rot in the streets, and they really ponged (the streets!). As water was so short the noble English still tended not to bathe that much. If you were rich you might wash your clothes once a month; if poor, you wouldn't bother. Consequently, diseases like smallpox, typhus and 'jail fever' were all the rage.

Mind you, the French were no better. There's a lovely ancient English insult that goes – if you want to hide something from a Frenchman, put it under a bar of soap!

Health
Doctors were not much use. Most of them had no qualifications at all, and had no more status than any other craftsmen. Housewives would rely on passed down herbal remedies, superstition, or apothecaries. These guys were a bit like homoeopaths now, selling mostly herbal pills, potions and ointments of their own invention. Whether these quacks did any real good either then or now is something that might be wiser not to go into. Barbers at that time were also dentists and surgeons on the side. Sounds all rather

convenient. You could have a short back and sides, a tooth pulled, and your leg off, without leaving the chair. As anaesthetics hadn't been invented, you could choose a stiff drink or a bang on the head (anyone with any sense might just have had both).

Agriculture

Major changes happened in agriculture and therefore rural life in the eighteenth century (1700–1800). Up till then, if you'd gone up in your helicopter (which you probably wouldn't have had), you would have seen that the countryside looked a bit like a multi-coloured parquet floor, interrupted by little hamlets of a few ramshackle houses. Each villager would have several individual strips of land. The daft thing was that these ruddy strips weren't next to each other, so he'd often have to trudge long distances between them. Each village would have a largish area called the common land on which the common man could graze his common animals.

Enclosure Acts

The Enclosure Acts were invented to sort this nonsense out. Basically, a couple of guys called commissioners would pitch up at your village once an Enclosure Act had been passed on it. They would then take all the land from everyone and share it out again. The theory was that all the little bits would be lumped together into bigger bits that would be much easier to farm. The poorer you were, however, the more you got screwed on the deal, losing your rights to the much depleted common land to boot. The squires, rich farmers and the local parson (for whom the Lord provided extremely well) usually cleaned up. The country began to look much as it does now with large fields, or enclosures, hemmed in by hedges.

Also the rotation system of farming became all the rage at this time. A farmer would divide his land in, say, four bits and grow different things in each leaving one to lie fallow and just grow grass. Each year he'd swap them round.

Chapter 28:

The Great Land Grab! – 1750

After the war with France, and Bonnie Prince Charlie's abortive rebellion, there were a few rather nervous years of peace. Both Britain and France were scrabbling around, trying to nick land off poor unsuspecting natives all over the uncivilised world. At the same time they were both trying to curry favour (not flavour) with what was left of the great Mogul Empire in India. The French

managed to set up a load of froggy forts along the St Lawrence, Hudson, Ohio, and Mississippi rivers forcing the British colonies to stay along the coast.

By 1755 both sides really took their gloves off and decided to start the Seven Years War. The teams were Britain and Prussia versus France and Austria. The British started badly and were severely slaughtered in America.

1756 – Minorca Goes

The wars went from bad to worse until – shock, horror! England finally lost Minorca (again). This, of course, called for the most drastic action. Luckily a chap called William Pitt the Elder (elder than who? you might ask) joined the government. With the help of General Wolfe – who huffed and puffed and blew the French down – he got back India and Canada. It was called The Year of Victories and by the time the French put their hands up and signed the Peace of Paris in 1763 all they had left were two measly trading stations somewhere in India. Poor old George II missed the party, however, having died of a heart attack, aged seventy-seven, a couple of years before.

By the Way

When things were all going wrong up India way, a complete British garrison of 146 men were captured by the Nawab of Bengal and put in what came to be known as the 'Black Hole of Calcutta'. This was a windowless, ventilationless chamber only 20 ft square. It occurred on the night of 21st June 1756 and when the guards brought them their Cornflakes the following morning, only 23 had survived (which is why they *didn't* get in the Guinness Book of Records).

Chapter 29:

Tea Time!

In 1760 George II had been succeeded by – wait for it – George III who was far worse than his dad or grandad. He wanted to wear his crown every day and rule properly like the olden days, not having to listen to any soppy old Cabinet. This spelt the end for the Whigs who'd been sitting pretty for more than fifty years. It was time for the king and the 'king's friends' to have a go. The king's best friend and adviser was Lord 'Scotch' Bute. The London mobs hated Bute and the king, who they thought was a mummy's boy, so they burned boots (a bad pun on Bute) and petticoats (to represent George's mum) in a huge bonfire.

Pitt was dismissed, having long been regarded as a megalomaniac, but without his leadership, government after government failed. Relations with the colonies became frosty, to say the least, mainly because they refused to tax themselves and send the

cash home. It was a bit like asking someone to beat themselves with their own stick, but the government reckoned they knew best. In the end Parliament decided to do the taxing which steamed up the colonies even more. This row was to lead, eventually, to the American War of Independence.

1773 – Boston Tea Party

The king had hired a real crawler, Lord North, to keep Parliament quiet. He carried on mismanaging affairs of state – especially in America. Although lots of these taxes were repealed a huge tax on tea remained. The result was a huge fancy dress party in Boston when the drunken colonists, dressed as Red Indians, invented a vast, rather salty beverage by throwing £18,000 pounds worth of the East India Company's finest tea into the harbour.

George, who was thought to be going crazy, tried to make it up with Pitt, making him the Earl of Chatham. Pitt, though quite chuffed to be 'lorded' was still, unfortunately, totally opposed to government policy, as were the regenerated Whig party. It was all too late, however, for on the 4th July 1776 Congress issued a Declaration of Independence making George Washington their first President. To this day, Americans have a party, set off fireworks and light bonfires on Independence Day to celebrate breaking away from us lot. Luckily (maybe), Canada remained loyal along with a few of the middle American colonies. Britain occupied New York in an attempt to separate New England from the southern states, but our general (and, believe it or not, comedy playwright) Burgoyne, having advanced from Montreal, was forced to surrender at Saratoga to the revolting Yanks.

1777 – War with France No. 4

The sneaky French and Spanish, never ones to miss a chance of having a go at their oldest foe – the British – decided to make out they were real champions of American liberty and declared war on us. In 1780 the Dutch joined them, followed by just about everyone else. Even Ireland joined in and a 10,000 strong mob, led by the loony Lord George Gordon, took over London for four days. The uprising, famous for its widespread murder and destruction, was called the 'No Popery Riot'. For some idea of what it must have been like, stand outside the Goat and Shamrock at closing time on any Friday night! Lord Gordon (son of Cosmo Gordon) was famous for being totally eccentric. He libelled just about everyone including the French Ambassador, Marie Antoinette, and then the Queen of France. Personally I can't see what all the fuss was about, seeing as we hated the darned French anyway. In 1788 poor Lord Gordon was chucked into Newgate, a particularly horrid prison founded by Sir Dick Wittington, where he languished for the rest of his days. Mind you he was lucky! Many of the rioters were executed on a brilliant new 'Hanging Machine' (or gallows) which remained in Britain until relatively recently.

1782 – Peace Again

Our 'War Against Just About Everybody' had ended, and Britain was for once trying to keep on the right side of everyone. George III had managed to lose most of our new Empire except for India, Canada and Gibralta (which seems plenty to me).

If you ever wondered why our Queen doesn't have more say in modern Britain, you can blame old George. After his constant bungling the Crown was never allowed to poke its nose into the country's affairs again. The Cabinet was restored, with a Prime Minister who was head of the majority party in the Commons – just like now. George did, nevertheless, prefer the Tories to the Whigs and asked young William Pitt the Younger (old William Pitt the Elder's younger boy) to form a ministry. He was only twenty-four.

Mechanisation

Things were zipping along really fast in Britain by this time. Funny-looking, and slightly crude, machines and tools were constantly appearing in the country, helping farmers become more efficient. The beginning of mechanisation in industry meant that

LOVE YOUR NEW MACHINE!

the rich were becoming richer and the poor much, much poorer. Never had the country been so obviously divided, and the natives were getting restless. The dear old Whigs who were all for reform were not to get a look in for fifty years. The Tories, on the other hand, were far too concerned squeezing cash out of the colonies to really lose any sleep over what was happening in Britain.

1789 – French Revolution

Everyone fell about laughing in Britain when they heard about the French Revolution. Watching your old enemy tearing itself apart is always nice from a safe distance. When they topped their King and Queen, however, and started attacking anyone in authority, the

smiles disappeared and the Tories realised that the same thing could happen here if they weren't extremely careful. Strangely enough, old George III was quite liked over here. In spite of everything, the British have never really gone in for Royalty bashing.

1792 – Censorship

The Tories weren't taking any risks, however, and banned the cheaper press. They wouldn't have had to worry if it was these days – our cheap newspapers don't have any news – unless you count what topless Debbie's up to on 'Page Three'.

Public meetings were forbidden and the Act of Habeas Corpus was suspended. This meant that they could shove anyone they liked behind bars or down under to Australia without trial. Young William Pitt, I must explain, had decided – as soon as our Cook discovered Australia in 1770 – that it would be a great place to send all our convicts (who now own the country, and half the world's lager!).

Chapter 30.

Napoleon Rules OK

Things were really hotting up in 'Gay Paree' with heads rolling from left, right and centre. Tumbrils (nice little wooden carts) carrying the poor nobility to – and their slightly shortened bodies from – Madame Guillotine, were as common as red buses in London.

This rough, tough way of setting up a Republic upset the rest of Europe, and soon France was at war with most of it – and doing surprisingly well. This was largely due to a funny 'petit homme' called Napoleon Bonaparte, commander of the new Republican army. This brilliant little fighter was soon to become Emperor of France in 1804 – and just about everywhere else. He was supposed to have had one of the highest IQ's ever recorded and only needed three to four hours sleep a night.

1800 – Britain Gets Nervous
You can imagine how jittery the Brits were getting by this time. Pitt realised that it was just a matter of time before those dratted

French looked over their shoulders and spotted their oldest enemy – us! He tried to do a deal with the Irish, combining the English and Irish Parliaments. This was no doubt because, in the past, the French had always used Ireland as a base from which to attack Britain. This drove poor, old, dopey George even further round the bend as he wouldn't have Catholics in the house, and flatly refused to have anything to do with it.

1801 – United Kingdom

After loads of cash went into the back pockets of the right people, this Anglo/Irish Union went through, and we became the United Kingdom. There was so much fuss, however, that Pitt resigned, and the strain of losing finally sent poor George completely crackers. He spent his last years wandering aimlessly through the huge empty

corridors of Windsor Castle, blind as a bat, deaf as a post, mad as a hatter and gibbering to himself. His white hair and beard hung nearly to his knees and he only ever wore an old purple dressing-gown. During these last years of his reign Britain was effectively ruled by the Dreadful Prince Regent (crowned George IV) but more of him later.

By the Way

It was around this time that William Brodie, a cabinetmaker, head of his union and member of the Edinburgh town council, became the subject of Robert Louis Stevenson's *The Strange Case of Dr Jekyll and Mr Hyde*. During the day he was a well-respected businessman but at night he led a gang of masked robbers. Both of 'him' were eventually caught and hanged.

Meanwhile

1760 – Kew Gardens opened.

1765 – A thirty-eight mile ditch was dug, filled with water, and called the Bridgewater Canal. Canals were soon to become real competitors to roads.

1766 – Cavendish discovered hydrogen to be lighter than air.

1769 – Arkwright invented the first water-powered spinning machine.

1774 – Joseph Priestley discovers dephlo-gisticated air. This was such a mouthful that they later, sensibly, called it oxygen.

1775 – James Watt uses a lot of this new oxygen up, fiddling around with his new-fangled steam engine.

1780 – The first fountain pen invented. Good for writers, and even better for geese (quills?).

1781 – The word QUIZ appears. A Dubliner named Daley bet he could introduce a new word into the English language. He chalked this strange word all over the city (first graffiti?) and everyone tried to guess what it meant. 'Quiz' was born – and its meaning obvious.

1783 – The Montgolfier brothers blew up a balloon, tied it to a basket, and flew away. They weren't the first, however, as earlier that year a sheep, a duck, and a cock had done the same thing watched by King Louis XVI and Marie Antoinette.

1785 – *The Times* newspaper appears for the first time.
1790 – Turner painted the first pictures that looked a bit the same either way up.
1795–1821 – John Keats wrote a lot of new poems which included Ode to a Nightingale and Ode to a Grecian Urn (please don't ask how much a Grecian earns). He should have got the poet's prize for the silliest girl-friend's name – Fanny Brawne!

Chapter 31:

Boney Gets The Boot

Pitt got it all wrong about Napoleon invading Ireland. Boney had a much more ambitious plan. Never one to do things by half, he planned to invade England by sea, air and would you believe it – tunnel. The air attack was going to be from huge, extremely dangerous looking troop-carrying balloons. The tunnel, planned in 1803, was supposed to pop up somewhere on our south coast and surprise us all. It's taken another 200 years to surprise us!!

1804 – War with France No. 5
Before Boney's boys had a chance to put the first spade into the French turf the whole business was scuppered by our very best sailor ever – Horatio Nelson. Although managing to lose things like his eye and his arm, and the contents of his stomach on each voyage he was no slouch when it came to sea battles. He first upset Boney, who was boss in Egypt, when he sank lots of his galleons in the Nile.

1805 – Battle of Trafalgar

Napoleon then thought of this great ruse. While the British fleet under Nelson was protecting the West Indies (which was like Britain's huge piggy bank) the French fleet would suddenly about turn and rush back to hit the unprotected British Isles. One day Nelson turned round and noticed – with his one good eye – that the French had gone, and quickly followed. The French fleet under Villeneuve unexpectedly met another British fleet under Admiral Calder coming from Britain, and was forced to Cadiz where they joined up with the Spanish fleet who were their mates. Nelson's ships caught up with Villeneuve and the Battle of Trafalgar began. By the end of the match the French and Spaniards had lost 4,400 men, with 2,500 wounded, and given 20,000 prisoners. Nelson only lost 450 men, with 1,200 injured, no ships and – oh yes – his life! His chums rather thoughtfully sent him home pickled in a barrel of navy brandy. Napoleon called it a day and gave up all hope of invading England. The Frogs I can safely say have never, to this day, forgiven us.

1808 – Revenge

Just to get his own back, however, Napoleon decided to blockade all British goods from the continental ports which he controlled (The Continental System). Silly little man! He'd obviously forgotten that although he ruled the land, we ruled the sea. The British thought – what's good for the goose is good for the gander. So we beat the French at their own game and stopped any of their goods going into these ports, effectively blockading them instead. This really got up the noses of the occupied continental countries who were getting more than a little fed up with this hook-nosed, red-haired French midget.

Meanwhile, back at the ranch, the Duke of Wellington was preparing an army to help the rebel Spanish nationalists, who'd had enough of French occupation. Wellington was a tough taskmaster, calling his lower ranks the 'scum of the earth'. He was none too impressed with his poncy officers either, who worried so much about their splendid, if somewhat sissy, uniforms, that they were often spotted taking umbrellas onto the battlefield so as not to get wet.

In 1813 Wellington dived into Europe and chased the French all over the place, finally catching and driving them out of Spain at Vittoria before crossing the Pyrenees.

1812 – Things Go Badly for Boney

Napoleon was having a rotten time invading Russia, partly because he had piles and could hardly ride his horse (not surprising); and

partly because when he finally reached Moscow everyone had cleared out apart from thieves and beggars. He'd lost 33,000 men getting there and on one day alone his senior surgeon had sawn off 200 shattered arms and legs (Frogs' legs?).

As they were leaving, the Ruskies set fire to their city and naughtily took all their fire engines. When the fire died down Napoleon realised how perishing cold Russia was and decided to get the first sleigh home. Unfortunately, it was cold enough to freeze the hind leg off a donkey so that his troops, who were fresh out of donkeys anyway, had to leg it (if they had any) home. Thousands died of exposure and starvation on the way back.

He fought on for another couple of years but by then the Russians had joined the Prussians and Austrians and were a formidable force. Meanwhile our boy Wellington was giving it plenty down in the South of France. The Russians captured Paris in 1814 so Bonaparte chucked in the towel.

The French decided they wanted a king again and little Boney was exiled to Elba, an island miles from anywhere.

Tired of beach life (strange for a Frenchman) Napoleon escaped back to France where Louis XVIII was enjoying being King for a bit.

1815 – Waterloo

The army – Boney was delighted to find – were still loyal to their funny ex-leader and followed him to the final showdown. This was the famous battle of Waterloo. Wellington started badly and nearly got the boot (sorry), but at the last minute the Russians arrived – like the cavalry in a cowboy film – and Boney was defeated once and for all. So ended The 20 Years War.

When Britain came out of the war, she found that she'd got a better Empire than ever. She now had Canada, Australia (though full of convicts), India, the Cape Colonies, Ceylon and Guiana. Of course we still had the scattered islands of the West Indies, but they were turning out to be more trouble than they were worth.

1816 – Back in Britain
Despite all this new-found wealth and power it didn't do the average working man in Britain much good. They were just exploited by the nouveau rich and the aristocracy. It wasn't as if they could do anything about it, as they weren't even allowed to vote or have meetings. Despite this the population was rising – probably because there weren't so many dreadful catastrophes to carry them off.

1819 – Bad Times
This post war prosperity was short lived, however. It's all very well churning out loads of wonderful new products but if, after a war, nobody's got any francs, liras or pesetas to pay for them it's all a bit pointless. The Corn Laws weren't much help either. These taxes on imported wheat had been running for years to make the home-grown stuff competitive. The tax at this time was now so high, and

OOH CHARLES, CAN WE AFFORD THE BREAD?

out wheat production so insufficient, that it meant that if you were broke, bread went off the menu. It must also be noted that, despite all the clever new diseases, the number of mouths that now had to be fed had risen to 7,000,000.

The Arts
Dr Johnson and Boswell, both famous writers, had formed the Literary Club – a right arty affair. Members included such all time greats as Oliver Goldsmith and Edmund Burke (fellow scribblers), Sir Joshua Reynolds and Thomas Gainsborough (good with the old paint brushes), Adam Smith (economist), Richard Sheridan (the playwright), Edward Gibbon (a serious historian!), and Robert Adam (builder of posh houses).

By the Way
When Napoleon died in 1821 his head was shaved and the individual hairs were given out as souvenirs. His heart was put into a silver vase and his stomach into a

pepper pot. A bit of his intestines, which ended up at the Royal College of Surgeons, was destroyed in an air raid in 1940. More bizarre still, his most private part, said to be only an inch long and looking like a sea horse, was offered for sale at Christies, the auction house, in 1972. It was listed as a 'small dried up object' but unfortunately failed to reach the reserve price. Apparently the little thing had been nabbed by his confessor priest (I wonder what he'd told him!). Who's got it now?

Meanwhile
1802 – Dalton finally found the atom which was rather difficult owing to it being a bit on the small side.

1803 – Fulton invented the first steamboat and the first torpedo (to sink it).

1807 – Slave trade abolished throughout all the British colonies (about time too!).

1810 – Bikes invented. They weren't much cop, however, as they didn't have any pedals.

1812 – Britain's first cannery set up in Bermondsey, London. Tin cans had only just been invented. Strangely enough, they didn't invent a can opener for another fifty years. I bet I can guess your next question!

1814 – Wordsworth regarded as our top poet. He wrote a daft rhyme about daffs.

1815 – Proper roads started to appear, running the length and breadth of Britain, financed by tolls which were charged at turnpikes. It's interesting to note that after 175 years of free road travel, there's talk of bringing tolls back – (that's progress?).

1819 – A ten-year-old blind boy, Louis Braille invented – Braille.

1820 – Macadam invented tarmac for roads. This made life easier for stage and mail coaches to travel at night. This in turn made life even easier for highwaymen like Dick Turpin, who robbed the rich to pay . . . himself!

YOUR MONEY OR YOUR WIFE.

Chapter 32

Gorgeous George

Crazy old George III finally gave up the ghost in 1820 – not that anyone noticed – as did Castlereagh in 1822, one of his top ministers, who'd also gone wacko. Although Castlereagh's chums had managed to keep him away from sharp objects (there weren't that many ways of killing yourself in those days) he managed to find a tiny penknife and . . . you can imagine the rest.

The Prince Regent, now George IV, had been a right trial to his poor mum and dad all his life. He was a gambler, spendthrift, womaniser and incredible drinker. 'Drunk as a Lord' is an expression directly attributable to our George. Even before he got his dad's gold hat on he had become despised by the British commonfolk, so much so, that he was always surrounded by soldiers, who caught most of the stones intended for him.

Mrs Fitzherbert

He was a sneaky beggar as well. He'd secretly married a widow called Mrs Fitzherbert. It had to be secret because she was a Catholic and all hell would have broken loose if his folks had got to hear about it. As it was, however, it was one of the worst kept secrets ever and eventually our noble Prince dumped her callously, knowing it would put the kybosh on eventually being king. She must have got over it, however, as she is one of the only people to go down in history as having died of exhaustion from a fit of laughing.

Caroline of Brunswick

He quickly married Caroline of Brunswick who, although a German, was definitely born on the right side of the sheets and managed for once to have a legitimate kid. He didn't fancy her for very long (surprise, surprise) and deviously spread tacky rumours about her honour.

While she was on holiday abroad, he wrote and offered her £50,000 not to come home – which sounds rather reasonable to me. She wouldn't hear of it, however, and came back to much public acclaim. George then tried divorce and, using the government like a blunt instrument, attempted to get her for adultery. The magic combination of no evidence and immense public popularity, however, got the case kicked out even though a divorce had been OK'd by the Lords. George then prevented her being let into Westminster Abbey when they were both due to be crowned in 1821. This was the last straw and the shock led to her demise shortly after. George, true to form, went on to live with (and kick out) lots more women.

Someone famous once described him as 'a bad son, a bad husband, a bad father, a bad subject, a bad monarch, and a bad friend' (not bad eh!). Having said all this, however, someone else famous said of him – 'he was very polished ... knew how to listen ... was affectionate, sympathetic and gallant ... with some wit and great penetration'. In fact, if you were his mate, most people thought he was a great laugh, terribly charming and extremely flash with his cash. His parties sounded really fab with no expense spared,

and it must be noted he was a recognised expert in food and wine. George was also extremely kind and supportive to artists and writers like Jane Austen and Walter Scott.

Unfortunately, his generosity didn't extend to his poorer subjects of whom he was, apparently, blissfully unaware. His extravagance was unequalled even though he was supposed to make do on what would now be £2,000,000 a year (Try me! Try me!). He built the rather gross Buckingham Palace as a little London pad, and the totally over the top (and brill) Brighton Pavilion for somewhere different to go at weekends.

1822 – Foreign Affairs

Meanwhile back to what was happening elsewhere. The king had long ceased favouring the Whigs, and a new Tory government was born under Lord Liverpool with three prominent liberal members –

Canning, Huskisson and Peel. Canning told the United States that Britain would help if any of those nasty European countries started any funny business. Huskisson repealed the Combination Acts which had made Trade Unions illegal. Peel invented the first proper police who were called 'Peelers' in 1829. Women (police) weren't thought of till 1920 but probably arrested anyone who referred to them by that name.

WHO INVENTED YOU?

1829 – Catholics

Catholics for the first time (incredibly) since 1673 were allowed to have high position. This was OK until they tried to get into Parliament which the Tories thought was well over the top. However, faced with a civil war in Ireland, they passed the Catholic Emancipation Act in 1829. This split the Tories so much that, at the General Election, the year after George IV's succession, they lost to the wiley Whigs. The Tory stranglehold on Parliament went down the drain after sixty years of power.

Chapter 33:

England Gets Into Training – 1830

Canals in England were becoming a bit of a liability. In hot weather they tended to dry up and in cold weather they froze. If this wasn't bad enough, the owners were beginning to get a bit greedy, charging pocketfuls of cash (as tolls), if you wanted to use them. The answer came with the invention of the steam locomotive. The first proper modern railway came in 1825 and ran between Stockton and Darlington. Five years later the famous Liverpool–Manchester line opened. This was largely due to George Stephenson who not only won a competition to build the best engine, but also made and laid the rails for it to run on.

Rail Travel
The good old class system was not forgotten. The rich travelled first class in comfortable enclosed carriages. The not-so-rich were seated, but travelled in the open air. The other poor souls travelled

in open trucks, like cattle, with no seats (not that cattle would necessarily want them). All this would have been fine if the track ran along the sunny Côte d'Azur, but Liverpool to Manchester – please!

The Rocket, as it was called, reached unheard of speeds of up to – wait for it – 29 mph. This really brassed off the folk whose homes and land lay alongside the new tracks. They claimed it would lead to no birds or horses (God knows why?), eggless hens, milkless cows, and general mayhem. Moan, moan, moan!! They should have seen our M25 . . . on a *good* day!

1830 – Huskisson Gets the Rocket

At the opening ceremony Huskisson, the ex-Cabinet minister, largely responsible for the building of the railway, had rather a horrid accident. He got out of his carriage while the Rocket was turning round and was gaily rabbiting with the Duke of Wellington. While being congratulated, someone yelled to him to get out of the way. Poor Huskisson panicked and leapt back straight in front of the brand new engine which ran over his legs (ouch). He died shortly afterwards (and probably didn't get his fare back).

Coaches

The Stagecoach companies soon went broke as tracks criss-crossed the land like the lines on the palm of your hand, but in the towns it was a different story. Steam coaches were becoming all the rage until boring old Parliament passed a boring old law that said they couldn't travel at more than 2 mph. Even then they had to have

some poor nerd walking sixty yards ahead carrying a red flag. I know some people that drive as if that law's still in force. Anyway steam coaches soon dropped out and horse-drawn coaches stayed (and messed up the streets) for many more years.

In the early nineteenth century only one person in a hundred had a vote and some newish cities like Manchester and Birmingham weren't represented in Parliament at all. The old Iron Duke (Wellington) thought this was fine and strongly disapproved of doing anything about it. Around this time (1820), revolution hung heavy in the air all over Europe. In England, the Enclosure Movement had forced loads of little farmers into the red and they were sucked into the towns where all the horrible smoke-belching factories were spreading like weeds on a back lawn.

By the Way

As Mrs Fitzherbert couldn't be seen in public with the Prince Regent, he had a tunnel dug between his flash Pavilion and her place, across the road.

Working Conditions

As supply was greater by far than demand, the unscrupulous owners only employed those who'd work for the least money (what's different!), so wages actually shrank. Whole families, including little kids, had to work long hours just to get enough to eat. If they got sick it was tough bananas as far as the factory owners were concerned. They were as happy as pigs in muck, living in huge country houses, not giving a damn about the conditions their workers were forced to suffer. Trade Unions took years before they had enough clout to tell these rich skinflints where to get off.

The natives were getting restless, however, and there were strikes and mini-riots all over the shop. The Whigs, who didn't have the same blinkered view as the Tories, realised that they'd better do something. Led by Earl Grey (of smelly tea fame) they managed to squeeze a Reform Bill through which started to sort things out.

The Reforms of this Era

1. To get rid of all the pocket or 'rotten' Boroughs which sometimes had carried as many votes as huge towns.
2. £20,000 a year was to be given to church societies who were educating young children (presumably not the poor miserable little perishers that were working).
3. The State assumed responsibility for the poor. They didn't do much, but they did assume responsibility!

4. The Municipal Reform Act. This meant that towns had to mind their own business through municipalities elected by the rate-payers.
5. The Factories Act was passed. This meant that kids of under nine shouldn't work and that when they did, it shouldn't be for more than nine hours. This was all very well, but it doesn't take the Brain of Britain to fathom out that they weren't working for fun, and that if they didn't, the family would be in a worse state than before.
6. The Poor Law Amendment Act was passed in 1834. Groups of parishes clubbed together to form Poor Law Unions with an elected board of governors. The net result of this turned out to be the infamous workhouses where, if you were a pauper and having a miserable time, you went there and had a worse one. They were, therefore, mostly full of widows and orphans who had little choice.

Chapter 34:

Just William

As far as monarchs were concerned, we'd had weak ones, strong ones, jolly ones, wicked ones, grumpy ones and gay ones but George IV had been the pits. The Crown had never reached such an all time low. When he died, the next one up was William, his brother. George's daughter, Charlotte, who would have been queen, had selfishly died in 1817. When William first heard of her death he realised that soon he would be king as old George already had one foot in the grave. At the time he was living with his housekeeper who looked after him (in more ways than one) and had given him several children. William realised she wouldn't do and that her time was up. He quickly changed her for a better model, marrying instead Princess Adelaide of Saxe-Meiningen who, although a bit of a dragon, had far more Crown 'cred'.

Country Couple

William IV had always been a bit of a sailor having started on ships at fourteen. He'd become a close chum of Horatio Nelson and was given the actual bullet which killed him, to treasure for ever (sick or what?). He hated cities, so when he married his Fraulein, they went to live in Windsor which in those days was all fields. Adelaide spent most of her time running a model dairy (you'd think he could have bought her a real one).

William was a bit of an old fusspot by all accounts – faddy, snappy, often grouchy, always getting uptight over the silliest things, and constantly repeating himself... repeating himself. Mind you the poor old beggar, who was in his sixties, had a right to be a bit fed up. When he succeeded to the throne in 1830 he discovered he'd been left mounds of paperwork to do, owing to the mess his brother had left things in. It's reported that he had to dip his hands in a bowl of hot water regularly because the constant signing of documents caused agony to his rheumatic joints.

1835 – More Reforms

William's reign, though short, saw momentous changes. He had eventually consented to the Reform Bills. Big deal! If he hadn't there'd have been a civil war. These bills, in retrospect, went a long way towards the process of government 'of the people, by the people, for the people' which we now call democracy. We might not have it – but at least we know what to call it!

At this time a whole new sort of people were emerging, neither particularly rich nor particularly poor. They were to grow into the dreaded Great British Middle Class.

On a lighter note, William was the first monarch to let Londoners stroll about in (and mess up) his huge back gardens which are now the Royal Parks.

Adelaide, his gripey and somewhat haughty wife, had a thing about kids (as both hers had died) and was always having loads of nephews and nieces round to their castle for tea. There was, however, one little girl who didn't get invited, as her mum, the Duchess of Kent, couldn't stand the Queen. She was a rather plain, strange and very serious kid who always played alone. She was to become the smallest but longest reigning monarch that Britain ever had.

Chapter 35:

V For Victoria

When only eleven Princess Victoria was told that one day she'd be Queen. She wasn't too wild about it at first and bawled her eyes out. When she had stopped snivelling, she sat bolt upright and swore to her governess, 'I'll be good'.

She was crowned when eighteen in 1837, a funny-looking little thing (five foot), with pop eyes and a tiny little cupid's-bow mouth. She wore sombre clothes from the word go and didn't seem to get the jokes much. She was guided by the Prime Minister, Lord Melbourne, who told her to take it easy at first and not rock any boats. She managed to keep her funny wee nose out of public affairs for a couple of years, but when Melbourne resigned due to his position being so weak, she had a real scrap with his successor, Sir Robert Peel. He'd told her that she must replace her Ladies of the Bedchamber who were Whigs – with Tories. She refused – Peel resigned – Melbourne came back – she said sorry to Peel – and everyone lived happily ever after.

1838 – Prince Albert

Well! not actually 'ever' after, I must confess. When approaching marriage, two years later in 1840, Melbourne gradually lost his influence with her and old Peely got in again. The object of Victoria's affection was Prince Albert of Saxe-Coburg, her cousin, who she'd quietly fancied for years. It beats me why they always seemed to marry Germans (fat lot of good it ever did us). It's interesting to note; because she was a queen and he was only a prince, she had to do the asking. All they really had to do to keep the support of the nation was to stay married and have loads of nice normal nippers. Court life, as you now know, had been a bit dicky for many years to say the very least. After all, the young couple followed a bad king (George II), a mad king (George III), and a total buffoon (George IV).

1840 – Hungry 40s

The years between 1840 and 1850 were called the 'hungry 40s'. This was because 1. wages were terribly low, and 2. the Corn Laws were still keeping bread prices terribly high. A loaf of bread cost almost as much as some poor devil's daily wage. When the potato crop failed in 1845, thousands of Irish died of starvation and the rest went to America where they all seemed to become slightly soppy policemen in films! Victoria wrote in her diary that the Irish famine was 'too terrible to think of' so – apart from cutting down on an extra slice of toast for breakfast – she didn't.

Things only cheered up when Sir Robert Peel, who'd taken over from Melbourne, chucked the Corn Laws in favour of free trade, bringing bread prices down instantly. Despite this Victoria still thought he was a creep, but realised that being the head of the Conservative (new name for Tory) party she had to either like it or lump it. Vicky therefore decided to like it and they eventually became quite matey.

IT'S THE LEAST I CAN DO!

1842 – Chartists

Britain wasn't alone with its widespread poverty. All over Europe the poor were on the verge of starving and revolution was again in the air. The growth in England of the middle classes and their representation in Parliament had really put the working classes' noses out of joint and they were feeling well fed up. A 'Charter' was prepared by six tame MPs and six workers, which again proposed 'Votes for All'. A monster petition was collected but, when Parliament predictably kicked it out, the only solution the 'Chartists' saw was to have a major punch up. 20,000 special constables were enrolled (including, believe it or not, the future Emperor Napoleon III) to meet a huge demonstration on Clapham Common, but in the end it rained cats and dogs and was a washout. Napoleon Junior, by the way, had crossed the channel with his Madame because his angry subjects were polishing up, and looking lovingly at, their dear old guillotine again.

1851 – The Great Exhibition

The British, as always, remained loyal and things started to cheer up a bit. Prince Albert organised 'The Great Exhibition' in Hyde Park which chuffed Victoria no end. A ginormous palace of glass and steel was erected and the British goods that we were trying to flog to punters from all over the world were displayed. If you can imagine a huge Ideal Home Exhibition – don't! It was actually quite tasteful. Victoria, unlike many of the Royals today, wasn't a snob

and preferred the simple life and simple folk of the country rather than knocking around with the fashion conscious trendies of London. She was happiest spending time with the old man and their nine kids either on the Isle of Wight or up in Scotland.

Albert the Diplomat

Prince Albert was gradually let in on all the affairs of State and turned out to be rather sensible. It was largely due to his intervention, that we didn't fall headlong into another war. A dispatch was about to be sent to the United States Government which was apparently so stroppy that there was only one way for them to react. Albert intervened, deleted the nasty bits, and saved our bacon. He was only forty-two at the time but, physically, seemed to have just about everything wrong with him. He died in the same year and Victoria never got over it. She built a daft memorial, a big bridge and a round hall; all are still to be seen in London and all are called Albert.

Poor Victoria put on a black dress and stayed indoors for over two years. She dealt with all the affairs of State from Buck House and when either the Liberals (new name for Whigs) or the Conservatives (new name for the Tories) wanted to see her, they had to go to the trades-men's entrance. She was hardly to show her face (or black body) again till the 50th anniversary of her reign in 1887. The crowd went barmy as she was still, strangely enough, really popu-lar. The lesson to all monarchs must be – if you want to stay on the right side of us common folk, keep your head down and don't give us anything to bitch about.

Chapter 36

Any More For More War!

Politically loads had been happening. When old Peel died both the Conservative and the Liberal parties were split, neither managing to get a majority. The first coalition government was therefore formed under Lord Aberdeen with Palmerston in charge of wars. In 1854 we joined the French (Mon Dieu! Can you believe it?) to fight the Russians who were giving the Turks a hard time up the Crimea, an area by the Black Sea grabbed by the Ruskies in 1783.

1854 – Crimean War

It was a particularly nasty scrap conducted in the nastiest of conditions. Although the allies were winning, the cost was terrible. Thousands of our boys, on one occasion, found out the hard way when the stupid Lord Cardigan, commander of the Light Brigade, decided to see whether swords and bayonets could beat cannon-balls at the Battle of Balaclava. The boys that weren't massacred suffered dreadfully from lack of food, and the freezing cold. Even the horses died from exposure (aah!). As if that wasn't enough, cholera came along and the death rate topped 100 a day.

Palmerston was made Prime Minister and stopped all the mucking about – winning the war in 1856.

1854 – Florence Nightingale

About the only person to come out of the whole thing with any credit, was Florence Nightingale who did wonders when she finally arrived at the military hospitals. Her actions inspired a whole new breed of women called Suffragettes who believed that they should have more say in how things were run and were to give the chauvinist politicians a great run for their money. Strange as it may seem, Florence was a terrible hypochondriac. When she got home from the war she went straight to bed telling everyone she had a terrible heart condition and that her life hung by a thread. It must

I STUPIDLY SAID I'D STAY TILL THE END.

have been a blooming strong thread as she stayed tucked up for another fifty-four years before eventually being proved right (aged ninety).

1857 – Indian Mutiny

The Crimean war was neatly followed by the Indian Mutiny. It appears the Indians were getting their turbans in a twist over the non-too-subtle introduction of western ways. Apparently, it came to a head when they discovered that their soldiers were being supplied with cartridges greased in the fat of the sacred cow or the abominable pig. They went crazy. (I doubt if the cows or pigs were that wild about it either!) We quietened them down, however, and by 1858 the British government had India safely under its rather expensive boot.

1861 – American Civil War

This bloody war was an attempt by the southern states to break away from those of the north. It curiously pointed out the rift in thinking between the British rich and poor. Despite a cotton famine the working classes supported honest Abe Lincoln and the north, while the upper classes predictably favoured the rich southern slave owners. Parliament sensibly (for once) sat on the political fence and left them to it. When Lincoln and the north won, however, Britain's relations remained somewhat cool.

1864 – Bismarck

Palmerston's last attempt at diplomacy finally landed him in the sh ... ade! Bismarck, head Prussian minister, wanted to grab two nice fat Austrian Duchies to add to his Empire. Palmerston jumped up and down and threatened him with God knows what. Bismarck went ahead – Palmerston did nothing – Bismarck triumphed – Palmerston died – and a tough new European power was born.

In 1871 the French Empire was eventually crushed by the Prussians (tee hee!) and we got their ex-Emperor (and ex-policeman) back, with his flash Spanish wife, Eugenie. Actually we shouldn't laugh because although we'd never been that pally with the French, it was certainly a case of better the Frog you know than the Kraut you don't. This, you see, really was the beginning of the German Empire and we all know what fun they were going to be.

Britain again remained neutral – not really surprising seeing as the Germans had married half our Royal family. In fact one of Victoria's girls was the wife of the new German Emperor himself. Had Victoria not been thick with Mr and Mrs Napoleon, who for some strange reason settled in Chislehurst, Britain might have got hitched to Germany (urghh – I hate sauerkraut).

Mind you Britain's Empire wasn't doing badly either during Victoria's reign. Our Empire's population expanded from 96 to 240 million people and the land it covered went from eight to twelve million square miles. You don't have to be Einstein to work out that one day there'd be a population problem.

By the Way

It is generally believed to be true that William Mildin the 14th Earl of Streatham was the inspiration for Edgar Rice Burroughs' *Tarzan of the Apes*. In 1868 he was reputedly shipwrecked on the West African coast when only eleven years old. He lived with a nice family of monkeys for fifteen years before being found and returned home (where he no doubt lived up a tree in the back garden).

Meanwhile

1827 – John Walker of Stockton-on-Tees invented matches and sells the first box.

1834 – Houses of Parliament burnt down (probably lit by a match). To be rebuilt as they are now.

1837 – Stocks banned. Stocks were a punishment used widely throughout Britain. The victim's arms and legs would be sandwiched between two heavy blocks of wood and he'd be left in a public place to be ridiculed by the hoi-polloi.

1837 – Charles Dickens wrote *Oliver Twist*.

1845 – Robert Thomson patented a hollow rubber tyre filled with horsehair (nice to know horses were still useful).

1848 – The Pre-Raphaelites started trying (rather badly) to paint pictures like early Italians.

1848 – Public Health Act passed to try to prepare for cholera which was on its way from all those foreigners.

1850s – Tennyson and Browning dominated poetry.

1853 – Press gangs were banned. These were gangs of savage sailors who grabbed ordinary men in the streets and forced them to be in the Navy.

1853–1856 – Livingstone crossed Africa (and got lost).

WHERE AM I?

1856 – Bessemer mass-produced steel.

1858 – Brunel's 32,000 ton ship the *Great Eastern* launched in London. It was the biggest ship ever seen – and the biggest flop.

1859 – Charles Darwin gobsmacked all Christians by writing *The Origin of the Species* in which he stated that God had got it wrong and that we developed from monkeys. Further proof of this can be seen in the P.G. Tips ads.

1870 – Home Rule was a term created for the Irish demand for self-government.

1874 – Levi Strauss invented jeans in America, I wonder if he realised that it was to become THE uniform.

Chapter 37:

Glad To Be Gladstone – 1865

Palmerston was dead and the two contenders for his job were Disraeli, the Conservative, and Gladstone, the Liberal. Disraeli kicked off, and in an attempt to woo the working class, passed another Reform Bill in 1867. The canny poor weren't having any of it, however. The following year they chucked him out in favour of Gladstone. This peeved Victoria because although she really liked Disraeli, she thought Gladstone a 'deluded old fanatic' (her words). She once commented, 'He speaks to me as if I were a public meeting,' which I think's quite funny for a queen.

Nevertheless, reforms followed thick and fast and were as follows:

1. Voting was made secret.
2. The army was reorganised so the rich and priviliged couldn't buy themselves commissions (to be officers).
3. Trade Unions were made legal (at long last).
4. A Land Act protected tenants from their unscrupulous landlords (at longer last).
5. The Anglican church chucked out of Ireland.
6. Universities were open to all (unless you were thick).
7. Primary schools were finally introduced in 1870 (but you didn't have to go).
8. Not really a reform I suppose. Victoria allowed the Anti-Homosexual Bill (poor Bill) to go through, but, as she couldn't even conceive that lesbianism was possible, struck out any female references.

Unfortunately, it was too much change too soon and poor old Gladstone had to swop with Disraeli again. Anyone for tennis?

1877 – Empress of India

Meanwhile, being just a queen was turning out to be a bit downmarket for Victoria. Disraeli, who was always looking for

different ways of being even more popular (creep), offered her the chance of being an Empress in 1877, which she jumped at. OK, it was only Empress of India, but you've got to start somewhere. Disraeli, now her favourite Prime Minister, took over a big chunk of South Africa in the famous 'Scramble for Africa', but Parliament changed ends again and spoilsport Gladstone gave it back to the Boers (Dutch farmers). Vicky even came out of retirement to join in the scrap.

1884 – The Irish Question
Everything came to a head over Home Rule for Ireland (so what's new?). The Liberals thought Ireland should mind its own business and the Conservatives thought we should mind it for them (in a nutshell). Gladstone's colleagues rebelled and the Liberals and Irish Nationalists were beat hands down. Gladstone resigned after fourteen years in office and the Irish question was left – all together now – unsettled.

1885 – Lord Salisbury
Disraeli was dead and Gladstone retired. Now we either had Lord Salisbury who, although a fine Conservative, is largely remembered for being the last Prime Minister to have a beard; or Lord Rosebery, who is largely remembered for being one of the first not to (no crummy Thatcher jokes please!).

Poor old Victoria was getting a touch ancient but Britain was strong, cocky and fighting fit. Apart from the Crimean War and that bit of trouble in India our Empire was behaving itself. Britain was becoming 'The workshop of the world' and 'abroad' was queuing up to buy whatever we made. London had by this time also become the world's financial centre.

1886 – Europe

By now, however, things were looking a bit different. America and the united countries of Europe (dominated by the horrible Hun), were catching up and nibbling at our heels. The thing that got the Europeans hot and bothered was that, unlike Great Britain, they didn't have any possessions abroad (to exploit) and they were dead jealous.

It was the Belgians (who are they? You might ask) who were sniffing around Africa and had already nabbed the Congo. We weren't doing too badly, having grab-bed Nigeria, Kenya, Nyasaland (now Malawi) and Rhodesia (now Zambia and Zimbabwe) and sharing the Sudan with Egypt. Only the Germans who'd bagged Tanganyika (now Tanzania) prevented us from controlling everything from South Africa to Cairo.

1886 – Africa

When gold fever hit the Transvaal – a Dutch Republic which the Boers set up to get away from the British – it was invaded by British 'cowboys' determined to make a killing (financially). When, with inimitable British cheek, these invaders demanded the vote, a huge scrap broke out which quickly developed into the Boer War. The whole world thought we were creeps but in the end we won and the Transvaal and the Orange Free State became ours in 1902. And what creeps we were! The British burned most of the Boer farms and herded the occupants into 'concentration camps'. Thousands died in these atrocious places much to the horror of the British at home. It has been said that these camps gave Hitler (coming soon) his very worst ideas.

1888 – At Home

At home the Local Government Act replaced a system unchanged since Tudor times. Education was made free. Even though the

Factories Act and the Housing Act were passed, most of the working class were still appallingly poverty stricken. Trade Unionism was crouched ready to leap in and kick the exploiting employers where it hurt most. In 1893 Keir Hardie founded the first Independent Labour Party and in 1900 a conference of the Trade Unions, Socialist Societies, and the new Co-operative Movement, formed the Labour party that we know today. In the same year Gladstone tried to get Home Rule for Ireland again. It was okay with the Commons but the Lords would have none of it and kicked it out.

By this time the European situation was looking extremely poorly. The struggle to snatch colonies had led to a full-blown arms race. Europe was split into two huge camps with Germany, Austria and Italy on one side, and France and Russia on the other. Britain stayed 'Splendidly Aloof' but watched nervously as the Krauts built a fleet to shoo us off the waves (which Britannia ruled), and started supporting the boring Boers, who were getting a bit fed up with being bossed around by the British in Africa.

By the Way
In 1888 the world's best known murderer, Jack The Ripper, was roaming the streets of East London. He murdered ten prostitutes, with names like 'Clay Pipe Alice' and 'Carroty Nell', in such a horrible way that the police thought he must have been a surgeon. His identity is a mystery to this day. At least ten movies and 200 books have described his lurid exploits.

Meanwhile

1876 – Alexander Graham Bell rang someone on the phone he'd just invented (and probably got a wrong number).

1877 – Thomas Edison invented the record player.

1877 – W. Hirschel invented fingerprinting in India to stop the crafty old army pensioners from drawing their pensions twice.

1878 – Cleopatra's Needle a 3,500-year-old priceless obelisk brought from Egypt in a specially designed ship called the *Cleopatra* (what a coincidence). It was erected on the Thames Embankment to commemorate our victory over Napoleon.

1885 – Karl Benz, a German, drove the first successful petrol-driven car (a Merc?).

1886 – Coca Cola is invented in America, and advertised as 'Esteemed Brain Tonic and Intellectual Beverage'. Bet they were glad when they thought of 'The Real Thing'.

1892 – Zip Fastener invented and called the C-Curity. Unfortunately, the inventor hadn't got it quite right and it was liable to spring open at any time (very embarrassing!).

1893 – First breakfast cereal, Shredded Wheat, invented by H K Perky (I bet he was).

1895 – First movie shown in Paris.

1895 – Marconi turned on the first wireless (and probably got the Archers).

1897 – Thomas Edison switched on the first light bulb.

Chapter 38:

Eddie For King – 1901

When poor little old Victoria died it was her dear son Edward's turn. He was sixty years old and, unlike his mum, liked to be seen out and about having a good time. It's fair to say that the British had had enough of a ruler who was always behind closed curtains. I suppose if you're paying all that money, you want to see something for it.

The country, by this time, needed very little maintenance from the top as it was now totally run by Parliament. This left Edward with loads of free time to indulge his many pleasurable pastimes. He was always to be seen at the race tracks, at the theatre, and with women who definitely weren't his wife.

It's fair to say that he wasn't the cleverest king we've ever had, hating anything that required the slightest bit of concentration. He once described the first submarine, which he had to inspect, as 'very complicated, with lots of brass'. Sounds like a man after my own heart.

He had married a Danish princess called Alexandra in 1863 who was not only popular with the great British public, but also with her mother-in-law (the queen), who by that time was a grouchy old misery and not at all easy to please. Edward's favourite pastime was one of the worst kept secrets in history and his lady 'friends' included Jennie Churchill (Winston's mum) and Lillie Langtry (the famous actress).

Edward VII and the French

Don't get the impression, however, that Edward was a useless king. As a diplomat he really did the business, especially over in France, where he was often to be seen – usually in Paris – usually having a 'bon' time – and usually with someone he shouldn't have been with. This popularity with the French (highly suspicious?) led to the Treaty of Alliance called the Entente Cordiale in 1904 which was to become 'trés' useful as you will soon see.

Edward's loose lifestyle caught up with him, and he was only to reign for nine years, dying in 1910.

By the Way

The Labour Party first appeared in Parliament in 1906 when twenty-nine MPs were returned. There were already twenty-two Trade Unionist MPs who, although attached to the Liberals, were really more inclined to Labour.

Meanwhile

1901 – Rudyard Kipling wrote the *Just So Stories*.

1903 – First aeroplane flight by the Wright brothers in America.

1905 – Hubert Booth invented the first vacuum cleaner (horse-drawn). When first used in London it was so noisy it caused the horses to bolt (with the vacuum cleaner!).

1909 – Henry Ford manufactured the first production line car – the Model T. You could have any colour, he said, as long as it was black!

1909 – Bleriot managed to fly the English Channel.

1910 – Huge balloons called Zeppelins used as the first commercial air service and later to bomb London. Why didn't we pop them?

1911 – Ernest Rutherford found a proton (a who – ton?).

1912 – *Titanic* hit an iceberg and 1513 poor passengers drowned.

1912 – George Bernard Shaw wrote *Pygmalion*, a story about a common young miss what gets posh.

1913 – Stravinsky's *Rite of Spring* booed off stage in London.

1914 – Ernest Swinton invented the tank for Britain (came in useful).

1917 – The Russian Revolution. Tsar Nicholas abdicates. Lenin and the Bolsheviks take power. Royalty went out – Communism came in.

Chapter 39:

War Of The World

At the time of Victoria's death the Prime Minister was Balfour, a Conservative, but by 1906 the Liberals had swept him away.

They had promised the grumbling workers they'd put a stop to the rising prices and falling wages. Campbell-Bannerman, and later Lord Asquith, went a long way to achieving this and also brought in free grub for school children; slum clearance; and fixed minimum wages (they were ridiculously low, but at least fixed). You don't get anything for nothing in this life, and cash had to be found to pay for the many reforms. They looked, for the first time, towards the rich landowners and decided to tax them properly – and about time too.

When Lloyd George (who looked a bit like Charlie Chaplin) proposed a further super tax, swiftly followed by – shock – horror – a land tax, the House of Lords boiled over and squealed like stuck piglets. They rejected the whole new budget, and most of the reforms for good measure.

1910 – George V

By this time we had a new king (George V), who seemed quite a reasonable bloke. Lloyd George appealed to him to help squash the power of the loaded Lords. This, surprisingly, he did and the Lords, even more surprisingly, put their aristocratic hands up and gave in. From then on, the House of Lords has only been somewhere warm to go for a few doddery old ex-politicians and the rather inbred relics of our nobility's glorious past. The House of Commons, from that point in history, called all the shots as Britain's sole legislative body.

1911 – Politicians

In 1911 MPs started to be paid. In the past, all politicians were either self-made men, or had come from old money. Either way, they were definitely not short of a few quid. By giving them a salary of £450 a year (now £20,000) it meant, at last, that ordinary working chaps could (if voted for) get a seat in the Commons. The Trade Unions were also allowed to shove cash in their candidates' back pockets – a decision which was to change British politics to this day.

When the reforms came, however, it was a bit like locking the stable door after the horse had bolted. Britain was in the full flow of social turmoil or, in other words, fed up to the back teeth. There were serious strikes, particularly of the miners and railwaymen; the Suffragettes started chaining themselves to railings as a protest, fed

up with waiting for the women's vote; Welsh non-conformists were baying for the dis-establishment of their Church, and the Irish Nationalists were demanding Home Rule yet again. By 1914 the southern Catholics were on the verge of civil war with the Protestant Orangemen of Ulster (the same old problem).

When the natives become restless, there's nothing like a Royal wedding or a war to unite them. As Britain's royalty had no one to marry off, it seemed like the trouble brewing in Europe could be rather timely.

1914 – Trouble with Germany Again

Germany was still up to its old tricks, trying to expand its Empire by bullying defenceless little countries; and Austria had upset the Russians by snatching Bosnia and Herzegovina. The arms race changed gear and in 1914 when a silly Serb murdered the heir to the Austrian Empire the powder keg finally blew.

Austria declared war on Serbia – Germany on Russia and France. When the Krauts invaded Belgium (which Lloyd George called a 'little five-foot five nation'), Britain drew its guns and declared war as it had done years before when France and Spain had tried the same thing.

Britain's Allies

If it seems a bit like David challenging Goliath, it wasn't. Luckily we had some big tough boys to stand behind us. Canada, Australia, New Zealand, South Africa, and even India and Ireland, were in our gang and prepared to roll their sleeves up and get stuck in. Mind you, having said all that, they didn't have much choice did they?

Soon the whole world was tearing itself apart and, by the time the Yanks joined the fray in 1917, Britain alone had lost 1,000,000

FRENCH PIG

of its young men, mostly in the disgusting trench warfare of France.

Before long, however, Germany was on its knees. By 1918 they'd lost the war, all their colonial empire, a big bit of their European territory, all their fleet and all their money – and it jolly well served them right. But did it teach them a lesson? Wait and see.

1918 – League of Nations

Something worthwhile did seem to come from the Great War. President Wilson of the United States suggested an international association to prevent the same thing happening again (oh dear! oh dear!). Everyone promised to behave themselves except Russia and – can you believe it – the United States, who said it was too idealistic.

Wars are funny things. Apart from reducing the population in a rather dramatic way, they sometimes have surprising side effects. The British had become united against the common foe; the class system and the battles between the workers and their bosses being almost forgotten. The Suffragettes got the vote for all women – as a prize for being so helpful in the war. After the First World War business boomed for a couple of years and everything looked OK for a prosperous future, so we didn't have to have a Royal wedding!

1919 – Ireland Again

Things weren't so rosy in Ireland – surprise! surprise! Not only were they after Home Rule, but now the extremist Sinn Feiners wanted a totally independent Republic. The long expected civil war broke out, at last, and Parliament sent thousands of out of work ex-soldiers (called the Black and Tans) to sort them out. A good comparison could be made between their nickname and the Rottweiler dog's colouring. They were just as vicious and brainless, making things much, much worse.

Finally, to cut a long war short, Ireland was split in two. The southern Irish Free State in the south, and the rest in the north.

If only they'd thought of this in Tudor times, centuries of violent, Irish, argy-bargy might have been saved (or might not!).

The Depression

The post-war boom was short lived and the 20s and 30s brought a terrible slump. Anyone who did manage to make anything couldn't sell it as most of the 'civilised' world was flat broke. Even America was depressed (poor thing), and as for central Europe, it was on the verge of starvation (wars are jolly fun, aren't they?).

Britain was one of the last to fall, but when it did, it really scraped the bottom of the barrel. Hunger marches and strikes followed huge unemployment. Surprisingly, the figure of 3,000,000 out of work was about the same as it is now (OK I know the population was smaller!).

Labour, as always in hard times, gained more and more support, becoming the third great political party. In 1922 the Conservatives didn't want to play any more and left Lloyd George's coalition. Unfortunately, they took the ball with them, and Bonar Law (daftest name for a PM yet), followed shortly by Stanley Baldwin (who sounds like a northern footballer), formed a Conservative government. They prescribed protectionism as the sweet pill that would make everything better. It didn't, and soon, inevitably, the first Labour government, headed by Ramsay MacDonald, knocked them out, offering a different-flavoured pill to make everything better. It didn't work either, and Stan Baldwin came back with a vast majority. What happened to the Liberals? Don't ask! From that day on, Lloyd George, and the Liberals, were never to be a serious threat to the Conservatives or Labour again.

1924 – Winston Churchill

Baldwin's chancellor was Winston Churchill, who re-imposed import duties to protect ourselves from cheapo imports. Unfortunately, by returning to the gold standard (please don't ask), he made our products more expensive which made the depression even worse. By 1926 the cat was completely out of the bag and a General Strike hit Britain like a sledgehammer. It only lasted ten days and then collapsed taking the Trade Union Council with it. Acts were swiftly passed to keep these naughty unions in order, but this upset the workers so much that they voted Labour again, welcoming MacDonald back in 1929.

Then – shock, horror! – the American economy hit the deck, and the rest of the world's economy slipped further down the cliff. Old MacDonald formed a 'National Government'. This is a clever political trick that a not-very-good government uses when it hasn't got a blinking clue how to get itself out of the sh . . . ambles. It really means that by sharing the power with the other party you don't cop all the blame yourself. The joke was that this Parliament had 471 Conservatives but only 52 Labour members, so poor old Mac was left leading practically an all-Conservative government which was a bit embarrassing.

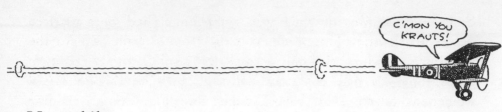

Meanwhile

1919 – Alcock and Brown managed to fly the Atlantic.

1922 – Broadcasting started from the BBC.

1926 – Baird invented something called a television.

1927 – Charles Lindbergh ran out of pals so flew the Atlantic alone.

1927 – First talking pictures. Cinema owners finally shot the piano players.

1928 – The great Walt Disney gave birth to the even greater Mickey Mouse.

1929 – US stock market collapsed heralding another world depression.

1930 – The first supermarket opened in New York.

Chapter 40:

Back At The Palace – 1936

When George V died his eldest boy Edward VIII was next in line and the British Empire, now called the Commonwealth, were delighted as he'd spent so much time visiting them. All except India who were fed up with the British and wanted them to clear out. Unfortunately, Edward had this American girlfriend called Mrs

Simpson, who was not only still married, but had been married before (tut! tut!). This went down like a lead balloon with the government, who told him it was to be her or the crown. Apparently it's just not done to have divorced AMERICAN women as queens. (I'd have thought anything was better than Germans.) Anyway, they obviously thought it was a flash in the pan and that he'd give her up. They were wrong for only ten months later he threw in the sponge and told the country they could have their goddam crown back.

1936 – George VI
Edward's younger brother Bertie (Albert), was a bit surprised to get a new job (King), and a new name (George). He did, however, have a nice wife (the now Queen Mother) and two little girls (our Queen and Princess Margaret) and was generally thought to be far more suitable than his naughty brother. Just to show no hard feelings he gave his poor elder brother the title HRH Duke of Windsor; and Mrs Simpson (when she'd got shot of Mr Simpson) became an all-American English Duchess. Her mother-in-law, however, the old Queen Mary, wouldn't have her in the house and was never to speak to her (that's mothers-in-law for you).

By the Way
During the period of poor Edward's abdication in 1936, he hit the brandy and soda so heavily that he had to have his stomach pumped.

Chapter 41

Bad To Worse

If you think Britain had been through some hard times, hold on to your seats. While we'd been absorbed in a General Strike, hunger marches and miscellaneous mayhem, Japan invaded Manchuria. The League of Nations wagged its corporate finger and told the pesky little Japs to behave. Japan promptly said 'shan't', and refused to play any more, promptly pulling out, followed shortly by Germany in 1933.

At this time news was coming from Germany of a funny little painter and decorator with a strange haircut and a daft moustache, who was promising his fellow countrymen a way out of the appalling economic mess they were in. His name was Adolf Hitler, and he was to win the 'World Bad Guy Record' of all time. His nationalism knew no bounds, and the National Socialist Party swept through the German nation like Beatlemania through Britain in the sixties. The Nazis, as they soon became known, hated anything remotely foreign, making the tall, blue-eyed, blond-haired caricature German a standard which they all had to aspire to. Strangely enough, Hitler himself was short and dark but no one dared mention that.

1935 – Hitler and Fascism
What his 'Brown Shirts', and later his Secret Service, did to the gypsies and Jews has no place in a 'funny' book, but one can say

that, years after, the rest of the world finds it very difficult to trust Germany again. Mind you, it would be untruthful to pretend that there wasn't fascism in Britain. In fact, a nasty bit of work called Sir Oswald Mosley spearheaded the anti-Jewish movement. He bought a load of black shirts for his fascist mates and tried to stir this hatred up in England, only to be arrested and thrown into jail.

By this time you had to be blind or stupid not to see the potential 'aggro' in Europe. Hitler occupied the Rhineland, and the Spanish Civil War had broken out between the idealistic Communists and the Fascists. Japan then declared war on China. Italy, probably realising it was going to join the baddies' side, pulled out of the League of Nations, leaving it like a toothless lion.

Hitler now really had the bit between his teeth and took on almost Godlike status with the sheeplike Krauts. He incorporated Austria with Germany and conquered Czechoslovakia. Mussolini (him of the silly pointy hat) led Italy to crush Albania and waited eagerly to see if Hitler would smash Poland (it sounds a bit like the World Cup!).

1939 – Chamberlain Asks Nicely

France and Britain promised Poland that they wouldn't let those nasty Germans get away with it. Neville Chamberlain, our new Conservative PM, went over to Germany to ask Herr Hitler, nicely, to promise to be a good fascist and leave Poland alone. He came back wreathed in smiles saying that Hitler wasn't really a bad bloke and that everything would be all right. Hitler obviously thought he was a right wally and on September 1st 1939 he invaded Poland, sticking two fin-gers in the air at Britain and France (remember? Go forth and multiply). This was the last straw and on the 3rd, we both declared war on Germany and the fight really started.

151

Chapter 42

World War II

THE SIDES

The Allies	Axis Countries
Great Britain	(the Enemy)
France	Germany
Russia	Italy
South Africa	Japan
Australia	
New Zealand	
Canada	
America	

It seems rather unbalanced when looked at this way, but at the very beginning of the war it was very different. If you are wondering what happened to all the other countries, they were mostly overrun by the Germans or the Japanese very quickly.

1939 – Bleak Prospects

Things started badly and by 1940 the Krauts had ousted British troops from France who quickly surrendered. Nevertheless the Brits were united as never before, largely due to Churchill's rousing oratory – 'Never have so few owed so much to so many' – or words

OLIVER CHURCHILL   WINSTON HARDY

Spot the Difference.

to that effect. It didn't take long before everyone had taken sides and the fighting had spread all over the world. Hitler had conquered most of Europe and was concentrating on Egypt and the western Deserts. At first our 'Desert Rats' really showed the Italians how to fight in these dreadful conditions but when Rommel and the infamous German Afrika Korps turned up it was a different story and we really had the sand kicked in our faces. It was a combination of our brilliant little General Montgomery and the arrival (just in time) of the Americans in their fab Sherman tanks that eventually caused the Germans to surrender their buckets and spades and leave the beach. Gradually the allies started getting the upper hand and when Hitler tried to invade Russia in 1941, the 'Great Bear' shook itself and joined in the fray.

1941 – America Joins In

One of the great turning points had been when the Japs attacked and destroyed a large part of the American fleet at Pearl Harbour. This had really caused the Yanks to explode and their mighty army, who'd been standing by, sprang into action. Suddenly everything looked very different. Italy finally surrendered in 1943 having not really had a very good war.

By the way, here's an old wartime joke:– What's the shortest book in the world? Answer: The book of Italian war heroes!

Meanwhile at home the British were having the fight of their lives:

The Royal Air Force

On our side we had the amazing little Spitfires and Hurricanes, but they were greatly outnumbered by the Messerschmitts and Stukas of the mighty German air force which was called the Luftwaffe.

The air battles that took place over England supplied the British film industry with material that was to keep it busy for the next thirty years. Our boys were always portrayed as brave, good looking, clean shaven, Biggles types who were kind to their wives, children and pets.

The filthy German pilots, on the other hand, had mean, unshaven faces and were always played by the same brutish actors who, had we ever followed them home, would have cheated on zeir Frauleins and vipped zeir Dachshunds.

The Royal Navy

The same was true at sea. Our officers were all shown as pipe smoking, duffel coated, frightfully upper class Nigel Havers types. Below decks the lower ranks were quaint, honest cockneys, who knew their place and when shot or drowned, died quietly (clutching pictures of their mums), without complaining.

The horrible Hun, on the other side, skulked around in their U-boats, sneaking up behind our brave lads and shooting them in the backs (typical). When they were sinking (which was pretty regular), the Germans made dreadful fusses, shouting and screaming like nobody's business, and cursing the far-too-clever British navy (three cheers!).

These were the films, however, and it must be said that, though their cause was rotten, many of the Germans were astounding soldiers.

Invasion?

Again the war had come just in time to help the British populace forget how much they hated each other. At one stage it looked very likely that we might be invaded for the first time since William the Conqueror in 1066. (Hitler the Conqueror?)

It was just as well the German stormtroopers didn't get to Britain, as all we had to stop them was our funny little Home Guard. These were volunteer 'soldiers', usually of advanced years, whose job was to protect our women, children and pets with not much more than garden tools.

Advance at your Peril!

Chapter 43

England Digs In

When it looked as if the German invasion was imminent, the bombing raids became as regular as milk deliveries, and the British put up a fight the like of which had never been seen before or since. Huge, Zeppelin-like balloons hung over major cities, not to tell where the party was, but to make sure the attacking planes couldn't fly too low. Most city families dug shelters in their back yards. Those that didn't have back yards, dived into communal shelters as soon as they heard the air raid sirens. These dreadful sirens made such a horrid eery din, that they were almost as frightening as the raids themselves.

In central London, which obviously caught the brunt of Germany's fury, everyone hurried into the Underground for late night protection. Funny really – nowadays protection is the last thing you'd get! City children were evacuated to stay with their country cousins, but they were often like oil and water – the streetwise city kids finding country life difficult to cope with. This, combined with terrible homesickness, caused many to drift back to their families before the end of the war. Food, clothes and petrol were rationed and luxuries like fruit, chocolate and nylon stockings were not to be seen again for years, apart from those given as presents by the American soldiers when they eventually arrived.

They gave their chewing gum, cigarettes and stockings, from their military bases, to all our best-looking girls (while our boys were away).

Our new Royal couple, George and Elizabeth, proved a great boost to the morale of the British people. They spent much of their time in the centre of London, regularly visiting the homeless and injured, even though their own home (Buck House) was hit nine times.

1940 – The Bombing

Thousands of homes, and the people in them, were destroyed by the appalling night bombing raids, but the British refused to give in. Never in our history did we think the suffering so justified or the enemy so revolting.

Towards the end of the war the ghastly Germans developed the nastiest weapon that had ever been seen – or not seen! It was a petrol-driven guided missile called a V1 (later the V2), launched from somewhere in Holland. They were the first totally unmanned attack vehicles and were nicknamed 'Doodlebugs'. Everyone was terrified of them as, although they could be heard approaching, at the last minute the engines would cut out. It was anybody's guess where (and on who) they might land.

1944 – The Grand Finale

France was liberated in 1944, Hitler then kindly killed himself (about time too!) and in 1945 Germany gave in. They had lost 4½ million people and most of their cities were destroyed. America, just to make sure, dropped the biggest bomb ever seen on Hiroshima and the Japanese put their hands up.

The war was over. The horrible Hun was beat. Good had triumphed over evil – and Britain could now get back to its internal (and eternal) feuding again.

THE
VERY BLOODY
HISTORY
of BRITAIN

1945 to now

Introduction

If you were one of the three people (excluding my mother) who struggled through my last mighty work, you will have discovered that, as a historian, I would have made a very good baker. You might remember that I found history, as it was taught at the half school, half prison camp that I 'attended', just a string of obscure dates that seemed to have as much relevance to my little life as a book on etiquette to a professional wrestler.

Part I of my Very Bloody History of Britain (without the boring bits) covered everything from when your great, great (× 600) grandparents grovelled around in the primeval slime waiting for something to happen, to our finest hour when we showed

When are you going to evolve?

the horrid Hun (in their worstest hour) where to get off in World War 2. This book will drag you through the last fifty years to the present when, with a bit of luck, our future will one day merge into someone else's history.

So where do we start and what will we cover?

After the horrors of war, Britain looked optimistically (if a bit apprehensively) to the road ahead. Our young chaps, fed up with Kraut crushing, took a break from wondering if they were ever going to live beyond their teens, and girls, having shown what they could do in the war, began to anticipate something approaching equal opportunities (and more men to choose from).

In some ways, however, wartime had been quite straightforward, both for humble peasants (like what I am) who, let's face it, only had to worry about coming out of it in one piece, and their leaders who, for once, could forget party politics and just get on with the job of flattening foes.

Peacetime, unfortunately, just ain't that easy, as everyone from the managing director to the dustman has a perfectly valid opinion on who should run their country – and how. No one could deny that in 1945 Britain was at a major crossroads with so many options that even a clever clairvoyant could only guess which way we'd go. . . .

Firstly, and most importantly; what was going to happen to the Empire that we'd ruled over (and milked) for so many years? Just like the French, who'd had to let go of Vietnam, or the Dutch, who were facing revolting Indonesians, Britain was hearing the faint, but ominous, beat of distant drums from India and Africa. Those natives were certainly getting restless. Indeed many countries throughout the world regarded us as a dangerous imperialist power on a par with Russia (which seems quite a hoot now!). Even the Yanks, who'd been the very first of our colonies to tell us where to get off, were now none too happy about the whole idea of a 'mighty' British Empire (probably, because they wanted one!). Understandably, a few politicians (like Churchill) seeing the writing on the wall, thought we should cuddle up to Europe, though admittedly, at this stage, for defensive rather than economic reasons.

Poor Britain was, therefore, to find herself in a fine mess as, not only was she getting it in the neck for being this wicked imperialist but, if she waved goodbye to any of her colonies, she'd be seen to be losing her grip.

The other great problem to face Britain, after the all-for-one-and-one-for-all war, was class. Could the huntin', shootin' and fishin' set still hang on to such a huge portion of the country's loot in a country showing signs of creeping towards the left, or would they end up short in the head department (metaphorically speaking) like some of their ancestors or French rellies?

Unfortunately, however, problems (and answers) are seldom as straightforward as this, and world events always put the spanner in the works of any plans a country might have for its future. If you want to see how all these and many other plots thickened, and how we got ourselves into the other fine mess we're in today, take a deep breath . . . and with the best of British luck read on.

Battling with Peace

Churchill, that fabulous fat man with the fabulous fat cigar, had shown the British what a brilliant leader he could be when his back was against the wall. When, therefore, he went into the General Election on 26th July 1945, he had every reason to expect that the shell-shocked nation he'd saved from the slavering jaws of the horrid Hun would welcome him, and his Conservative cronies, back with open arms. But you can always trust the fickle British to do the exact opposite of what is expected – bless 'em. They knew Churchill was fab at wars, but weren't at all convinced he knew how to cope in peacetime.

The war had had a strange effect on the British. For the first time in their history, the rich and privileged had stopped treating the working class like another species and had joined with them to fight the common foe (and those Krauts sure were common!). Countesses had worked next to shop girls making munitions, driving trucks, and working on the land and the bosses had rolled up their immaculate sleeves and joined the peasants on the shop

I say! Isn't work fun?

floor. When the war was over the lower orders (the middle class hadn't really been invented) were none too keen to return to the them-and-us, cap doffing, 'the guvnor's-always-right' system, which had flourished under the Tories before the war. So, much to the anger of Churchill and his none-too-merry men, they replaced the wartime coalition government (a mish-mash of the Conservative, Labour and Liberal parties) and voted in the Labour Party with the biggest majority in its history (before or since!). Foreigners were nothing less than gobsmacked at the result and one incredulous American political commentator reckoned the British population must have received a severe blow to its corporate head.

The practically unheard of motley crew of old lefties was led by a puny little pipe-puffing politician called Clement Attlee backed up by the brash but brilliant ex-miner Ernest Bevin as Foreign Secretary. The country they inherited, it must be said, wasn't that much of a going concern, but Britain knew that it had to dust the counters down, and open 'Great Britain Ltd' as quickly as possible.

Cutting the Cake

Before turning their attention to internal affairs, however, Attlee and a little posse of politicians went off to Potsdam (a dead posh house where all those horrid German leaders had once lived) to join Churchill, the head-American President Truman and head-Russian Stalin (him of the big, black moustache) in the squabble over how to slice up the seriously crumbly Kraut cake. The Western lot didn't like the idea of the puppet Poland (manipulated by Russia) taking a huge chunk of Germany and kicking out millions of its punch drunk inhabitants, while the soon-to-be-hated Stalin wouldn't entertain (surprise, surprise) the idea of free elections in the Eastern European countries.

Churchill, shrewd as ever, used the term 'Iron Curtain' which he accused the Ruskies of lowering, or rather slamming, down against the West. This was the beginning of what became known as the 'Cold War' which was to threaten world peace for years. On a happier note in April, after 2,000 nights of blackouts, all the lights went back on throughout Britain and our parents and grandparents found yet another excuse to have a huge party (some thought it more fun with the lights out). In Croydon alone, which had been particularly heavily bombed (what could the Krauts possibly have had against Croydon?), 7,000 streets lights went on at once.

The UN is born

On 25th April, delegates from all over the world gathered in the San Francisco Opera House, not for a sing-song but to plan a new peace-keeping body to replace the League of Nations. The United Nations, as it was to be called, was formed on a cloud of optimism to make sure that a world war could never happen again. On 26th June delegates from 50 States signed an agreement to supply soldiers to an international force controlled by the new UN General Assembly. It basically meant that if any one of them started pushing their weight around, the other would cut him down to size. In other words it was 'peace with teeth'.

VJ Day

On 14th August, those pesky Japanese finally put up their hands and surrendered. Had the Yanks not dropped their ever-so-clever, but hideously effective A bombs (2000 times nastier than anything seen before), totally obliterating Nagasaki and Hiroshima and killing 7000 Japanese, the Japs might have fought on longer. Far from feeling guilty about our ally's dastardly deeds, we British had yet another huge party.

The Ex-Premier of Japan, General Hideki Tojo, was so miffed at the prospect of being given the third degree by the conqueror's court that he shot himself in the heart. It really wasn't his year, however, as he 'missed' and had to stand trial like everyone else.

Nuremberg Trials

Meanwhile back in Germany, the allies opened the trials of all the now ex-Hitler's German mates at Nuremberg, where the Nazis had held all their flashest rallies (rubbing their noses in it or what?). Unfortunately (for them), guys like Goering, Hess and Ribhentrop, in their Germanic passion for thoroughness, had kept copious records of all their dirty deeds which, when retrieved, were enough to sign their death warrants.

Lesson One: If you're going to commit terrible crimes against humanity – for goodness sake don't keep a diary!

Meanwhile

January: The train takes the strain. The first boat-train for five years left for Calais.

June: Vampires in Britain! The RAF unveiled the Vampire Jet capable of a never-before-reached 500 m.p.h. A little late I'd have thought.

July: The BBC lightened up a bit too, with its Light Programme.

August: One of Germany's nastiest war criminals, Walter Schellenberg (the 'Butcher of Berlin'), was arrested by the Allies. He was almost more famous for having 'invented' Madame Kittie's, the brothel in Berlin famous for having every room wired with

Darlink! I sink I have vays of making you talk

168

recording equipment, in order that trained 'frauleins of the night' could elicit secrets from high-ranking foreign visitors.

October: George Orwell made the immortal comment in his brilliant, but scary *Animal Farm*: 'All animals are equal, but some are more equal than others.' (I bet the humble slug could have written that.)

Hit of the Year: 'We'll Gather Lilacs', a soppy song about . . . gathering lilacs.

1946

Britain Goes Short

Just as your forefathers (and mothers) were beginning to look forward to a life of plenty, the grumpy government told them that things could quite possibly get worse, despite a whacking great loan from the States (which was nearly spent by the end of 1947). The war had cost Britain a quarter of its national wealth – some £7 million – and we'd lost two-thirds of our export trade. Overseas investment? Forget it, we'd hocked just about everything but grandmother's false teeth to fight the war. And if that wasn't bad enough, there were other unforeseen problems connected with smashing the baddies, one of which was what to do with all those left, in this case 30 million peckish Germans. Britain found that having successfully ruined German agriculture, she then had to feed its people. You really can't win 'em all.

A world food shortage meant that rationing had to get tougher. This even stricter rationing was hard to take for a nation fed (or not fed) up with going without for so long. Bread, now much darker owing to a lowered wheat content, was rationed rather bizarrely according to how much energy you consumed at work. (I imagine civil servants got almost none.)

Churchill, now terrific in opposition, wagged his cigar, and claimed it jolly well served the British right for voting in the lousy Labour Party.

And Now the Jews

As with the Germans, there then emerged the problem of what to do with the Jews. A carefully considered Anglo-American report came out in May which hit the double jackpot by upsetting not only the world's Jews but the world's Arabs as well. It reckoned that the Holy Land (Palestine) should be regarded as the Jews' natural home but should not be regarded as purely Jewish because it lay at the crossroads of the Arab world. Unfortunately the Arabs didn't see it that way, saying that if it was anyone's natural home, it was theirs (well they would, wouldn't they?). It was a bit like someone coming up to your front door and demanding they live in half your house. They were, consequently, just a little miffed when in just one year, 100,000 of the Nazis' victims were plonked in what they reckoned to be *their* back yard. It was then added that the British mandate should continue till Arab-Jewish hostility disappeared. Nice one! I wonder what they'd have said if they'd had any premonition of what was going to happen. Let's face it, descendents of those Arabs and Jews have been fighting like Tom and Jerry almost ever since.

By August 1945 Britain, much to the annoyance of the Americans (who didn't want any more of them in their country), was actually keeping the Jews who exceeded the agreed quota *out* of Palestine by putting barbed wire across the harbour at Haifa, effectively imprisoning the poor refugees on ships that had become floating slums. Nobody seemed to have any idea what to do with them.

Love and Marriage

One of the more embarrassing effects of our prolonged war was exemplified by the fact that 40% of all girls under twenty had to have their wedding dresses let out for their wedding day (in those days having a nipper out of wedlock was almost unheard of). Let's face it, there was a limit to what our brave lads could do (that didn't cost much) during those home visits and one cannot deny that those flash American GIs often left our gullible girls with a lot more than chewing gum and nylons to remember them by.

Luckily, it was reckoned in those days to be as easy to get a marriage licence as a dog licence. This was all right as long as the youngsters were still friends after the war but unfortunately couples were often virtual strangers after those long separations (not to mention the black outs!) and found that getting rid of their partner was not as easy as getting rid of Rover the dog. In 1946, there were some 50,000 shotgun marriages waiting to be dissolved with simply not enough courts to deal with the crush, so they had to like it or lump it until their number came up.

Rover – do you take Harold to be your lawful master?

Nationalisation

Now that the Labour Party had got its feet safely under the table, it decided to hot up its nationalisation programme (just as the Tories these days are hellbent on denationalising everything). Nationalisation means that the State takes over large industries so that

    a. the profits can be shared amongst the population and

    b. they can run more efficiently.

That's the theory anyway. So, in that case, we ask ourselves, why aren't the railways brilliantly efficient and hugely profitable? Apparently railways were even more dreadful before nationalisation so they, with road haulage and ports, were the first to go, followed by coal mines. (At least our Tories don't want to denationalise the mines – they just close 'em.)

Shock Horror! Less Beer

In an attempt to hang on to the disappearing wheat stocks, beer production was halved. Far less serious, meat was rationed to one shilling's (5p) worth a week. Mind you, it was probably not as bad as you think. These days you couldn't buy a pig's ear for 5p. Then you could probably get a couple of pounds of sausages.

Meanwhile

February: Bananarama! A long lost visitor from foreign parts, the banana, turned up at our ports. Many children didn't even know how to eat them (unfortunately three year old Dorothy Shippey did – she ate one over the three, and died).

March: Black day for post-war squirrels. The government issued a recipe for squirrel pie. Take one large, fresh squirrel . . .

June: John Logie Baird, the inventor of the box, went into his. Not only did he invent the telly (what a responsibility), but also a weird electronic gizmo that detected objects in the dark. (A mechanical nose?)

August: A report came out claiming that the black market in chocolate, nylons and perfume was flourishing. Someone had to fill the gap after the flashy American soldiers had gone home.

October: At Nuremberg, twelve evil Nazi chiefs were sentenced to death and Rudolf Hess, who had claimed loss of memory, got life. C'mon Rudi, even the Brits wouldn't buy that one.

November: Hungarian journalist Ladislao Biro was on the ball. He invented the ballpoint pen which was a small sensation when it got to Britain even though it cost 55 shillings (£2.75). Was it called the Ladislao or something else? Answers on a postcard.
• IBM invented an electronic brain capable of doing in seconds what would take the average human brain hours (or, in my case, days). It was called the Electronic Numerical Integrator and Computer. To people's amazement, science fiction writers talked of a distant future when computers would be used in every field of science and business. Not that distant, we think.

December: Buffalo scientists (or should I say scientists in Buffalo) came up with what was thought to be a cock and bull story that smoking cigarettes might be connected with lung cancer. How right they turned out to be.

Britain Pulls Out

Talk about kicking a country when it was down. The 1946/47 winter was colder than a Siberian fridge and the post-war fuel shortage brought the already tottering British to their chilly knees. Any fuel that was available was piling up at the pits because transport had come to a snowy standstill. When the great thaw came, things got even worse especially if you were a sheep or a loaf! Two million poor little bleeters were washed away by the ensuing floods, and a month's bread was wiped out when 500,000 acres of wheat were all but destroyed.

Who gave you that loaf?

Way Out East

Over in hotter climes, the British were becoming really fed up with trying to keep people from killing each other. Jewish terrorists were now having a go at our soldiers who were only trying to keep those angry Arabs at bay by controlling the number of Jews flooding into Palestine.

If that wasn't bad enough, other troops were being run ragged trying to keep the peace in an India shortly due for independence. Lord Mountbatten had been given the dubious honour of becoming the Viceroy of India but could only watch helplessly as the Moslems and the Hindus curried – sorry – carried on slaughtering each other willy-nilly, as they couldn't seem to agree over who should have what territory. In May 1947, the British cabinet finally agreed to Mountbatten's idea of pulling them apart (called partitioning), a bit like you do with naughty kids. The Moslems would be put in the north west (where most of them had been anyway) to be called West Pakistan, and the Hindus would have the great big bit below to be called Hindustan (later India). Apart from this, there was a corner at the bottom right which was to be known as East Pakistan, also predominantly Moslem, and a bump on the top right hand corner to be called Kashmir (predominantly Buddhist), the border of which was still being disputed.

So, did the colonials like this whole partition idea? Of course they didn't. For a first, the huge Indian army, with all its ships and planes and camels would have to be split up (an almost impossible task); for a second, nobody could decide whether or not the new countries should be in the Commonwealth and, for a third, many of the disgustingly rich maharajahs who, quite understandably, were perfectly happy being disgustingly rich (and had huge private armies to keep things that way), wanted to declare independence instead.

On 15th August the British crated up their cocktail cabinets, emptied their elephant guns, paid off their thousands of servants, and cleared out to leave the Indians to fend for themselves. All except Lord Louis Mountbatten who was made Governor-General of the largest part – India (and made an earl to boot). This left the Moslems and Hindus to get on, uninterrupted, with tandoorying each other which they did with increased vigour. By the time the 8,500,000 Moslems and Hindus had a nice border between them, 400,000 had come to a sticky end and a further 100,000 had almost died on the journey, from either exposure or starvation. Obviously their gods moved in mysterious ways.

...and Palestine?

Within a few weeks of all this, Britain also decided to let the Jews and Arabs fight unhindered and cleared out of Palestine. On 30th November, the UN General Assembly inadvertently set up a lovely little scenario for an Arab-Jewish war by backing the British and American plans to partition Palestine formally so that the Jews could have a proper home of their own. Surprise, surprise, the Arabs were even less thrilled than they'd been before with the idea of lending half of what they thought was theirs anyway.

Elizabeth's Greek Take-Away

On a cheerier note, the Princess Elizabeth (our present Queen) announced that she was going to marry a young, unusually handsome Greek lieutenant called Philip Mountbatten (or, more probably, Mountbattenopoulous) who was the nephew of the aforementioned Indian Governor-General, Lord Louis Mountbatten. Great! Now we had Germans (our royal family) marrying Greeks in order to lord it over us British. Democracy?

At their highly expensive and glamorous wedding in November, the Archbishop of Canterbury said

> Notwithstanding the splendour and national significance of the service in this Abbey, it is in all essentials exactly the same as it would be for any cottager (?) who might be

married this afternoon in some small country church in a remote village in the dales. The same vows are taken, the same prayers are offered, the same blessing given.

That's as maybe, Bish, but I bet Liz and Phil didn't go back to fishpaste sandwiches and brown ale.

Meanwhile

January: The most popular programmes on the radio were 'Dick Barton Special Agent' (a really hammy detective series) and 'Woman's Hour' (a mumsy magazine programme).
• Al Capone, the best, or should I say worst, hoodlum in the world died.

March: Unbelievably, the Government banned all midweek sport so that the workers, bless 'em, wouldn't tire themselves out.

April: The Public Morality Council claimed artificial insemination was illegal as it was deemed to be adulterous. Obviously a case of better the husband you know than the test tube you don't.

September: The one-day-to-be-great Harold Wilson joined the cabinet aged 31, the youngest minister yet.

August: Princess Elizabeth had to go on her honeymoon without a trousseau, owing to the clothes' shortage. The poor dear must have been chilly wearing only a ring.

• British women were asked to economise by keeping their skirts short to save cloth! Predictably British men seemed relatively happy at the idea. This all proved a bit of a drag when Christian Dior's 'New Look' swept in from France. Although very flattering to women, especially after the austere utility wartime look, one of its main features was a hemline only inches from the floor.

1948

Health for All

The National Health Service was perhaps the fabbest thing that the new Labour Government (or any other, for that matter) had been responsible for. Almost unbelievably, everything from diarrhoea to dandruff or cancer to carbuncles was treated absolutely free. You could even get a wig on a prescription from

Well Mr. Jones – if you're absolutely sure.

your local doctor. It was largely achieved by Minister of Health Aneurin Bevan and was to make him one of the great figures of the history of British politics.

Everyone seemed over the moon with the new service, apart from the people actually carrying it out – the doctors – who were more concerned about losing money than anything else. They voted 766 to 11 against the NHS which is funny when you think that nowadays they are getting their stethoscopes in a twist at the prospect of it all changing back.

Nationalisation
Meantime, you must be dying to know how the new nationalisation programme was getting on. A bit early to tell but maybe the fact that the brilliant new Coal Board lost £5.44 million in the last quarter of 1947 gives you a clue.

Trouble Out East
1948 had started with the sad news from India of the assassination of Mahatma Gandhi, the funny little Hindu leader known for wearing only tiny round glasses and a tablecloth. The poor little chap-ati had only just finished fasting for Hindu-Moslem unity and was probably in a hurry for a curry down-town, when this guy jumped out of the crowds and shot him three times. When it was discovered that it was a Hindu who'd done the dirty deed, fresh riots broke out across India and Pakistan. The good news was that, just like all the continuing mess in Palestine, it just wasn't our problem any more. So there!

You Scratch My Back and I'll Scratch Yours
On 17th March Britain, France and the Benelux countries (Belgium, Holland and Luxembourg) signed a treaty promising that they would all jump to each other's defence if anyone big and horrid threatened any one of them. Nobody named names but few had any doubt that the threat was more than likely to come from that great bear – Russia. Hardly was the ink dry on the agreement, when the Russians slammed a blockade on all the

Western aid to Berlin, which it had had its beady eye on ever since the end of the war.

Birth of a Nation
On 14th May a new state, to be called Israel, was proclaimed by the Jews as their new home. All the British quotas were abandoned, making it a free for all for anyone (provided they were Jewish) to go and live in the Palestinian sunshine. The Arabs, predictably, went simply mad and Egyptian forces raided the gun cupboard and instantly massed on the southern border, looking extremely ugly.

Britain to the Rescue Again
On 30th June, back in Berlin, the RAF and the Western Allies broke the by now serious Russian blockade with only one month to go before the bewildered Berliners would have run out of grub. A mighty airlift to the western zone of the city smashed within a couple of months the Russian efforts to starve the Berliners into submission. The Cold War had reached freezing point.

Rubber Trouble
Nasty things were happening up Malaya way. Chinese Communist rebels had a new hobby – murdering British rubber planters. Britain bounced back on 30th July, sending a force of soldiers to sort the Commies out. At first the 'rubber bandits' ran away like scared bunnies, but it wasn't to be that easy. It seemed that the murders were only the beginning of a much bigger Communist plot to take over the country. The British had involved themselves in something a lot more serious than chasing a few terrorists away.

Babies Go Bonkers
The only area of production really booming was the baby business, probably due to the end of enforced wartime separations. Nippers were piling up at a rate never before imagined, and added to that, far fewer were lost due to the brill new National Health Service. This pushed the birth rate 21% higher than was actually needed to

keep the population stable. Even Princess Elizabeth got in on the act, and in December gave birth to two big ears with a baby boy (called Charles) in between.

I say Phil, where d'you think he got those features from?

Meanwhile

March: 'Orrible Oswald Mosley and his home-made, brown-shirted Fascists were silenced by a ban on all political marches in London for three months. Theirs was planned for 1st May.

April: The General Certificate of Education (GCE), that scourge of so many future generations, replaced the School Certificate.

June: Despite the Commons voting to suspend hanging, those bloodythirsty peers in the Lords chucked out the bill and the scaffold survived to service more criminals.

July: A brilliant little car called the Morris Minor was born.

August: Freddie Mills, who looked like everyone's idea of a cartoon boxer, managed to kerb his frantic, swinging style to win the World Light Middleweight Title. Poor Freddie was later murdered (to death) in a gangland killing.

November: The sugar-sweet child star Julie Andrews sang before the Queen. Let's face it, being royal does have its drawbacks.

1949

The Natives Get Restless

The Labour Government was beginning to lose its bottle over the nationalisation plan, realising that it was beginning to get right up the nose of the common man who was slightly weary of the economic state (especially the ever-reducing rations). Tate and Lyle, the huge British sugar refiners, decided to take on the Government who had been trying to nationalise their industry. They invented a

daft little character called Mr Cube (original or what?) who appeared on 2,000,000 sugar packets, and all their delivery trucks, declaring in his sweet, cubular way how much he didn't want to be nationalised, thank you very much. The steel industry, also, saw the chink in the government's armour and took the Labour Government on with huge help from other private companies scared stiff that they might just be next.

Churchill, never one to miss the chance of jumping on a bandwagon, took the mickey out of the government, saying that every industry they'd got their horny hands on had gone from profit to loss in less time than you could even *say* nationalisation. Bevan waded into the slanging match, calling the Tories lower than vermin (rude to vermin I'd say), and a roly-poly battle-axe of a Labour MP – Bessie Braddock – screamed that she didn't care if the other side starved to death. Nice words from a party claiming to be striving for a more humane society.

On 18th September, the sh...illing hit the fan when Sir Stafford

Cripps, our particularly grumpy Chancellor of the Exchequer, announced that the poor, long-suffering quid was to be reduced in value by 30%. This meant that the battered British had now, on top of everything else, to face a substantial rise in the cost of living.

A survey was released proclaiming that Mr and Mrs Britain were spending more on booze (and who can blame them?) and less on food, than ten years earlier. Crime was on the increase (naturally!), but convictions for drunkenness were less than half. This could, of course, have meant that the cunning British had decided to get drunk at home (or the cops were sloshed too).

NATO Gets the OK

Updating the former agreement between European nations (to pitch in if anyone got into bother), Britain, America, Canada, France and the Benelux countries agreed on 8th March to a new peace alliance called the North Atlantic Treaty Organisation (NATO). Basically, if anyone took a swing at any one of the member countries, it would be construed as an attack on the whole lot. Many people were scared stiff that this might prod the sleeping Russian bear and make him cross. The far left, particularly in Britain, who still hung on to a loony admiration for Russia, saw the agreement as blatant bear-baiting. Many westerners slept happier in their beds that night, however, little knowing that, when push came to shove, NATO would prove a toothless wimp.

The Ireland Bill on 11th May, which finally recognised Eire as a republic, was passed almost unanimously by the British Parliament. Rather oddly, the Irish Republic didn't become foreign but something in-between. The people of Eire, for instance, were still allowed to vote in our elections, which even Attlee admitted was a bit cock-eyed for a new republic.

The Royals Revealed

The rot started here. For the first time in recorded history a member of the Royal Household spilt the beans (by appointment,

of course). Marion Crawford (Crawfie) spoke to the *Ladies Home Journal* in the States. OK, it was pretty innocuous by today's standards. She said that the two princesses (she'd been their governess) were mad about horses and that the Duke of York (now king) had made a rare joke in which he claimed that his sister Mary had actually *been* a horse until she 'came out'. 'Coming out' was a cunning practice among the noble classes, in which girls of around eighteen were presented to the Queen and launched into society. It was really a sort of posh meat market where the 'debs' (short for debutantes) were paraded in front of eligible men much like they do, strangely enough, when selling thoroughbred horses. Just another way of keeping the bloodline pure I suppose.

China Chooses a Chairman

A cold wind blew in from the East on 1st October with the news that a chap called Mao Tse-tung had just become the boss of 40 million Chinese. He was the Chairman of the Communist-ruled People's Republic of China. The rest of the world showed very wobbly smiles as they grudgingly recognised the new regime, except Australia, Canada and America, who liked communism as much as snowmen do sunshine.

Dean Acheson, the American Secretary of State, said 'Communism is a very emotional subject in our country right now.'

Emotional! You're not kidding, Dean! I've never heard pure unadulterated hatred called that before. Britain, hypocritical as ever, didn't hesitate to recognise the new regime and didn't even put any conditions down. This just might have had something to do with the £3 thousand millions' worth of commercial interest they'd got running with the old regime. Velly funny how a litte cash can ease a greedy country's misgivings.

Meanwhile

January: The new micro-groove 7" discs came out in the States. This really hacked off established music-loving punters, as it meant buying completely new equipment in order to play them.

While the debate on hanging was still raging, the first woman for 12 years, Ruth Allen, was hung for murder.

February: The understandably sensitive Jewish community got itself worked up over the first showing of the movie *Oliver Twist* in Berlin. They weren't too happy about the way old Fagin was portrayed as a money-grabbing, Jewish crook (which he was, of course).

March: Bad news for British teeth. Rationing of chocolate and sweets ended. Also rationing on clothing finally ended. People generally got fatter and clothes generally got bigger.

April: Sir Alfred Munnings, famous for painting flat looking horses with small heads, called modern art 'silly daubs and violent blows at nothing'. Unfortunately for poor old Alfred, the statement caused exactly the wrong result. The Great British Public dashed to the Royal Academy to see what all the fuss was about.

May: If you didn't have a telly, you could watch your knickers getting in a twist at the first launderette in Bayswater, London.

June: Knickers again! American tennis player Gussie Moran showed hers (lace trimmed) at Wimbledon and upset the stuffy All-England Club.

July: The cost of health. The Government admitted that the NHS was costing 2/6d (12$\frac{1}{2}$p) a head per week, 1/4d more than they'd reckoned.

August: Starlings on the minute hand of Big Ben made it lose four and a half minutes. (A mystery to me. If they slowed it when it was going up one side, why didn't they speed it up when it was going down the other?)

September: Boy, are we British good at building white elephants. This time it was silver and called the Bristol Brabazon – the largest plane in the world. Unfortunately, it was so heavy and lumbering that it was put out to grass almost immediately.

Hit of the Year: 'Baby, It's Cold Outside'.

1950

The Fab Fifties
We are now half way through the century and it must be said that the British were still not happy bunnies. Much as we didn't want the Tory toffs back, we were none too thrilled at the performance of a Labour party that always promised so much and never delivered a bag of beans. This was proved by the results of the General Election in February. It turned out to be neck and neck to the finishing post, with Labour winning with the weeniest majority for fifty years. The British, however, were fed up to their back pockets with being used like laboratory rats, suffering the experiments – both social and economic – of, admittedly well-meaning, mad professors in the guise of politicians. They expected results from Labour.

Cold Comfort
Overseas, some chilly news crept under the rusty Iron Curtain. On

Do you do take-aways?

15th February 1950, Russia and China announced that they had jumped into the vast Commie bed together and were to unite against the world – which meant the West (that included us, folks!). It was a match made in heaven for them – and hell for us, as it meant that now old Joe Stalin could protect his endless frontier with Asia, whilst building up his military might in Europe. We Westies gulped nervously at the new Mao/Stalin love affair and wondered where it would all lead.

I Spy

All this East/West sparring and posturing required monitoring – and so began the spy era. Funny little grey men with wire-framed glasses, called Norman or Cyril, sat in their front rooms in Ruislip tapping out not-very-secret secrets on their crystal sets to their Commie controllers. Thousands of miles away, identical little fur-hatted grey men called Ivan and Boris, in Moscow suburbs like Ruislipovich, were sending similar stuff back to us. Occasionally, just to confuse future TV script writers, they'd pretend they were working for one side when they were really working for the other (double agents) or pretend they were working for one side while convincing the other that they were working for them too, while really working for another side entirely (triple agents), or occasionally they'd prete . . . oh, you get the picture!

Reds under the Bed

Communism had become the buzz word for everything that was horrid and not quite cricket (or baseball). Senator Joseph McCarthy in the States launched a crusade to wheedle all the filthy reds that were lurking not only under the bed, but in their insidious way throughout the federal government and, seemingly, throughout the entertainment industry as well.

First Blood

Just to kick things off nicely, over in Korea, the Communist northerners invaded the independent southerners and the Western allies put their hands to their holsters and prepared to interfere – or should I say – intervene.

The United Nations – who were all the nations that weren't Russia (who wouldn't come to meetings) or China (who weren't asked) – decided to chuck everything into defending the little Republic of Korea. Suddenly, like a cast-aside toy that suddenly becomes desirable when another kid shows interest, the whole world was getting worked up over the fate of a tin-pot country that weeks before they hadn't heard of (see the Falkland Islands). What had started out as a little foray by a few cheeky Communists was to turn into another full-blown, rip-roaring war which would eventually wipe out 5 million men, women and kids.

Troops Go In

On 29th August, the first of 4000 British troops landed in Korea to back up our dear old mates (and fightin' pardners) the Yanks. As they left Hong Kong, they were ordered by their Commander in Chief, Lieut. General Sir John Harding, to 'Shoot quickly, shoot straight, and shoot to kill,' which must have been about as useful as telling a trainee lion tamer to keep his eye on the wretched lions.

On 28th November, the troops of the United Nations paddled ashore off 260 ships, (scaring the wits out of the smallish North Koreans) and went on to occupy most of Korea in less than six weeks. Just as they were getting kinda comfy, they had to run for their lives as huge waves of Chinese troops started sweeping over them. Suddenly, the big boys were being threatened by the little boys. By 6th December over 200,000 Chinese had swarmed across the border catching not only the soldiers, but also the politicians at home, with their trousers well and truly down. Here we go again.

Fat Pharo

Just to make things even more complicated for Britain, the dreadful old Egyptian King Farouk pushed aside his many wives and, out of the blue, demanded that all the British troops, who were keeping the peace in the Middle East, scarper immediately. This demand was met with a chilly response by the British Parliament with the backing of the Americans. (You Limeys scratched our backs so we'll scratch yours.) Here we go again . . . again!

Out Goes Cripps

Life politics-wise was also becoming a touch tricky at home. Sir Stafford Cripps, the austere, vegetarian Chancellor, was finally 'sent off' due to ill health. The 'sub' was an ardent young man called Hugh Gaitskell, who was to become a familiar figure in British politics for many years. To be honest, the Labour Government was as good as clapped out. Along with Cripps, Bevin was shortly to retire, and Dalton, Morrison and Attlee were beginning to look likely candidates for the 'home for old lefties'. It was all a bit tricky for a party with such a tiny majority. In fact, the situation got so bad at one stage that some poor sick Labour MPs had to be dragged into the house on stretchers, just to boost the numbers at make-your-mind-up-time.

Cross Channel Telly

On 27th August, Auntie BBC beamed pictures across to our screens from France for the very first time. Richard Dimbleby, father of all serious TV presenters (and David and Jonathan) whizzed across from Calais on a cloud of micro-waves to be collected up and transmitted to our own front rooms.

Dimbleby only missed, by a few days, passing over Florence Chadwick, an American, who'd chosen a slightly slower route across the Channel. She broke the woman's cross-channel swimming record by an hour (see pointless things to do). Her poor appropriately named chum Shirley France wasn't so lucky; she was plucked from the Channel hysterical, and blue as a tit, eight miles from the English coastline.

Scotland Gets Stoned Again

You might remember from my last book (available at all good bookshops) that the English nicked Scotland's very own Coronation stone called the Scone of Stone (or something like that) in 1296 and, despite many promises, had never quite given it back. It had since stayed tucked under our Coronation Chair in Westminster Abbey much to the annoyance of the stroppy Scottish Nationalists who saw it (and porridge) as a symbol of their independence. On 25th December a person (McSuperman?) or persons unknown broke into Westminster Abbey and relieved us of the 458 lb rock. Our brilliant police, with almost uncanny insight, put out an alert for a car looking – wait for it – decidedly back-heavy, driven by person or persons unknown with Scottish accents (how do you spot a Scottish accent?). The stone eventually turned up in another abbey in – no prizes for guessing – Scotland – Arbroath to be precise.

Meanwhile

January: Britain asked its rich chum America if it could spare us a pile of atomic bombs. We could have asked Father Christmas.

February: Sir Harry Lauder, everyone's caricature Scotsman, died aged 79. Among the deep and lyrical songs he penned was 'Stop Your Ticklin', Jock'.

March: The lengths some people will go to settle an argument. Thor Heyerdahl, the famous Norwegian explorer, reckoned that the Polynesians must have originally sailed from South America. His chum said no way, so Thor built a raft out of old balsa logs and, 101 days after setting sail, won the bet. *Kon-Tiki* (the name of the raft) became the subject of an all-time best selling book called *The Kon-Tiki Expedition*.

• Roger Bannister, a medical student, broke the world record for the mile with what seemed like an impossible time of 4 minutes 1.48 seconds.

• The British weren't half dirty, they were 48% dirty. In a survey it was revealed that only 52% of our households had bathrooms.

June: The National Coal Board thumbed its sooty nose at all its critics by announcing a profit in 1949 of £9.5 million.

August: The Royal stork stopped at Buck House again and dropped off Princess Anne.

November: The amazing George Bernard Shaw, one of Britain's greatest playwrights and author of *Arms And The Man* and *Man And Superman* (he reckoned he was better than Shakespeare) died aged 94. This stroppy, red-bearded Irishman, who lived on vegetables and wore daft clothes, was loved or hated by all who met him.

Hit of the Year: 'I've Got a Luverly Bunch of Coconuts'. (Roll on rock and roll!)

1951

Bevan Bows Out

Aneurin Bevan, that bad old boy of the Labour left, blew his Welsh top and quit the Government in a right paddy, on account of his colleagues' decision to make a mockery of his darling NHS by charging for false choppers and glasses. His resignation was also a slap in the face for new boy Gaitskell (the new Chancellor of the Exchequer) and became the high point in the destructive right v. left punch-up within the Labour Party that still goes on today.

Churchill Goes into Labour

Churchill's opposition to the tired Labour Government was really hitting them where it hurt most – in the lobbies (ouch!) – and on 26th October, he and his Tory mates beat the Socialists (i.e. the Labour Party) in the General Election, putting the smell of fine cigar smoke back in No. 10. Old Winny (as he was affectionately

labelled) was back, aged 77, fighting fit, and champing at the bit to undo all the harm that the lefties had done. There was no doubt that the old campaigner, never one to hide his light under a bushel, would have a far larger television audience than when he'd been

PM before. In 1951, telly sales had gone straight through the roof and the manufacturers were planning to make 250,000 in the following year.

Trouble in China

Velly, velly tlicky. 1951 opened with the approach of a full scale war with the yellow peril, China. To be honest, if you were to compare the conflict in Korea to a soccer match, at this point the score would probably have been 0-0, with the United Nations United threatening to break through with a goal at any minute. By March, General MacArthur was having a head-on collision with his boss, President Truman, owing to his belief that the Allies should take the battle to the enemy, and nuke China. This was dead popular with the anti-communist fanatics who saw it as a way of chop-sueying the Chinese once and for all. But Truman and the UN didn't go for this plan too much as they hoped to come to some political deal with the Chinese (and not risk having 3 million of 'em on their backs).

Big Mac Gets the Push

On 11th April, President Truman finally came to the end of his personal tether with the warmongering General MacArthur. Two other generals had whispered that the way MacArthur wanted to do things would lead to the wrong war, at the wrong place, at the wrong time, with the wrong enemy (China)! Truman obviously thought, this time, that four wongs didn't make a wight, and promptly fired him.

Watch Out! There's Mau Mau About

Just as we British were working out the possible consequences of all the Egyptian mess, trouble broke out in Kenya, one of our more prestigious (and profitable) colonies. The Mau Mau, a group of particularly unpleasant natives who nobody knew anything about, had decided they'd had enough of the thousands of white settlers (mostly British) who were doing very nicely, thank you, farming the fertile highlands, using African labour and, more to the point,

African land. What started as the odd burglary turned into arson, intimidation of peaceful tribespersons who wouldn't take the oath to drive out the whitie, and eventually widespread pangaring, using pangas (horrid sort of curved hatchets). One of their daftest, if somewhat spine-chilling, oaths went like this: 'When the reedbuck horn is blown, if I leave a European farm before killing the owner, may this oath kill me.' I don't suppose the poor reedbuck thought much of having his horns blown either.

By October 1952, the situation had got so out of hand that Britain was forced to dust down a load more troops and ship them out to Kenya. One of the colony's top men, Senior Chief Warahui, had been speared to death in broad daylight so the President of the Kenya African Union, Jomo (nicknamed Burning Spear) Kenyatta, and 500 further suspects, were rounded up and given the third degree. By January 1953, the whites (and the reedbucks) were in a state of total panic as whole areas of the Kikuyu tribes reserves had fallen under Mau Mau control.

Kenyatta (compared by some to Hitler) was eventually jailed for seven years for being head Mau Mau man. Poor Mr Spear (Burning to his friends) claimed rather feebly that the Mau Mau weren't really anti-white (of course not, Jomo!) but were just trying to get a better deal for African people.

Canal Caper
Just as life was getting a little quieter in Korea, due to a sort of

queasy unofficial ceasefire, trouble broke out in the East. Britain had a treaty with Egypt which was due to run out in 1956. This treaty had been of immense strategic importance to us during and after the war, as the Suez Canal allowed a nifty short cut between the Mediterranean and Indian oceans. In 1951, the Egyptians didn't want to play any more. They proclaimed King Farouk of Sudan (see Great Mistakes in King-Making) as their monarch, and started making life very tricky for our soldiers on the canal bases. The British then offered a jolly decent concession by suggesting a Middle East defence pact backed by France, America and the US, which included handing their base back. The Egyptians, however, had their blood up and replied with a gesture rather similar (but completely different) to Churchill's famous wartime victory sign.

So, out of the blue, British forces crept up the Canal Zone one night and surprised the Egyptian soldiers guarding it. When the sun came up, Britain held the key points. It was pretty clear, however, when all the wives and kiddies were suddenly shipped back to Britain a couple of weeks later, that the whole area was a powder keg that could go up at any minute. Finally, in November, the British agreed to withdraw from three towns, and the Egyptians agreed to stop their terrorism (but they didn't mean it). By January 1952, the situation was almost out of hand and British people were being murdered left, right and centre.

By July of that year, the legendary (and infamous) playboy King Farouk, who had by now suspended parliament, had hightailed it out of Alexandria, ousted by a military coup. Everyone had finally had enough of his over-the-top lifestyle and far-too-obvious links to corruption in high places. His nine month old son was left to rule the country with just a little help from General Neguib the army leader.

Britain the Brilliant
Before going under, the Labour Government had tried to divert the country's attention from the all-pervading gloom. No royal weddings this time (thank God). Instead, they went one better. They invented something called The Festival of Britain, a huge

extravaganza to show the rest of the world (and the menacing masses) just how clever we all were and just how well the country was doing. Herbert Morrison (a Labour Cabinet Minister) called it 'the people giving themselves a pat on the back'. Heaven knows what for. Probably for putting up with him and the rest of his geriatric cronies for so long. Mickey-taking apart, this festival was truly magnificent, bringing together some of the finest design and manufactured goods to be seen for many a long year. It occupied a 27 acre bomb-shattered site around Waterloo Station (which now looks rather similar again). Spanning a large percentage of this area was a vast dome called, just a little pretentiously, The Dome of Discovery. One of its most remarkable features was its almost invisible means of support (much like the British economy!).

Mint Spies

On 7th June a juicy scandal broke that was to set the scene for many to come. Two frightfully-frightfully British diplomats, Guy Burgess and Donald Maclean, suddenly disappeared much to the puzzlement of our brilliant police, who searched high and low to no avail. Eventually the two chums thoughtfully sent a postcard home, telling everyone that they'd gone on a long Mediterranean holiday. Even the police didn't go for that one (as the two absentees hadn't taken their swimming costumes) and so the search continued.

It took till 1955 for the penny (or should I say rouble) to drop. The naughty pair had been telling those horrid Russians all our best secrets for years and then, before they could be found out had, most unsportingly, hightailed it off to Moscow, to live happily.

Meanwhile

February: Good King George got a well-earned (notice, well-earned) pay rise, the first since putting on the big gold hat.

April: Taste hits the deck. Miss Sweden became the first winner of a contest to find the most beautiful (and most boring) bimbo in the world. Since then, every year, a troupe of multi-national bimbos has disrobed to never-to-be dampened swimsuits and white high-heeled shoes, in one of the most kitsch, politically incorrect shows ever to sully our telly screens – 'Miss World'. It's so bad it's good!

July: A survey pronounced that the average housewife in Britain worked 75 hours a week, let alone the overtime put in at the weekend. It was thinly disguised that she was simply a slave to the kitchen and the kids.
• World Middle Weight Boxing Champ Sugar Ray Robinson, arguably the finest fighter ever, was beaten by British boxer, Randolph Turpin, to the surprise of just about everyone (including Randy).
• The Admiralty rather sensibly banned the 'Snort' breathing tube on British Submarines as the one on the *HMS Affray* was found to be faulty. They weren't kidding; the *Affray* was found, full of water, 250 feet down under.

October: A single footprint was found halfway up a mountain in the Himalayas and reckoned to be that of the Yeti or Abominable Snowman. Either the thing had one leg or he sure had hopped a long distance. They never found another.

1952

King George Becomes Ex
The dreaded curse of the grouchy grouse struck again. It was reported that, after a pleasant day's shooting those rather dim dickies, on February 6th King George VI died in his sleep. Young Princess Elizabeth, the new Mrs Edinburopoulus, on safari in

Africa with Phil the Greek, woke up to find herself fatherless and a queen – or should I say *the* Queen. Her ex-dad was sadly mourned by nearly all the British people as he'd earned mega-brownie points by refusing to run for safety during the war with his wife (our Queen Mum), and sticking out the horrendous bombing with the rest of the brave but terrified Londoners.

Nuclear Peace

Churchill dropped his own bomb on 26th February by announcing that Britain now had a nice shiny atomic one. Our new toy was welcomed by America, whose spokesman proclaimed it would be a major contribution to world peace as a deterrent (which was a bit like Mr Nobel offering his famous peace prize after inventing dynamite). The tests were to be carried out from the top of a pylon so that, according to Downing Street, 'there would be no danger to people or animals' (providing you didn't mind them buzzing or glowing).

Shooting for Peace

In another weird attempt to promote peace in Korea, allied fighter-bombers obliterated the ancient city of Suan on 8th May with bombs and napalm. I suppose wiping out all the opposition is, after all, one way of assuring peace.

Back in Africa, just as the situation was beginning to go off the boil in Kenya, the first stirrings of racial unrest were seen down in the south. Black people and Indians began non-violent demonstrations against South Africa's apartheid laws (which had been designed to keep the blacks and the whites 'apart', or rather to keep the blacks under the 'protective' boot of the whites). By November, the situation took a dive when seventeen Africans were shot dead while throwing stones which, you must admit, doesn't sound altogether fair. An Irish nun and an insurance agent (sounds like the beginning of a dirty joke) were killed in the cross-fire.

All Change at Home

A tragic death occurred on the London streets on 5th July. The last, much loved, electric trams were taken out of service and scrapped, due to that favourite old government pastime of removing any trace of indigenous tourist attractions.

But that was not all that was a-changing. The economy was beginning to pick itself out of the gutter and with this awakening prosperity, social patterns were on the move too. On 11th July, a survey revealed that the British were:

a. Living longer (maybe not being shot at and bombed by Germans every five minutes had something to do with it)

b. Marrying earlier (10.00 a.m. instead of 12 p.m.)

c. Divorcing more often

The British were also drifting away from a lot of the traditional manufacturing industries (like tram-making, no doubt). Also, twice as many people were living alone compared to twenty years before, which doesn't take a genius to realise might have something to do with the divorce rate. Women were demanding the unheard of equal pay to men for the same work. Their cry was taken up by a Labour Party trying to tart up their shambolic image, which had been caused by the internal punch-ups, between the left and the right, the right and the centre and the centre and the left. Poor old Attlee, however, was far too close to his personal wits' end to concern himself with the women's issue.

Meanwhile

January: British headmasters criticised the new GCE examinations saying they were too hard for some kids. Isn't that the point of exams?

• The driver of a bus which killed 23 military cadets got a £20 fine and was banned from driving for three years. Life was obviously cheaper in those days.

April: In an effort presumably to wipe out mice, the cheese ration was reduced to an ounce a week.
• The Queen, in her infinite wisdom, decided to stick with Windsor for the family surname. Shame – we'd have liked some other town like Bootle or Scunthorpe for a change.
• The Queen, again in her infinite wisdom, gave Benjamin Britten permission to write about the relationship between Queen Elizabeth I and the Earl of Essex. See! Even our Queen's got one of Essex's girls somewhere in her ancestry.

June: The Government announced that they would introduce flashing orange lights to help zebras cross the road (or something like that). Actually, it was the first pedestrian crossing.

August: The first 'short, sharp shock' detention centre was opened for 'big, bad boys' in Oxfordshire.

September: John Cobb, the famous speedster, was killed when he hit 240 m.p.h. (and maybe the monster) in his faster-than-usual motor boat on Loch Ness.

October: More tea vicar? Tea rationing finally ended.

November: Talk about backing the wrong horse. The only left-wing Bevanite to get into the Shadow Cabinet was Nye Bevan himself.
• *The Mousetrap* by Agatha Christie, opened in London. It must have had something going for it – it's still running.

December: The Queen's Christmas Day speech in which our sovereign addressed us like naughty children, was broadcast for the first time.

• Anyone who thought that the A bomb was the ultimate weapon was in for a big surprise. American scientists exploded their new Hydrogen, or H bombs (hundreds of times more powerful), on a small island in the Pacific. Unfortunately, it destroyed the island completely. Whoops!

1953

That's Crowned It

This was the year that our Elizabeth was officially made queen and finally got to wear the sparkly hat on 2nd June. It had been a fairly uneventful five months leading up to the Coronation. Uneventful, but generally encouraging economically. The Tory Government under old Churchill were finally forging ahead and the British were beginning to enjoy the end of all that crippling austerity. Winston had surrounded himself with a brilliant young posse of super-posh, ex-public schoolboys. Macmillan, Butler and Eden were to become household names for many years. Harold Macmillan had been told, when put in charge of housing, that the job would make or mar his career. The former soon became the case as in 1953, 327,000 houses were knocked up for the public sector, far exceeding what Macmillan had been asked to achieve. Despite coming from a well-loaded family, Macmillan knew how to roll up his sleeves and get his hands dirty (metaphorically). He once said of Rab Butler – the colleague of whom he somewhat disapproved – 'He's one of those men who can't cook without meat! I, on the other hand, can cook with bread and water.' I bet he could . . . as long as someone else had to eat it.

Whites Only

The British and other white people in Africa, though pompous, exploitative and mean, weren't daft. They'd long recognised the dangers of keeping a whole continent under their manicured thumb and on 5th February decided to strengthen their position even further. A master plan for a new British state with a population of over 7 million, to be called the Federation of Rhodesia and Nyasaland, was published in London. 'Of course,' it claimed, 'the interests of the African people will remain paramount.' It didn't say, however, that that was as long as they were happy to work their butts off for the whites and help them get stinking rich.

Russian Roulette

The man who saved Russia and then punished it for years, old Joe Stalin, died of a brain haemorrhage on 5th March. Unfortunately (for them) Russian leadership was so often a case of better the devil you know than the devil you don't. Old Joe had been responsible for the most appalling treatment in his less than welcoming labour camps (to which he sent anyone who disagreed with him) but he had also been a key figure in the creation of the USSR, and had been reckoned to be one of the most brilliant military commanders of the war.

After bitter wrangling and in-fighting, his replacement, comrade Nikita Khrushchev, struggled to the top of the pile and was to prove to the West certainly worse than the devil *we* knew.

Coronation Fever
One of my strongest memories as a child was how everyone went totally bonkers over the crowning of Queen Elizabeth on 2nd June. Millions, throughout the world, saw the ceremony on huge black and white tellies (with tiny screens). It was the first Coronation ever to be televised. Kids got commemorative gifts at school; flags and bunting were draped from our humble houses and the procession route was full to bursting with a population who still knew their place.

Ain't No Mountain High Enough
It really was the month for going crazy over events. On the day before the Coronation, Everest, the highest mountain in the world, was finally climbed by a New Zealander called Edmund Hillary and a Nepalese sherpa (guide) called Tensing. The expedition had been led by Englishman Colonel John Hunt. Truly, there was more fuss made than when, later, men walked on the moon. These days, so many people go up and down that damn mountain that I'd be surprised if some entrepreneur doesn't open a tea shoppe on the top before long.

Winston Poorly
Later in the month, almost as if all the excitement had been too much, poor old Winny Churchill, now 79, had a severe stroke and could hardly speak (unlike later PMs who could hardly stop) and was ordered to take it easy. The seriousness of his condition was

kept secret by a press that in those days had something approaching integrity. Churchill didn't really take over the reins again properly and was replaced by Anthony Eden in 1956.

Korea Goes Quiet

On 27th July, the guns were put back in their boxes at 10 p.m. A month later everyone returned their prisoners, and everything went back to exactly as it had been before. Great, the only problem was that it had cost 2 million lives to get absolutely nowhere. That's war for you.

Baby King Deposed

Over in Egypt, poor little King Fuad was tucked up with his cuddly camel when the news was announced that he wasn't king any more. Still, what you never knew you had, you probably never miss. General Mohammed Neguib, the guy who had chased off his dad (see p.31), became President and Prime Minister and Colonel Gamal Abdul Nasser (watch this name) became his deputy.

Here Come the Kennedys

On 12th September in the USA, the brilliant senator with the film star looks, Jack (later John) Kennedy, married a pretty girl called Jacqueline Lee Bouvier in Newport, Rhode Island.

Young Jack was destined to become the most powerful and influential (and naughty) person in the world as President of America. The world stage was nearly set for one of the most fascinating and dangerous periods in history.

Meanwhile

January: An almost replica accident to the appalling *Herald of Free Enterprise* disaster occurred in the waters off Belfast. Someone didn't close the front doors after having loaded all the cars on to the Princess Victoria ferry, and the heavy seas burst in. Captain James Ferguson, in typical daft British fashion, saluted as he went down with the ship and 128 passengers and crew.

February: A young starlet called Marilyn Monroe shocked America by appearing on a calendar wearing nothing but a coy smile. Despite cries of 'Filthy!' and 'Disgusting!', she came to represent all that was glamorous in American womanhood.

• Red letter day for kids, and black day for teeth. Sweet rationing ended.

April: Two Cambridge scientists discovered deoxyribonucleic acid. If that doesn't mean much, it became better known as DNA and unlocked many of the mysteries of how living things reproduce themselves (no rude comments please!)

June: One of the most famous murderers, in the history of famous murderers, Reginald 'no dick' (as he was nicknamed) Christie, was sentenced to hang. The funny little man with the round, steel-rimmed glasses had gassed four women (one of them his own Mrs) and hidden them behind a false wall and under the floorboards of his home in Notting Hill, London. Apparently two meticulous police searches failed to notice that his garden fence was propped up by a human thigh bone.

October: The cheapest four cylinder car on the world market, the dear old 'sit-up-and-beg' Ford Popular, was sprung on a surprised British public. If a prize could be given for the most ugly and austere looking motor, the 'Pop' would have won wheels down. Take one look at what manufacturers were doing, car-wise, in the States, however, and you'll realise how they must have regarded their poor brothers across the pond.

November: The skull of the Piltdown man, thought to be the missing link between man and monkey (no football hooligan jokes please!) turned out to be a hoax.

• Smog, one of the curses of British urban living, was proved to be a killer to asthmatics or people with weak chests. Masks costing one shilling were offered on the NHS.

December: Young people flocked to their radios every Monday night to hear a programme that broke totally new ground. 'The Goon Show' featuring Harry (of dubious Highway fame) Secombe, Spike (of dubious sanity fame) Milligan and the late lamented Peter Sellers finally showed that you didn't have to be grown up to get the jokes.

Hit of the Year: 'Diamonds are a Girl's Best Friend' by Marilyn Monroe.

1954

Plenty for All

This was the year that saw the end of rationing for our long-suffering relatives. No sooner had it stopped than a report was published saying that the diet under rationing had been much healthier than their normal diet. Many adults were now smoking a great deal, but the habit was then regarded as rather good for weight control. On 12th February however, another report hit the headlines claiming that smoking was likely to make you much thinner than you might ever have bargained for, being now a definite cause of lung cancer. Oddly enough, yet *another* report

claimed there was no proof of this, but lost a little credibility owing to having been issued from the Association of Tobacco Manufacturers.

More Mau Mau

You might be wondering how things were progressing up Kenya way. Events had taken a strange new turn as, on 4th April, British troops arrested 40,000 African suspects, on the premise, presumably, that if they managed to keep all the Africans in custody there wouldn't be any left to cause trouble. It was called the General China operation, after one of the Mau Mau's self-styled leaders. A bizarre little note which was supposed to have been written by one of the Mau Mau negotiators, who failed to show up to meet the security forces, was found in a cleft stick. It asked if the British would fly 'sky-shouting aircraft' over the forest areas equipped with loudspeakers to tell 'other terrorists' not to kill anyone that wanted to negotiate. We did fly aircraft over the forests – but they just fired rockets and dropped bombs. The bomb is mightier than the loudspeaker methinks.

Rock Hits the Brits

News came from America of their 'Rockingist Rhythm Group',

Bill Haley and the Comets. On 12th April, they recorded a number called 'We're Gonna Rock Around the Clock' which became a worldwide hit. Young Bill was an unlikely star, being a slightly podgy 29 year old with a daft kiss curl on his forehead. The sound, however, completely knocked British teenagers for six and at last it looked like there might be some alternative to all that dreary stuff (loved by their parents). Suddenly all those beehive-haired, big frocked songstresses like Eve Boswell and Alma Cogan looked and sounded decidedly past their sell by date. Not only that, but no longer did teenagers have to listen to naff songs like 'How Much is That Doggie in the Window?' or 'The Toothbrush Song'. The more fanatical followers of 'the devil's music', as some senior churchman called it, wore strange Edwardian clothes, weird haircuts and called themselves Teddy Boys. They didn't stop at music: their other great passion was cutting each other up (or anyone who got in the way) with old fashioned cut-throat razors.

We Love Billy

Another import from America came with the purpose of saving our souls. A clean cut, surprisingly handsome, hard-selling evangelist called Billy Graham hired anything from theatres to football stadiums to 'persuade' his wide-eyed converts to come forward and give themselves to the Lord. Thousands did but, unfortunately, the effects mostly wore off on the bus ride home.

Leave the Commies Alone

Back in America, MacCarthy's great Commie hunt was called off when the US Senate rapped him on the knuckles and told him that he'd been going over the top (a bit like Billy).

Suez Pull Out

After 75 years of occupation, British troops finally quit the Canal Zone following an agreement with Colonel Nasser who, as everyone had predicted, was now Head Egyptian. The British base was simply put into mothballs and maintained by civilians just in case of any more bother.

Meanwhile

April: British troops gave up trying to arrest all the Kenyans. The General China operation failed.

- At least as great a driver as Nigel Mansell (and relatively interesting), Stirling Moss won a race at the first ever motor racing event at the new Aintree course (now only used for horses).

May: The first electronic brain, or computer, by IBM, was moved into an office situation. Guaranteed to speed up calculating a thousand fold, the new machines looked positively elephantine compared to the stuff we use today.

- They all said it couldn't be done. Roger Bannister finally trotted a mile in under 4 minutes (3 mins 59.4). Who could have guessed that half a minute would still be chopped off that time?

June: Lester Piggot, who didn't always look like a dried prune, was the youngest rider to win the Derby at 18. He was to become the most famous jockey of all time.

- The old test for drunk driving was walking a straight line or reciting tongue twisters. Doctors suggested that there might be a more scientific way of working out whether one was out of one's box.

July: Bad year for bunnies. The rabbit population of Britain was in severe danger of total wipe-out owing to a sledgehammer-to-crack-a-walnut virus called myxomatosis introduced from Australia to keep the numbers down. Maybe they should have tried condoms.

Packet of 300 please.

September: The Federation of British Sun Clubs held its first annual meeting. All clothes had to be left in the lobby.

• Suckers for punishment, the Labour Party voted in favour of the re-armament of Germany. An audible chuckle was heard to come from Hitler's grave.

1955

Churchill Says Goodbye

Sir Anthony Eden

After half a century in politics, Winston Churchill finally sat down and let the younger Sir Anthony Eden, a kind of latter-day Bertie Wooster, have a go as Prime Minister just before the General Election. It was a smart move to keep the job in the family (Eden was married to Churchill's niece). On winning the vote, Eden made his old mate Harold Macmillan, Foreign Secretary and Rab Butler, Chancellor of the Exchequer. Rumblings were also heard at the top of the Labour party when Attlee bowed out in favour of Hugh Gaitskell.

Cyprus in Turmoil

Britain, still playing its part as fatherly protector of the world, had its work cut out keeping the Turkish and Greek Cypriots from making kebabs of each other – let alone the Greek Cypriot terrorists (EOKA) from attacking the British, who still ruled the island. Greek Cypriots had always resented this British rule and wanted the island to be part of Greece (obviously). The Turkish were not too delighted at this prospect (also obviously) and looked to Britain for protection. In other words, we were in another right mess.

Britain Invaded
According to some of the more red-necked, nationalistic Britons, we were undergoing our own mini-invasion. Hoards of black immigrants from the West Indies were storming our shores having been given the impression (probably from us) that this was the land of milk and honey (or rather money). When they got here, however, it was a different story. We might have wanted them to do all the nasty jobs but we certainly didn't want them living in respectable areas or (worse!) mixing with our sons and daughters. Consequently, the milk soon turned sour and the honey glued them firmly (and permanently) at the bottom of the social ladder.

Still Hanging On
The last woman to be hanged, ex-model Ruth Ellis, went to the gallows after shooting her racing driver boyfriend, David Blakely. It was the murder with everything, and the British public, who can always be relied upon to luxuriate in other people's misery, lapped it up. The case did, however, throw the barbarous act of the ultimate rope trick into public debate again. Whilst, in the past, it had been all right to hang weird-looking pervs like Christie, there was uproar about pretty ones like poor Ruth Ellis.

Gathering No Moss
Still, everything has a bright side. At least Stirling Moss had one less driver to beat. On 1st May, he became the first Briton to win the Mille Miglia, a tortuous road race through ordinary Italian roads and rather too often over ordinary Italian people. It was later banned for that reason (such spoilsports, the Italians). Motor

racing was obviously not the best spectator sport that year as a little later there was an appalling crash at Le Mans, when a Mercedes and two other cars left the track at 150 m.p.h. decapitating some eighty people. The Germans, still a touch sensitive about their reputation for killing innocent people, never raced again.

Warsaw Packed

Leaders from the Soviet Union, Poland, Czechoslovakia, Hungary, Rumania, Bulgaria, East Germany and Albania crowded into Warsaw to sign the Warsaw Pact, a treaty to balance NATO (the club formed by the West). All the signatories promised faithfully to be ever so good and not to solve any of their problems with violence, and to work towards eventually throwing all their nasty guns away. Unfortunately, no one looked behind the Russian delegates' backs to see if their fingers were crossed. Yugoslavia, ominously, didn't sign.

Jean Genie

If you ever wondered when the fashion started that was responsible for making everyone look exactly the same the world over, it was 1954. Like most crazes, the blue jean phenomenon came over the water from America and took our manufacturers completely by surprise.

Telly Sales

On 22nd September, the poor, long-suffering British were regaled with world-shattering messages like 'Murray Mints, Murray Mints – the too good to hurry mints' or 'The Esso sign means happy motoring'. Advertising had hit telly screens with a vengeance. Strangely enough, despite the huge fuss that had preceded commercial TV, the actual event was a bit of a damp squib.

Crying Out for Cash

The last famous singer of the old ballady school, American Johnny Ray, was reported as having earned half a million dollars in the last year. Oddly enough, he is more famous for breaking down and sobbing during his act. Even oddlier enough, British women went crazy for this dorky-looking crooner who wore a hearing aid. Rumour has it he turned it off while singing.

Elvis Who?
Back in the States, a young truck driver called Elvis Presley was becoming, known rather embarrassingly, around Memphis as The Hillbilly Cat. Never mind Elvis, we've all gotta start somewhere. His shellshocked manager 'Colonel' Tom Parker told the press that the girls were literally tearing his clothes off, much to the annoyance of their parents.

Margaret Ducks Out
The Queen's rather wayward sister, Margaret, called off her wedding to Captain Peter Townsend on 31st October. She gave some lame excuse that, due to her duty to the Commonwealth, and the fact that the Church didn't go a bundle on divorcées, she felt she must do the noble thing and not go through with it. The fact that she would lose all the loot that she got from the Civil List, and her place in the queen queue, had absolutely nothing to do with it (and my name's Henry VIII).

My Bomb's Bigger than Your Bomb
The year ended with the chilling news that not only had the Ruskies got themselves a hydrogen bomb of their very own, but it was bigger and better than the Americans'. To be fair, they did tell us they only had it for national security (and to blast anyone who didn't believe them to kingdom come).

Meanwhile

January: Shock of shocks! Petrol went up to 4/6d (23p) a gallon.

July: Ullswater, in the Lake District, positively throbbed to the roar of Donald Campbell's (son of the late Sir Malcolm) hydroplane *Bluebird,* as he broke the world water speed record at 202.32 m.p.h.

August: A yuckily slick painting of the Queen was unveiled at the Royal Academy. It was by Italy's modern old master Pietro Annigoni and made him very famous – luckily only for fifteen minutes (see p.211 on Andy Warhol).
 • A horribly embarrassed and embarrassing Irish TV host, Eamonn Andrews, compered the first horribly embarrassing 'This is Your Life' TV show on 3rd August. It doesn't seem possible that we're still putting up with it. It's interesting to note that the other great telly host, Terry Wogan (who we're also still putting up with) was born on the same date 17 years earlier.
 • It's also interesting to note that yet another syrupy chat show host, Jimmy Young, was Top of the Pops that October with the appalling 'Man from Laramie'.

November: No more soccer by candlelight. The first floodlit international football match was played at Wembley.

September: Role model for a million spotty teenagers, James Dean, kicked off his legend by killing himself (and his brand new Porsche) in a crash just outside Los Angeles.
 • *Health Warning:* Legendary status is not guaranteed by this course of action.

December: Not only had those Ruskies developed their pesky hydrogen bomb, but now they claimed to have a rocket which could deposit it 4000 miles away.

1956

Cyprus Hots Up

It was the same old British piggy, but in a different middle. Stuck bang in between the age-old hatred of the Turks for the Greeks (and vice-versa), it was beginning to look like a no-win situation. More and more British troops pitched up on the island of Cyprus to patrol the streets of the main cities of Limassol and Nicosia. The British Governor, Field Marshal Sir John Harding, secretly met the Greek Cypriot leader, the formidable farmer's son Archbishop Makarios (who looked like a demonic negative of Father Christmas), but there was absolutely no way that he was going to allow the Greeks (who outnumbered the Turks four to one) the independence they were clamouring for.

Bring the Cows In, Dad

It was reassuring to know that Britain was on the ball as far as nuclear attack was concerned. It was announced that we were to get a really fab early warning system. Members of the Royal Observer Corps were to be spread around the country at 15 mile intervals, linked by an underground telephone. When it came right down to it, however, one can only suppose that they were to look out of their bedroom windows and, presumably, ring up their colleagues and Central Office if they saw anything suspicious coming. They would then rush out in the streets and tell everyone to go indoors and shut all the windows, as radiation could apparently be rather unpleasant (it could cause one to feel a little dicky for up to three months they claimed). Farmers would be asked to go out and get all their animals in and, no doubt, cut all their crops quickly. Meantime, one can also only suppose that the approaching rocket would either park up and wait for us all to be ready or go round the block a couple of times. 'Dad's Army' lived again.

More Cyprus

Cyprus was becoming a nightmare chess game. Whichever way the British authorities moved seemed to get them into check. Finally, Sir John Harding, who was near the end of his tether, made a move that really stirred things up. He removed the Bishop (Makarios) and deported him to the sunny Seychelles (it's a hard life). EOKA the Greek terrorists, then went totally crazy, whipping up riots and bombing anything that stood still long enough. Hugh Gaitskell, the opposition leader, leapt in and ridiculed the move as 'an act of pure folly'.

On 25th March, reports came through that poor old Sir John had literally been sleeping on top of his own personal time bomb. One of his servants, an EOKA supporter, had put one under his bed (you just couldn't get the staff in those days). Fortunately (for Sir John) his unfaithful servant had set the time wrong and the device was later exploded harmlessly in his back garden.

Damn alarm clock

Khrushchev Comes to Visit

Nikita Khrushchev, having rocked the world by renouncing old Joe Stalin as a brutal, despotic and criminal murderer (weren't they qualifications for the job?), came to Britain to have a friendly pow-wow with our Government. Everything went well until the wonderful George Brown, a Labour Shadow Minister famed for getting pi . . . e-eyed and saying the wrong thing, got into a furious argument with the Commie boss at a rather boisterous dinner party. Unbelievably, Nikita responded by saying that if he was British he'd vote Tory, which was like George saying that if he was Russian he'd try to reinstate the Csar.

The Case of the Disappearing Crabb

While Khrushchev was visiting with us, a scandal broke that embarrassed the pants off the British Government. A naval frogman, Commander 'Buster' Crabb, was caught 'doing underwater tests' underneath the Russian ships that had brought their leader. The Russian newspapers accused Britain of 'shameful underwater espionage' and accused us of undermining international cooperation.

Poor old 'Buster' was never seen again and although the press suggested he'd drowned, most people thought he'd been nicked by the rotten Ruskies. A year later, speculation ended when Buster was found (unfortunately *sans* head) near where he'd disappeared. The question then was – how did he lose it? And was it now on Khrushchev's mantelpiece?

Naughty Nasser

On 13th June, Colonel Nasser waved goodbye, with an insincere smile, to the British troops who'd been occupying the Canal Zone. Thirteen days later, he dropped a bombshell by nationalising the Anglo-French controlled Suez Canal Company, saying, rather rudely, that if they didn't like it they could jolly well 'choke to death on their fury'. And fury there was, particularly from the

Colonel Nasser

French who'd built the canal. Nasser then said he would spend all the cash that he was going to charge foreigners for using the Canal on building the Aswan Dam, which doubly miffed the Brits and the Yanks who'd reckoned they could make a killing by financing and building the damn dam. It almost makes you think that international affairs are really only about money.

Eden, who nearly blew a gasket, said that we couldn't allow a creep like Nasser to 'have his thumb on our windpipe'. In truth, the crafty old Colonel had us by a much more delicate part of our anatomy.

Oh dear, oh dear – the next thing the poor long-suffering British heard was that their forces and the French forces had jumped into the gun boats and were heading for Suez. On 9th October the Israeli army, always ready to have a pop at the Arabs, stormed across the border and headed towards the Canal from the other direction. Nothing to do with helping us, however: they were just retaliating against Egyptian attacks across their border. The plot thickened!

On 31st October, all hell let loose when Anglo-French aircraft dropped their guts on to the Egyptians before they could even put their camels away. They'd given Egypt and Israel twelve hours to get all their soldiers out of the Canal Zone but although the Israelis did as they were told, the Egyptians (surprise, surprise) ignored the warning. For the first time in recent history, Britain and France were chums. The UN, America and even Russia were refusing to have anything to do with this reckless action. After a rather ragged little war, the Anglo-French troops captured the Canal Zone on 6th November: but that was, by no means, to be the end of it.

On 12th November, there was a ceasefire, brought about by the UN who set the terms (and threatened to send in 6,000 troops if they didn't agree).

The Canal was by now clogged by loads of sunken ships; Britain was shunned by world opinion; relations with the States were at their worst ever; sterling was near collapse; Sir Anthony Eden was suffering from exhaustion; Britain was accused of setting up the Israeli invasion; and the Government was in total disgrace. Not bad going, eh?

Dear old Eden's famous quote of the year went: 'We are not at war with Egypt – we are in armed conflict.'

Hungary for Freedom
On 26th October Hungary rose as one to show two fingers to their Russian oppressors. The brave Hungarian people fought the

occupying Soviet troops with their bare hands, and thousands were killed for their trouble. When the huge bronze statue of Stalin was chopped off at the knees in Budapest, it looked as if the people had got away with their bid for freedom. No way! On 5th November, the fireworks really went off and the dream became a nightmare when a thousand surly Soviet tanks rolled in and over Hungary. All that could be heard from Budapest radio was 'HELP, HELP, HELP' as the merciless Russian bear literally squeezed the life out of the opposition. But the United Nations, when push came to shove, was too chicken to pitch in, and by midday the brave revolution was ground into the mud.

In Britain, the little Communist Party was left with so much egg on its already red face that a huge proportion of the almost quaint bunch of idealists quit the party, totally gobsmacked by their Russian idol's gross actions. It was never actually to be the same again.

Meanwhile

January: The Astronomer Royal, known to have his head in the clouds, said that the whole idea of space travel was 'bilge'. Only ten years later he would have been able to watch the moon landing on television.

• For the first time (surprisingly) in Britain's history, the import and export of heroin was banned.

February: A piece of wood shaped very roughly like a mule went on British TV. Needless to say 'Muffin the Mule', the mute puppet, was a huge success with us deprived kids.

May: Self-service shops were seen for the first time in Britain. Critics feared overspending, pilfering and the death of the small shopkeeper. It was a watershed in retailing history. These days we are hard put even to find a shop assistant – alive or dead.

June: Every red-blooded man's toes curled with envy when the gawky playwright with the Buddy Holly glasses – Arthur Miller – married their favourite fantasy, Marilyn Monroe.

August: The man who made fame and fortune splattering paint against his canvases, Jackson Pollock, splattered himself against a tree when his car ran off the road. I wonder if he was a James Dean fan?

September: The film *Rock Around the Clock* proved to be too much for the hordes of Teddy Boys who flocked to see it. Near riots rocked around Britain's cinemas as the lads in the drainpipe trousers and drape jackets jived in the aisles and ripped up the seats. What would they have done, we ask, if they *hadn't* liked it?

October: Frozen pea-man Clarence Birdseye finally went to the great freezer in the sky.

1957

All Change on Top

Who says it's fun to be prime minister? Even after a long holiday in Jamaica, Sir Anthony Eden came back brown but knackered. He resigned on 9th January, both as Prime Minister and, two days later, from parliament. 62 year old Harold Macmillan (who by now looked like a kind but worried walrus) got the top job, putting poor Rab Butler's nose out of joint. (He'd been favourite with the bookies.)

Fool's Gold

Poor old Britain really was having a hard time abroad. The British ruling classes (God bless 'em), though realising they would have to give up their lucrative dominions one day, weren't prepared to rush into it. They thought independence should wait until the 'natives' had proved they could handle it – a policy which history has proved to be not that daft.

On 6th March the British Gold Coast decided to drop the 'British' bit . . . and then the 'Gold Coast' bit – becoming the all-black state of Ghana. The brand new President Kwame Nkrumah told the cheering crowds that at last they were free from the chains of imperialism (which meant us, folks!). He also told them he wanted to get back to the dim distant past when black Africa had all the power and cash.

No sooner had they all stopped jumping up and down in Africa, than a new cry of joy went up in Malaya as they ended their 170 years of British rule. They, however, were not so dismissive of their old masters, thanking us for recently saving them from the slavering jaws of communism, but presumably *not* thanking us for exploiting them rotten for years.

Britain Misses the Boat

On 25th March, France, West Germany, Italy, Belgium, Holland and Luxemburg signed the Treaty of Rome, so forming the European Common Market. It was formed to banish tariffs and promote the free movement of people, goods and money. Britain, who still thought it was a great major power, had decided not to join the flash new club, preferring to stick with the dear old Commonwealth. Many people (including the Prime Minister) were not at all sure we had done the right thing and wondered if we should talk some more . . . The French, always ready to get one over on the British, could hardly conceal their Gallic glee, saying like cocky enfants that we should have thought of it earlier and that we couldn't join in their game . . . What's French for 'Yah Boo Sucks'?

You Lucky People

There's nothing like a good old, top-of-the-pile, true blue, millionaire Tory Prime Minister to dish out patronising statements. On 20th July Mac (as he became known) told his loyal subjects 'Let's be frank about it. Most of our people have never had it so good.' Maybe Mac (and even Frank) was doing OK, but a lot of us Brits, especially the newish immigrants, felt like ramming those words down his aristocratic throat. To be fair, however, the standard of living for the newly invented lower middle-class was one hell of a lot better than when the Tories had gained power.

Dogs Rule OK

3rd November was a red letter day (literally) in the canine world. A Russian dog called Laika had been booted into space by his Communist masters and was now doing mega-walkies round the world without leaving his tin kennel. The good news was that

222

Laika became the most famous dog in all history. The bad news was that the spacecraft, six times heavier than the first satellite (called Sputnik 1), was not designed to come home, so poor Laika eventually ran out of oxygen (and dog biscuits). They should have called him Pluto as, for all we know, the poor mutt's still in orbit, like a little planet, in what became a flying coffin. Ah well, it's a dog's life!

Lordesses

On 30th October the Government proposed the creation of life peerages and baronesses (women lords). The former meant that, for the first time, the privileged classes (toffs) would no longer have a stranglehold on the House of Lords. Common folk could, if they did really well in their working lives, sleep all day on those lovely red leather benches like the others. Little did the Government know that one day it would let in the likes of cocky, pulp novelists like Lor . . . (I can't even say it) Jeffrey Archer.

Rock On

Far more important, Bill Haley and his Comets finally hit a rapturous London. There were even lofty, murmurs of approval from our more than stuffy Royal Family. Mind you, it was Princess Margaret who did the murmuring, and she always said and did the wrong thing.

British teenagers were now wallowing in the waves of American rock and roll talent that were gushing over them. Elvis was in full flow; Fats Domino, Frankie Lymon, Paul Anka, Jerry Lee Lewis, The Everly Brothers, Buddy Holly and Little Richard to name but a lot, heralded what became known as the golden age of rock and roll. In retaliation (and trying to cash in) British singers like Tommy Steele, Lonnie Donegan, Marty Wilde (Kim's Dad), Adam Faith and Cliff Richard squawked valiantly to make themselves heard, but their sound, to us 'experts', was positively weedy compared to all the fab imported stuff.

Meanwhile

January: No more free telly. GPO detector vans became a common sight in Britain's streets designed to catch licence dodgers.
• Everyone's favourite prince, Charles, went to school for the first time.

April: Tom Finney became famous for having the biggest shorts in soccer (and as Footballer of the Year).
• The 'Sky at Night' presented by the man who always looked like he dressed while escaping from a fire, and spoke faster than anyone could think – Patrick Moore – was broadcast for the first time.
• Only Yanks could invent something called the Drunkometer, designed to measure the alcohol on the breath. Was this an omen?

July: MPs voted themselves £750 a year increase on their expenses. Great idea, I vote we should all try it.

August: Despite plenty of work at home, 2000 British people a week were heading off for somewhere better (like Australia or Canada) to live. Their boats probably passed all the foreigners on their way here to find somewhere better to live.

• Chelsea Football Club caused a sensation by playing 17 year old Jimmy Greaves. Unlike most footballers, Jimmy refused to go away and has now joined the ranks of all those other boring TV sports 'experts'.

September: The Wolfenden Report came out of the closet saying that homosexual acts between consenting adult men should no longer be against the law. Lesbians carried on gay-ly.

October: Christian Dior, the man most responsible for making women look like women after the war, died in Italy.

1958

Talk's Cheap

1958 heralded the age of economical, speedy communications over far greater distances. At last, you could call your Auntie Ethel in Scotland without having to go through some surly operator. Also a new phenomenon called a motorway was built to by-pass Preston (no comment!). This eventually came to mean that, instead of sitting alone in a traffic jam, you had cars either side of you. The first bit of the, later-to-be-awful, M1 was opened in December. Huge new traffic signs had to be designed that could be read at 70 m.p.h.

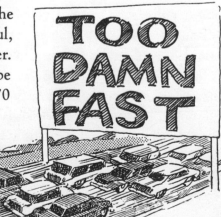

The Dreaded Meter Maids

While giving with one hand, the Government, typically, took with the other. Suddenly our urban roads sported gaily painted yellow lines which meant, for the first time ever, that one couldn't park where and when one wanted (provided there was a space). The downtrodden driver was allowed, however, to stop in *some* places but would, also for the first time, encounter horrid little meters which demanded payment for the privilege of doing just that. And if you didn't pay? Lurking on street corners, dressed in yellow and black battle gear, like psychotic wasps, were the instantly recognisable (and instantly despised) traffic wardens, whose only pleasure in life seemed to be stinging the motorist. The British, of course, accepted these new infringements on their liberty without a whimper.

Ban the Bomb

One group who didn't mind telling the government exactly where to shove its politics, formed the Campaign for Nuclear Disarmament or CND. Led by the one-day-to-be-PM Michael Foot; the brilliant, if somewhat potty philosopher, Bertrand Russell; the author J. B. Priestley; and the late, great journalist James Cameron, they were to become a force that would one day embarrass the hell out of the Government and *nearly* influence its nuclear policy.

'Ban the Bomb' became the battle cry of just about every socialist, student, or anti-establishment rebel in the country. Unfortunately, their famous scruffy marches looked so much like queues for soup kitchens that, predictably, their message tended to be ignored by the Great British (Oh dear, we'd better not make a fuss) Middle Class who thought that anyone who didn't wear a collar and tie was either a drug addict or on the payroll of the KGB.

Blacks Break Out

It just had to happen. On 9th September our coloured brothers, fed up with being taunted by white racists, suddenly blew their cool

226

and fought back. The Notting Hill race riots dragged to the surface the sort of tension that had been bubbling away in the States for years. For the first time, petrol bombs were lighting up British streets and from this point blacks, hacked off with being taken for granted, were seen to be on the case as far as racial discrimination was concerned. It was also, interestingly, the first time the press was censured for whipping up an already tense situation in order to make their story a bit sparkier.

Would you mind picking a fight with those chaps?

Nasser Rattles His Sabre

On 30th July, the Middle East erupted yet again. A gaggle of young Iraqi soldiers (heavily whispered-to by Nasser) overthrew their boss King Faisal. This put the wind up Iraq's neighbours Jordan and Lebanon, who immediately rang up America (on reverse charges) and asked for help. The Yanks, never ones to miss the chance of flexing their mighty muscles (especially where oil's concerned), got 1700 marines out of bed and rushed them to Beirut the following day where, instead of being fired at, they were greeted by a gaggle of bikini-clad Beiruti beach bimbos who offered them ice-cream and all sorts of other things.

Not to miss the party, and following our destiny as the world's co-prefect, 2000 British troops landed in Amman, Jordan to help King Hussein. The plot to invade Jordan by Nasser's United Arab Republic troops (really Syrians) had been cut off at the pass.

Nasser and his new best mate, the Soviet Union, were well miffed and ordered the UN to tell the British and Americans to leave the pitch for an early bath.

In England, Aneurin Bevan made a right prat of himself when he declared that Britain really shouldn't do anything to upset the Ruskies, while Khrushchev sent a postcard to Nasser saying that Soviet 'volunteers' could be available if required. Let battle commence.

Pick-a-Pope
The world's Catholics heaved a sigh of relief when, after twelve false starts, the Vatican managed to decide on a new head man and yellowy white smoke was seen issuing from the chimney (their way of telling the world that a decision has been made). Pope John XXIII, as he became affectionately known, was a surprise choice as, owing to his leftish views, he'd got right up the noses of the ultra-conservative Papal Court up Venice way.

De Gaulle est le Boss
Over in France, General de Gaulle, who looked more French than frog's legs, became the first President of the French Republic by an overwhelming majority. As far as we were concerned, this was 'pas bon' as it was well known that the ridiculously tall Frenchman thought we British were creeps.

Thalidomide Horror
The year ended with the horrendous discovery that the 'wonder' drug thalidomide, used to treat pregnant mothers for morning sickness, may have seriously deformed thousands of newborn babies.

Meanwhile

January: The net was closed. The first radar speed checks were used on London streets.
• Jerry Lee Lewis, the dynamic rock piano thumper, shocked a still

puritanical world when he announced that he'd married his cousin. Tricky, but not as much as the fact she was only thirteen. (Great balls of fire!)

• Civil servant Irene Ferguson cracked how to be the first woman to be paid the same as a man. She turned herself into one!

February: Probably the most talked-about air crash in history. The fabulous Manchester United football team was all but wiped out when their plane crashed on the runway at Munich Airport.

March: Always guaranteed to put his foot in his mitre, the late Bishop of Woolwich claimed that women who went out to work were the enemies of family life. Blimey Bish, it's a good job you've gone to the other place; you'd be hard put to find a mum that *doesn't* work these days.

May: Christopher Cockrell shocked the car, boat and aviation world by making a cross between all three. His 'Hovercraft' was the first vehicle to float on a cushion of air.

July: Nasser gets nasty. In Baghdad, King Faisal, the Crown Prince, and Iraq's prime minister were murdered in one of Nasser's more unpleasant plots.

August: High Fidelity, or Hi Fi, was the new buzz word in the record world. Would you believe it, you had to use two loudspeakers placed at either end of the front room, as well as the equivalent of your radiogram, somewhere in between.

October: Surprise, surprise! The USSR agreed to loan Egypt $100 million dollars to build the Aswan dam. Funny how things turn out.

• Just about the daftest looking machine ever built, the Bubble Car, went on display at the Motor Show in London. One variety of the car, designed to foil urban traffic congestion, required the driver to sit in front of his passenger and climb out of the roof.

The other type had the driver sitting next to his passenger and exiting ... through the front. Either way, both driver and passenger looked pretty damn stupid. The first were built by BMW who now own what remains of Britain's car industry. Now what does that tell you?

1959

Carry on Cuba

2nd January saw an event which at first looked as if it would have very little to do with Britain. The glamorous rebel leader Fidel Castro (him of the big beard and trendy fatigues) proclaimed to the world that he'd taken over Cuba after two years struggling against the infamous and desperately cruel dictator Batista. So far so good. Nobody likes dirty dictators and Britain was one of the first to suck up to – sorry, 'recognise' – the new regime.

Despite refusing to side with America against Russia in the exciting new game called Cold War, Castro laughed off any suggestion that he was a communist (what a porkie!) and even became the toast of Washington when he buzzed over there to convince them. Can anyone guess where this is going? Wait and see.

Cyprus Deal

More seriously, a deal was finally worked out for Cyprus. The new republic would have a Greek-Cypriot President and a Turkish-Cypriot Vice-President (that's diplomacy for you). Britain ducked out after 80 years of rule (most of them miserable) but was allowed to keep one or two military bases on the island. EOKA (the terrorist organisation) jumped up and down when they heard the details of the agreement and claimed their boss, Archbishop Makarios, would never either agree to the deal, or to be president. They couldn't have been more wrong. He did – and was . . . on 12th December.

You want the tooth fairy? What about the truth fairy?

Supermac Makes Moscow

Looking like a pint of Guinness in a too-tall white fur hat and a long black overcoat, Harold Macmillan landed in Moscow on one of his famous goodwill trips. After a brief meeting, Khrushchev claimed he had toothache and couldn't carry on with the discussions. Nice one Nikita – don't they have dentists up Russia way? British officials were not amused.

Good Cod — It's War

On May 6th Britain had a go at Iceland because they were using bully boy methods to enforce their new 12 mile fishing limit. This dispute had come to be known, rather obviously, as the Cod War, but had become a bit serious when Iceland's patrolling gunboats actually started firing live ammo at our trawlers (still using the old four mile limit). This simply wasn't cricket (or fishing), though I don't suppose the individual cods gave a monkey's *who* caught them – they'd end up as fish fingers either way.

Got Any Spares?

Hammer films came to life on 25th June when doctors at Hammer-smith Hospital announced that they were setting up a spare parts department. It worked like this. If you were unfortunate enough to be snuffed out by a road accident (for example), a chap would come along in a refrigerated van and whip out your liver and lights before you were cold on the road. These personal bits would then be stored back at the ranch until needed by someone whose own were knackered. Meantime, you'd be buried somewhat lighter. That was the theory anyway.

Mini Madness

One of the vehicles that could well turn you into spare parts if you crashed it, was the new Mini Minor, manufactured by the BMC (British Motor Company) to fit nicely under a speeding juggernaut. This four-seater motor, designed by Alec Issigonis, looked rather daft when it first came out, but the shape soon caught on and, to this day, has been a common sight on British roads. Its most remarkable feature is that it is actually bigger inside than out. Perhaps it was Issigonis who later designed Doctor Who's 'Tardis'. Dead clever these Italians.

Mac 'n' Ike

Carrying on his crusade to be mates with all and sundry, Harold Macmillan appeared with President Eisenhower (Ike) of America on the 'Downing Street Show' on telly, casually discussing world events in a manner that seemed about as natural as warm ice cream. It was, strangely enough, a huge hit, and the two old campaigners, flushed with success, proposed to do the same thing, a little more formally (if that was possible), with De Gaulle and Khrushchev.

Telly Takes Over

Distressing reports from the cinema industry claimed that telly was beating them hands down in popularity. This wasn't helped by Auntie BBC buying 20 American feature films. It was around this time that cinemas began mysteriously turning into a brand new scourge – the dreaded bingo hall.

Mac Does it Again

8th October saw a new General Election, and Supermac, 'never having had it so good', pulling one of the hugest majorities ever seen. Gaitskell, the loser, put his failure down to squabbling within his party. He did agree with Macmillan, however, that the class war was dead. Dead? They obviously didn't read *The Tatler* or *The Lady*.

Europe Does the Splits

Just as the European Common Market Club was settling down with a self-satisfied feeling of superiority, Britain, Austria, Denmark, Norway, Portugal, Sweden and Switzerland formed a club of their own, effectively showing two digits to the others. EFTA (European Free Trade Association) as it was called, made no secret of trying to upstage the rival gang. Talk about a damned cheek – they even asked the others to disband and come over to their clubhouse. Who was to get the last laugh! Read on.

Meanwhile

January: Sit-ins on London Underground's Northern Line prompted the powers-that-be to warn against strikes. 35 years later the line's still a disgrace.

• Being overweight was reckoned for the first time to be more of a problem in Britain than malnutrition. Simple! Why didn't all the thin people eat the fatties? Next!

• Henry Cooper, a much loved British hero, with a face like his own punch bag, became British and Empire Heavyweight Champion on 12th January, aged 24. 'Our 'Enery is still, thankfully, alive and kicking (or punching).

February: A brat is born. A black day for all those tennis fans who like a quiet life. John McEnroe entered the world.

What's with you two? Are you blind? Can't you understand plain English? You must be stupid....

April: The Queen Mother and Princess (I dig rock and roll) Margaret had an audience with the Pope. I've heard of being desperate to get your daughter married off, but this was ridiculous.

May: Talking of marriage. The state of Alabama banned a kids' book in which a black rabbit married a white rabbit. They were probably far too young to get married anyway.
• Talking of rabbits, two American monkeys became the first living creatures to return to earth in one piece (or should I say two pieces) when they splashed down in the Atlantic. They'd just been cruising around 360 miles above the Earth.

August: A survey reported that the average British household spent 18s 1d a week on food. These days that would hardly pay for the plastic bags to carry the stuff home in.

September: One of the funniest events in world politics occurred when Khrushchev lost his rag (red) because the Americans (for security reasons) wouldn't let him visit Disneyland. Sad really – he could have got a job as a Dopey (of *Snow White* fame) look-alike.

November: Talk about jobs for the boys. Fidel Castro astounded the Cubans (and the rest of the world) by making his old revolutionary chum, and pin-up, Che Guevara, Head of the National Bank. It was a bit like making Ronnie Biggs (see page 86) Chancellor of the Exchequer.

1960

Mac's Wind

On February 3rd, good old Supermac came out with another famous one-liner. He pronounced in a speech to the South African Parliament, referring to black unrest, that the 'wind of change' was blowing through the continent, whether we (notice the we) 'liked it or not'. Oh boy, did that go down like a lead balloon with the whities. He then went on to say that, if they weren't careful, all the African countries would shack up with the Communists who, in the short term, had so much more to offer. Let's face it, it doesn't take the best offer in the world to attract people who have little more than they stand up in.

It was no pie in the sky prediction either. Those saucy Soviets were definitely huffing and puffing at the African hut doors and they knew they wouldn't have to blow that hard. Hardly had the words left Mac's mouth when the appalling Sharpeville massacre gruesomely underlined what he'd been saying. 56 Africans were mercilessly slaughtered and 162 injured, at a rally in Sharpeville in the Transvaal. The police had waded into blacks demonstrating against having to carry pass cards. This was very much the thin end of a wedge that was to widen for years to come.

The Cold War Bites Harder

The Russians were now really throwing their weight around and everyone in Britain and the rest of the West was getting pretty nervous about what they might do next. Over in Germany, floods of people (mostly farmers) were crossing over from East Berlin following the Communist enforced collectivisation of small farms. Then, the summit conference, planned the previous year by Mac and Ike with De Gaulle and Khrushchev, fell through owing to the shooting down of an American plane (flown by Gary Powers) which the Commies outrageously claimed had been spying on them. Actually, to be totally truthful, it had (tee hee!).

Kennedy Gets In

The whole of the western world was delirious at the news, on 9th November, that the handsome John (or was it Jack?) Kennedy had beaten the sleazy Richard Nixon to the presidency of the United States. It effectively made this boyish-looking, youngest-ever, president, the most powerful man in the world. It would not be exaggerating to say that young people, throughout the free world, believed that he was the one person who might prevent us all from being blown to kingdom come by the follies of our elders and worsers.

Maggie Marries

The 60s also opened with the world-shattering news that Princess Margaret, after all that earlier fuss, was going to marry a common person after all. The lucky man was Anthony Armstrong-Jones who, although only a mere photographer (passports and wedding photos to the nobility), was actually rather posh. The rest of the Royal Family didn't make as much fuss as the last time because he wasn't divorced and they were no doubt beginning to wonder if they'd ever get poor Maggie off their hands.

Ship Ahoy

One of the great events to take our minds off all that Russian breath on our necks, came to a finale on 21st July. Francis Chichester (later to be Sir'd), a 58 year old Briton, suffering from lung cancer (and, as some people thought, total insanity!), successfully sailed the Atlantic alone, in the new world record of 40 days. His little boat, which looked not much bigger than a bath-tub, became almost as famous as its driver-sorry-captain when it went on display in London.

Pornographic Penguins

An even better worry-diverter was the hilarious trial of Penguin Books who were charged with the publication of an 'obscene' book, *Lady Chatterley's Lover*, by D. H. Lawrence. There's nothing more likely to make a book a bestseller overnight than to suggest that it's dead rude. Sales of this otherwise rather weedy book rocketed and schoolboys in every playground in Britain could be seen huddled in corners hoping the book would spring open at the dirty bits.

Mr Mervyn Griffith-Jones, prosecuting, came out with a classic remark. He asked the jury if it was a book that they would wish their wives or servants to read. Barristers were then, as now, not always completely in touch with the common man. Joking apart, if you were fortunate enough to have a wife or a servant, they'd probably have already read it. Case dismissed!

The Choice to Fight

Even more good news was announced on 31st December, unless you were one of the poor unfortunate lads to receive the last National Service call-up cards. No longer would youngsters of eighteen be press-ganged into playing soldiers for two years with the vague possibility that if they did well they could get killed for Queen and country.

New Old-Fashioned Music

Traditional jazz, with its almost quaint plinky-plonky charm, had been like an underground music amongst trendy art students. These Beatniks as they were labelled were the very first to wear high pointed boots, long hair, heavy make-up and black Gothic style clothes (and that was the boys!). Suddenly trad. jazz leapt across to the hit parade and bands led by Acker Bilk, Chris Barber and Ken Colyer couldn't believe their luck (or their bank balances). But it wasn't to last. Rhythm and blues, sweeping through all the clubs and bands, led by guys like Georgie Fame, Long John Baldry and Alexis Korner soon made Acker Bilk and his mates look like tired old muso-saurs.

Meanwhile

January: The sale of pep pills, like Purple Hearts, much loved by the modern teenager, were given the thumbs down by our caring Government.

February: Top of the hit parade was a song called 'Teen Angel' sung by American Mark Dinning. This little ditty was all about a guy singing to his recently-ex-girlfriend who has been smashed to bits in a car crash. Charming!
• The star hovered again over Buck House heralding the birth of Prince Andrew (later known as 'Randy Andy' for reasons unknown).

April: Ace racing driver Stirling Moss lost his licence for a year. He'd been driving his ordinary motor, on the ordinary roads, forgetting he wasn't on the race track. Thirteen days later he won the Monaco Grand Prix . . . remembering that he was.

May: Those naughty Teddy Boys were creating such a stir that the government passed a bill to clip their wings, or D-A's (popular abbreviation for their 'ducks-arse' hairstyle).

July: To give you some idea of what British record buyers were into in 1960, Rolf Harris (that ghastly professional Australian) had a major hit with his heart-rending version of 'Tie Me Kangaroo Down Sport'. At that stage grown-ups, as one might guess, still represented the lions' (or kangaroos') share of the record-buying public.

August: Two Russian dogs managed to get home to earth alive after their outing in space. This encouraged their masters to have a go.

1961

South Africa Quits
You might have thought that when South Africa told us that, like most other Commonwealth countries, it wanted to become a republic, the British Government would have jumped up and down with relief. Macmillan, on the contrary, stated in his most sincere, paternalistic voice, that he was sorry, maintaining that being mother of the Commonwealth was the only way we could influence the lot of the poor down-trodden black Africans.

Horrid, cynical people might claim that Mac's motivations were not quite that big-hearted. South Africa was one of our major trading partners and worth shed-loads of loot especially as the two countries enjoyed preferential treatment as Commonwealth members. The solution was simple. South Africa would go it alone politically, but tradewise would cooperate with Britain in all possible ways. In other words, we're all right, Jack, tough luck on the natives.

Cuba Libre!

Meanwhile something very ominous was going on up Cuba way. That definitely 'non-Communist' Fidel Castro and his brave boys were fighting off an invasion by the exiled lot that used to control the country. The Cuban Revolutionary Council, as they called themselves, had apparently set up an airstrip at the Bay of Pigs. Big deal you may say! Yet another tin-pot revolution. Why should that be any concern of ours? It was when we realised that all Castro's planes, tanks and armaments were being supplied free from communist Russia, and that much of the weaponry used by the old regime was American, that the piquancy of the situation became clearer and more scary.

Khrushchev had a furious argument with President Kennedy demanding that the Yanks should, like them, help Castro. New boy Kennedy told him, in no uncertain terms, that if Russia poked its snubby East European nose into Cuba, or anywhere else for that matter, it would get severely bloodied. For a while they pushed and pulled at each other like two snotty kids in a playground, while the rest of the world wondered if we were teetering on the edge of the long-awaited World War 3.

Postscript: The invasion failed, and on 1st May Castro proclaimed Cuba as a socialist nation and, surprise, surprise, banished elections.

Walled In and Out

Yet another huge event that indirectly made our knees wobble happened on 31st August. What had seemed like a nice little brick wall, separating East and West Berlin, suddenly grew and became covered in barbed wire. All the 50,000 East Berliners who worked in the Western bit were turned back, and anyone who tried to cross over was promptly shot. The only ones who did escape were the few East German guards who saw that it was their last chance to get out. There was absolutely nothing the other Berliners could do about it. By October, British and American tanks literally faced Russian ones across the border.

Children's Hour Axed

Britain's children were also getting a rough deal. Auntie BBC had decided to take 'Children's Hour' off the wireless and away from her nieces and nephews. To be honest, it wasn't the greatest loss to us sixties' kids as it was hopelessly out of date, catering for nice children of a bygone age: the telly was much better!

Rock Rolls On

Although British artists like Cliff Richard and Adam Faith were making a few quid they were still small potatoes compared to the hip-swinging Elvis, bug-faced Roy Orbison or the super-smooth Everly Brothers, who were dominating the charts. The greatest news in music this year was that Little Richard, the totally-round-the-bend High Priest of Rock and Roll, came back into the business after four years as a proper preacher. Praise the Lord!

Meanwhile

January: The 1,000,000th Morris Minor trundled off the production line. In slight contrast, the Jaguar E Type, maybe the prettiest car ever, had a very easy birth. It cost an unbelievable £2196.

• There was an investigation as to why the poor Queen's personal

train was held up for an hour. Perhaps she needed a break from all that coal shovelling?

April: The Soviet Union put the first human, Major Yuri Gagarin, sneakily into space. The Americans congratulated them with forced smiles, well aware that they'd lost the man-in-space race. They quickly bunged up the first person they could find with an astronaut's suit, a month later.

June: The first push-button pedestrian crossings were seen in London.

July: With not a little embarrassment the British Government, cap in hand, asked if we could join their Common Market. The special terms, asked for by Macmillan, really miffed the French (can you believe?) who threatened to spin out the talks for as long as possible or use their veto to keep us out.
• A report was published, saying that Britain's population had rocketed by 2.5 million in the last ten years. It now stood at 52,675,094.

August: The GPO announced that the tower they were planning in central London was going to be much taller than at first planned. This white elephant, the Post Office Tower, now has a mere handful of people working in it.

September: The first chain store to deal with the Baby Boom – Mothercare – opened in Kingston, London.

15,000 people demonstrated in London against the possession of the nuclear bomb. Dear old Bertrand Russell was jailed for 'inciting a breach of the peace'.

October: The Queen was obviously not that wild about having a 'commoner' brother-in-law, so she made Anthony Armstrong-Jones, Princess Margaret's new hubby, the Earl of Snowdon. Wasn't there a story about a princess who kissed a frogotrapher and got a prince?

December: Adolf Eichmann, a jolly nasty German, who had helped in the extermination of thousands of Jews, was finally sentenced to his own extermination after a lengthy show trial.

1962

Mac's Spring Clear Out

The most exciting event for years in British politics occurred when Harold Mac-the-knife-Millan cut a third of the cabinet in one slash. It followed an appalling by-election result, in which a Liberal overturned a Tory in Orpington. The party was pretty shaky anyway, and we British were becoming disillusioned with continual Tory promises of good times. It's nice to know some things never change!

Jeremy Thorpe, the up-and-coming Liberal MP, came up with the best joke about the Cabinet sackings when he said of Mac, 'Greater love has no man than this, that he lays down his friends for his life.' Ironical really – the same was to happen to Jeremy years later.

Blacks Stays Back

Now Britain had most of its unglamorous jobs filled (prime minister, etc.), the British Government were unkeen to have all those eager immigrants turning up from the Commonwealth, cluttering up our Labour Exchanges (now Job Centres). They

therefore searched for a way to get themselves out of the promises they'd made. Enoch Powell, at the Ministry of Health, didn't mind if the immigrants were skilled doctors or nurses as he was running a bit short, but he was getting a bit worried about the 'outrageous' habit the underprivileged ethnic minorities had of living together in little inner city communities and carrying on their customs. In July, therefore, the Government brought in the Commonwealth Immigration Act which stated, in so many words, that to get into these fair isles an applicant should either:

a. Have a job to come to.

b. Be able to do something that was needed in this country (see spying).

c. Have enough cash to be able to support themselves. (In which case, why would they want to come here?)

The opposition parties called it a nasty little piece of racist legislation as it was fairly obvious that the Act was directed at 'coloured' immigrants.

Satire at Last

At home the British had a new craze: taking the mickey out of itself. A new telly series called 'That Was The Week That Was', hosted by a sharp, young, clever David-called-Frost, broke new ground by lampooning everything pompous and anachronistic about our Establishment. (It's interesting to note that he is now *Sir* David Frost and part of the very Establishment that he used to laugh at.) It was around this time, too, that a new magazine called *Private Eye* hit the newsagents. The *Eye* (as it was known) also debunked the system and anything that stood still long enough.

Vietnam Looms

The beginnings of the Vietnam War were set in motion when that 'hope for world peace' Jack (or was it John?) Kennedy sent 5000 troops into Siam to check the expanding Communist military offensive. Nobody in America quite realised what he was getting America into and, anyway, the wonder-boy President could do no wrong.

World on the Brink

Everyone in Britain held their breath on 28th October when John (or was it Jack?) Kennedy put his hand to his holster and challenged Khrushchev once more to a draw. A high, spy plane flying over Cuba (again) had spotted lines of missiles pointing straight at the United States. America had never been threatened before and they sure didn't like it. Before you could say 'Coca-Cola', they'd put loads of ships round Cuba and stopped anything going in or out. Kennedy then demanded that Khrushchev took his missiles and shoved them anywhere he liked – as long as they weren't in Cuba. For one whole day the world swayed on the edge of nuclear war with nobody knowing which way Khrushchev would jump. In the end, he saw that 'peacemaker' Kennedy wasn't going to chicken out and backed down himself. Castro was most cross when he realised he was just a pathetic pawn in a much larger power struggle, and really smarted when he had to watch American observers supervising the dismantling of his lovely, shiny new toys.

Jobs Vacant

If you wanted a job that offered loads of cash, plenty of foreign travel, extreme danger but loads of excitement, then the big word down the local Labour Exchange was 'espionage'. Seriously, the early sixties was open season for spies. Every country was spying on every other country and every spy was spying on every other spy.

On 22nd October, an Admiralty clerk, William Vassall, was jailed. It turned out that the filthy Russians had found out that poor William didn't like girls much (know what I mean?) and invited him to a rather gay little party where they took lots of rather explicit photos (use your imagination) while he wasn't looking. They then blackmailed him into selling secrets about the navy and, no doubt, what colour underwear certain politicans wore.

On 22nd November, the Russians got their own back for his arrest and captured British businessman Greville Wynne, who'd gone to Hungary to demonstrate caravans (and my name's Marco Polo). The Soviets then began to prepare a major show trial.

Meanwhile

February: A little known group called The Beatles were turned down by the huge Decca recording company, who thought they'd didn't stand a dog's chance of making it into the charts.

• *The Sunday Times* brought out the first colour supplement. Critics, like those of The Beatles, turned it down saying the idea would never catch on. These days, even your local parish newsletter has a colour supplement.

• By now, both Russia and America had fine collections of each other's spies, so it was time for swapsies. Russia traded Gary Powers (of spy-plane fame) with KGB Colonel Rudolph Abel (America's most valuable prisoner). It wasn't really a fair swap as

Powers was only doing ten years as opposed to Abel's fifty.

June: Anyone want to bet on where Britain's first legal casino was situated? Brighton wins the money.
• The first edition of 'Police Five' was broadcast. Shaw Taylor, its presenter, became known in the underworld as 'Whispering Grass' proving that even crooks have a sense of humour (even if Mr Taylor didn't).

August: Yet another country rejected its mother. Jamaica gained independence after 307 years of British rule.
• Tragic news for male movie fans. Marilyn Monroe, arguably the most glamorous lady in the world, died in mysterious circumstances. Since then, the official verdict of suicide has been thrown into serious doubt and 'connections' with at least two of the Kennedys have come to light.

December: London's air was known to be filthy and, as if to prove it, a three day pea-souper fog caused the death of at least 60 people.

1963

Another Day — Another Harold

18th January was a black day for the Labour Party – literally. Hugh Gaitskell, the controversial leader of the party, died of a mystery virus infection. Harold Wilson, who looked like a slightly secretive pipe-puffing hamster, got the job after a savage fight with the brilliant, if unconventional, George Brown, who'd been Gaitskill's deputy (and who presumed he'd one day be sheriff). Brown decided to stay on as number two, but all their mates had a sly bet on how long they'd last before a major tiff.

De Gaulle Puts 'Le Boot' In

At an enthralled Paris news conference, President Charles de Gaulle delighted the agog frogs when he finally came out of the woodwork and trashed Britain's hopes of joining the Common Market. He told them that as far as he was concerned England would always act like a little two-bit island nation and, therefore, had no business trying to get into the big boys' 'gang'. Also he quite rightly recognised that we were not about to chuck away what was left of our Commonwealth (even though most of the Commonwealth countries were trying to chuck us). The final insult came when he looked condescendingly down his huge Gallic hooter and suggested that maybe Britain could be offered some paltry junior associate status. Macmillan, highly miffed, accused de Gaulle of trying to dominate Europe. Who said the Battle of Agincourt was forgotten?

Super Scandal Begins

There had been rumours flying around London for some time that the immensely boring-looking Minister for War, John Profumo, was carrying on with a pretty young model (not that boring eh?). Like all MPs caught with their pinstripes down, Profumo tried threat, bluster and writ at first, and must have thought he'd got away with it after his boss Macmillan called the matter closed. When, however, the 'model' Christine Keeler, who admitted doing a little more than just disrobing, was also connected (in the biblical sense) with Russian diplomat, Eugene Ivanov, the whole delicious concoction started fizzing again.

On 5th June, Profumo finally admitted that he'd been telling privileged porkies and promptly resigned from the Government and Parliament. The silly chump had been shopped by a rather suave West End osteopath Dr Stephen Ward, who was later charged for living off the earnings of up-market prostitutes like Keeler and her drop-dead-gorgeous chum, Mandy Rice-Davies, the epitome of the new term 'dolly bird'.

It was fab reading; the more that came out, the more the British public realized that just about all areas of lowlife and highlife (including royalty) were somehow intertwined. During his trial, the dirty doc, Stephen Ward, described a world where aristocracy mixed with drug addicts and sexual perverts (so what's new?). At one point, you could count the influential people who *weren't* involved on the fingers of one foot. The gutter press, who usually didn't require more than a whisper to create a scandal, could hardly believe their ears or luck. But Ward was very much the scapegoat and the whole sleazy business took a sad turn when, while waiting to be sentenced, he topped himself.

Macmillan, who'd tried his level best to sweep the whole thing under his plush Downing Street carpet, could hardly be seen for all the egg on his face. The poor chap was blown away by the affair and resigned as Prime Minister. The end of a perfect scandal.

New Home for Alec

Our favourite Prime Minister was replaced by Sir Alec Douglas-

Home, putting poor Rab Butler's nose out of joint even further. He'd been waiting in the wings (like Cinderella) for the star part for two years but had been kept from going to the ball by a secretive little in-group later labelled 'Mac's Magic Circle'. Ian Mcleod and Enoch Powell obviously thought Douglas-Home was a right prat and refused to work with him, accusing the poor toff of being lightweight, which was not surprising as he looked a bit like a skeleton dressed in MP's or rather PM's clothing.

The First Great Train Robbery
On 24th March, Dr Beeching, the man brought in by the Government to run their train set better, did something that not only changed the face of Britain, but literally ruined thousands of people's lives. He closed 2128 stations, mostly on branch lines. It effectively stranded the very people who needed their railways most.

This was the beginning of the end of the great battle between road and rail and heralded the car becoming the god it is today. If you want to blame anyone for all those hideous smelly multistorey car parks or those horrid, traffic-free shopping centres, full of the sort of people you only see in horrid, traffic-free shopping centres, then it's all down to Doctor Beeching.

The Second Great Train Robbery
On 4th August, another crime occurred that is still talked about today. A group of fifteen hooded hoods held up a train in a manner better suited to a bad cowboy film. They jumped the train knowing it contained over £1,000,000 in used (thereby untraceable) banknotes and got clean away. Most British people, it must be said, had a slight admiration for the audacity of their crime. Even so, over the following years, the police had caught up with most of them. Only one, Ronald Biggs, managed to escape and hole up in Brazil. Despite numerous attempts to extradite him, Ronnie continues to thumb his nose at the British authorities while cavorting with tanned Brazilian bimbos on Acapulco beaches. Who says crime doesn't pay?

Beatlemania

The last great robbery of 1963 involved the stealing of the hearts of practically every teenage girl in Britain. The Beatles, that group that Decca said would never make it, suddenly did, and were hotter than Bill Haley or Elvis put together. Many of us boys were to become sick of the sight of John, Paul, George and Ringo; firstly, because our girlfriends fancied them more than us, and secondly, because we were fed up to the back teeth of always hearing about how fab Liverpool and the dreary Mersey Sound were.

Not bad Kevin – but what about the accent?

Bye-Bye John or Jack

The year ended with news that made everything else, including Beatlemania, pale into insignificance. On 22nd November, John Kennedy's brief career as President was cut short by the assassin's bullet. Everyone, the world over, froze at the news, and the prospect of a world without him. The controversy over who shot him still rages on. The man who was instantly arrested, Lee Harvey Oswald, was himself plugged by a gangster with Mafia connections called Jack Ruby, who then in turn died three years later of a mysterious 'bloodclot'. There's always been a strong rumour that the dreadful 'Commies' might have had a hand in it (at least it couldn't have been Marilyn Monroe).

The Bomb Gets Banned

At last the Brits, the US and the USSR hung up their egos and signed the Moscow Treaty, banning the testing of nuclear weapons in the atmosphere, outer space, under water or in back gardens. De Gaulle wouldn't join in – probably because everyone expected him to.

Meanwhile

February: The worst learner driver in Britain, Margaret Hunter, was fined for 'erratic' driving after her instructor jumped out, claiming it was pure suicide to stay in the passenger seat.

April: British 'caravan' salesman Greville Wynne (see page 82) was sentenced to three years in a Russian prison followed by five in a labour camp for spying. Guess they didn't want any caravans.

June: Our 'Enery (Cooper) stopped all our hearts when he floored Cassius Clay – probably the best World Heavyweight Champion in the history of boxing. Trouble was, Cooper always had dodgy eyes and was pulled out in Round Five with a bad cut.

July: Viscount Stansgate became the first peer to renounce his title so that he could be common like us (well, a bit like us). Anthony Wedgewood Benn, bless him, has been a thorn in the side of the rich and privileged ever since.

November: Whether the BBC were 'leant on' or not, we'll probably never know, but 'That Was The Week That Was', which had reached cult status, was suddenly axed.

December: Poor Christine Keeler (who only wanted a fair day's pay for a fair night's work) was jailed for nine months for conspiracy and perjury.

1964

Labour In

This was the year that the Labour party, despite its hobby of inflicting wounds on itself, beat the floundering Tories after fifteen years of rule. Harold Wilson, the new PM, won instant popularity because, for once, Britain had a leader who hadn't been born with a silver  spoon in his mouth (but didn't he let us know it?). 'When I was a lad we were so poor . . . ' and so on, and so on.

The Socialists had an ambitious set of plans and a new determination to carry them out.

Vietnam Explodes

President Lyndon Johnson, who had eased into the dead Kennedy's boots, managed to get Congress to form a posse to hunt and contain those darn Communists in North Vietnam. His action followed an attack on US destroyer Maddox in the Gulf of Tokin, and the retaliation was fast, furious and extremely unpleasant. This was the official beginning of the Vietnam War, which was to influence and frighten the British for years (even though we managed to keep our noses out of it).

All Change

Nothing remarkable had happened since the war fashion-wise. Men and boys looked basically the same as they always had, and women were mostly influenced by what was happening in Paris. Trousers for ladies (popular during the war) had disappeared; hemlines had gone up and down (but always a decent distance below the knee); bras had changed from soft and rounded to wired and pointy; knickers had shrunk from voluminous to fairly brief; shoes had lost the clumpy look of before and during the war and were now stiletto-heeled and narrow. If anything, after the American-inspired big petticoats and bobby socks of the newly invented fifties' teenagers, grown-up women's clothes had become even more conventional, with hardly a dividing line between the post-teenagers and the older mob.

Nothing prepared the British female (or male for that matter) for the revolution that was to occur on 13th Jan 1964 when a young art student named Mary Quant suddenly launched a stinging attack on the whole French led *haute-couture* scene, saying it was *très* boring and out of date. From her small shop Bazaar in Chelsea, she started a look that was to take over the world including Paris (though the French would never admit it). At last girls could buy clothes that their mums would look silly in. Shorter than short skirts, bold patterns that hurt your eyeballs, pink lipstick, false eyelashes, clipped elfin-like haircuts and paler than skin colour tights (necessary if your bottom was practically showing). The swinging sixties were born.

Sex, drugs and rock and roll were becoming available to all. If your mum and dad didn't like it . . . all the better. It was a period when anyone over, say, 25, was past it. At last British kids had found their own identity and even the Yanks, for the first time, started peering rather inquisitively over the water.

But it wasn't just in fashion that our youngsters began flexing their muscles. The Beatles had for some time been the toast of America, but now rhythm and blues, that had been filling all the British clubs and pubs, was becoming the honey on top. Bands like The Rolling Stones, The Animals, The Zombies, Rod Stewart and Alexis Korner were playing a kind of raw aggressive music that was not only knocking the kids sidewise but shocking Establishment America. Even when, the following year, the Labour Department of the US Government rescinded all visas for visiting British groups, it failed to halt their growing popularity.

Mods and Rockers

This new youth freedom had some sensational side-effects. A new cult group called Mods, who wore clothes inspired by Quant and her growing bunch of imitators, would speed in magnificent convoys to seaside towns all over the south coast. There, they would have magnificent punch-ups with their sworn enemies The Rockers, a group of sadly dated, motorbike-riding, leather-jacketed, greasy-haired, American-inspired tearaways (who lived with their mums).

It's interesting to note that racial prejudice between black and white youth was practically non-existent in those days. In fact, the racism displayed by their parents was yet another thing to rebel against.

Meanwhile

January: One of the first of the hilarious truly British sitcoms,

'Steptoe and Son', was declared Britain's most popular telly show. The first episode of the last series had claimed 9,653,000 viewers.
• Machines hit Underground stations. Automatic ticket machines that nearly ripped your fingers out of their sockets were first seen.
• Can you believe it, the average weekly wage in 1964 was £16 14s 11d.
• A gloomy month for Britain – *The Sun* newspaper rose in the east.

February: The Government announced the building of the Channel Tunnel. I think they must have had one Frenchman and one Englishman doing the digging from either end ever since.

March: Yet another baby for our parents to support. The Queen had a fourth sprog, called Edward.

April: The twelve members of the Great Train Robbery gang got 307 years in prison (but not each).
• A chap who was to be a thorn in the side of the British was made Prime Minister of Rhodesia. Ian Smith, a butcher's son, looked more like a strict Presbyterian minister than a politician.

May: Music fans, bored with the stodgy old BBC, had a new, deliciously illegal girlfriend called Radio Caroline. She was a 'pirate' ship parked somewhere off the east coast, blasting out non-stop-pop to the fury of the Beeb and most parents.

July: Never have so many people owed so much to so few. To one, in fact. Dear old Winston Churchill left the House of Commons for the last time aged 89.

August: A telly that didn't take ten men to lift was introduced to England. Having said that, it still weighed 26 lbs.

October: One of London's oldest institutions, The Windmill Theatre, was closed. It was famous for having naked women on stage. Typical of this country's loony obscenity laws, they could wear, or not wear, whatever they liked as long as they didn't move.

November: England got out its begging bowl and borrowed £1080,000,000 on the never-never from eleven nations.

December: Here's a well deserved Christmas present. Lord Beeching (Lorded for services to railway murder) was himself chopped by the Government. I bet he didn't have to travel home by train.

1965

Bye-Bye Winnie

On 25th January everyone who'd survived the war shed a tiny tear at the news that dear old Winston Churchill, the fat guy with the acid wit and the broad girth, had gone to the great parliament in the sky. He had been, no doubt, the greatest statesman that anyone could remember and few dared even a cynical whisper of criticism at his passing.

But life had to go on. The years of Tory rule were now dragged out and examined more closely – particularly Harold Macmillan's rash statement 'We've never had it so good'. It had finally dawned on the working class that the only people who'd 'had it so good', in the past ten or so years, were the lucky so-and-so's that had had 'it' in the first place. If, by chance, the common folk had shown any rise in their standard of living, it was due to their new ability to buy things on the never-never.

It now seemed, in retrospect, that the haughty Tory Government had spent more time losing sleep over whether Britain was still one of the world's big boys, than keeping their eyes on the ball at home. Okay, towards the end of their reign they'd waved their manicured hands around and sworn blind they'd do something about the state of our hospitals, schools and social services – but it had all been a bit too late, the horse had not only bolted but had taken the stable door with him.

Not only that, but due to several almighty cock-ups abroad, like the Suez fiasco; the refusal of those other Common Market countries (mostly France) to let Britain join their game; a seeming inability to be able to brandish our very own nuclear weapon (sorry 'deterrent'); and all the African countries giving us the old two fingers, Britain could be said to have not only lost its money and its empire but its role in the whole damn business.

Resignation

Alec Douglas-Home, realising he'd made a dog's breakfast of practically everything he'd got his skeletal hands on (and also that he didn't need the PM's salary), happily resigned, making way for a man who couldn't have been more different. Edward Heath, the new Opposition Leader, seemed a rather jolly Dickensian sort with a big, red, round face, a pointy nose, and shoulders that shook uncontrollably when he laughed. He hadn't been to public school (tut, tut) and came from unfashionable Broadstairs where he led the local church choir and was not married (not that those two things are connected).

Britain in Labour

The Tories had had 13 years to muck up the country and now Britain had a bright new (well! brightish, newish) Labour Government. Most people thought everything was now going to be all right (welcome to cloud-cuckoo land!). Wilson had been elected on a programme of 'purposive planning' (which could have meant just about anything), and his 'national economic plan' included the state control of steel, water and building land. Sidekick George Brown, now the new, posh-sounding Secretary of State for Economic Affairs, told his eager followers 'Brothers, we are on our way.' But which way?

Certainly not onward and upward. Having got rid of the skin-head Alec Douglas-Home and the Tory toffs, the poor, long-suffering Brits soon found that his replacement, the seemingly down-to-earth Harold Wilson, also suffered delusions of grandeur; believing that Britain was still a major world power and that he, therefore, must be a major world leader. In fact, it could be said that although some things were never to be the same after 1964, they never really seemed any different either.

It was all a bit pathetic really: we seemed to be world famous for things that, at the end of the day, people could actually live without: fashion, pop music and a booming tourist trade (based on the fallacy that London was actually 'Swingin'').

On 15th June, those pillars of society, The Beatles were informed that they were to be presented to HRH and given MBEs. (Actually that's nothing, she even knighted Jimmy Savile later.) I don't think the Queen actually liked the Beatles (or Jim for that matter). In fact, I doubt if her Majesty had even heard of them: but The Beatles were earning more foreign loot than the rest of industry put together and, besides the Government decides who gets the honours anyway.

Hilariously, some old buffers gave their MBEs back claiming, as Canadian politician Hector Dupuis put it, that the award placed him on the same level as 'vulgar nincompoops'. The Fab Four probably agreed with him.

God Loses to Telly

At this stage of Britain's history 94% of Britons belonged to a church and two thirds of that lot were Church of England. Only 2% dared risk being struck by a thunderbolt from above by saying they didn't believe a word of it, while the rest floated somewhere between heaven and hell, hedging their bets.

The statistic that made everyone sit up, however, was the fact that only 10% of those that claimed to be God-fearing actually went to church on Sundays. The rest stayed in and watched the new devil's tool – telly – probably making do with the, almost kitsch, 'God slot'.

On the TV in those days there were very few programmes that the devil might have enjoyed. 'Ready Steady Go', however, was certainly one (according to our parents), and by 1965 (its third series) it had reached cult status. It brought into our front rooms every pop group or star that had ever upset mum and dad. A lot of the music came from kids who were hoping to crack stardom and did, for only five minutes, but most of the later-to-be-huge British bands like The Rolling Stones, The Animal and The Who also got their early exposure on this icon of the sixties.

Trouble in Gib.

Britain had owned the strategically important Gibraltar since 1713 (and still does), which had really got up the nose of the arch-fascist Spanish boss, Franco, who thought that Spain should have *their* rock back as it was attached to *their* country. He, therefore, decided to put up a comprehensive blockade which effectively made life impossible for border-crossing workers and visiting tourists – not to mention all those baboons who, for some obscure reason, lived on the rock and thought they were British. The argument was not resolved until 1967 when a referendum decided over whelmingly to stay British.

Trouble in Rhodesia

Oh dear, oh dear, Britain only had one colony left in Africa, Rhodesia, and now even they hated us. Ian Smith, their new super-grumpy Prime Minister, issued a Unilateral Declaration of Independence on 16th November. Smith was to turn out to be only a lightly disguised dictator, imposing censorship on all media, rationing and any money going out of the country. The old Governor, Sir Humphrey Gibbs, furious at having been sacked by Smith, turned round and sacked him back; but Smith wouldn't take his turn. He was running the show and everyone knew it.

Our Harold Wilson called it a 'rebel regime' and refused to trade with them, but it was all a bit tricky, as many people in high places still had close relatives (and, more to the point, loads of dosh) in Rhodesia. Representatives of the 4,000,000 blacks (there were only 20,000 whites) beseeched Wilson to go in with guns blazing (à la Thatcher) but Wilson thought he could break Smith and his rotten regime by being reasonable and setting a good example (silly fool).

Smith then put the cat amongst the corgis when he claimed that our Queen, God save her, on the night before the breakaway, had asked him 'not to sell the white man down the river'. What she probably meant was – don't sell the white man down *my* river.

Saved from Sex

Britain had its own housewife superstar. Mary Whitehouse decided, without so much as a by your leave, to be the guardian of Britain's morals, by setting up the National Viewers and Listeners Association. She and her followers sat by their tellies and radios every night, searching for the rude bits – before kicking up a huge stink. It must be said, however, that many people would have had more sympathy for her views if they had been presented in a more open-minded manner.

Skirting the Issue

In November, Customs and Excise got themselves into a right pickle over skirts. It appeared that women's skirts were liable to a

10% duty if over a certain length. Anything less was regarded as children's wear and was therefore exempt. Some bright spark came up with the idea of including a bust measurement when measuring garments in order to differentiate between children's and women's skirts. This was all very well, but supermodels like Jean Shrimpton were noted for the shortness of their skirts and flatness of their chests. Back to the drawing board!

Meanwhile, mini skirts (at that time they were still only an inch or so above the knee) were condemned by our moral watchdogs (like old Mary) as reflecting the fall of standards and rise of the 'permissive society' (and so say all of us).

Meanwhile

January: It's nice to know that kicking an old bit of leather around a field can push you up the social ladder. Sir Stanley Matthews, him of the short hairy legs and big shorts, became the first knight of football.

February: Beatle Ringo Starr married a Liverpool hairdresser, Maureen Cox. Unfortunately she never managed to do anything about his stupid hairdo.

March: Goldie, London's zoo's favourite golden eagle (brilliant name eh?) broke out of jail and stopped the traffic for three days around Regents Park. At first they were worried about him starving to death until they noticed some of the park's ducks had gone missing too.

June: Major Edward White, a US astronaut, went for the first space walkies. He liked it so much that, like Goldie, he had to be coaxed back in by mission control.

June: The Japanese announced that they were going to have a go at motor racing, as a way of introducing themselves to the British car market. How silly! As if we British (who practically invented the car) would ever buy Japanese.

August: Elizabeth Lane was made the first female High Court Judge.

October: The Queen wrote ever such a nice letter to Ian Smith (Prime Minister of Rhodesia) saying that she hoped he was well and that they would be able to find a solution to the crisis in her country.

November: Britain stopped swinging. Murderers would no longer swing for their sins, as hanging was finally abolished.

December: Roy (call me Woy) Jenkins became Home Secretary, and Barbara (call me anything you like) Castle became Ministress of Transport.

1966

Wilson Gets Worried

Harold Wilson (of whom Aneurin Bevan said 'All facts, no bloody ideas.') turned out to be just about the most cocky Prime Minister we'd ever had. His inflated opinion of himself was further pumped up by being told by the country, at the May General Election, that he could hang on to the keys of Downing Street for another term. Despite his huge popularity with the common man (who misguidedly thought he was one of them), his government was allowing the economy to get into such a tangle that even those old Tories began to look good.

On 16th May, the situation came to a head when the National Union of Seamen downed ships and went on strike, effectively paralysing anything trying to float in or out of the London docks. This caused the £ to tremble and then slip off its precarious perch and forced Harold to announce a nice new 'state of emergency'.

Wilson had blown his cool and blamed Commie agitators for the unruly mess his party was in. It's funny now to think anyone could have been frightened of this quaint little Yorkshireman – but they were – and the seamen did, eventually, go grumbling back to their boats. But Labour's cred. was blown. This was just the beginning of the bloody battle between the unions and the Government that was to rage for years. So what did our Harold do about it?

First, he announced a wages freeze which made it illegal for bosses to pay their slaves any more money (which must have pleased them lots). He then, in an effort to stop anyone with any money shoving it abroad, forbade any more than £50 being taken abroad. This was a disaster for travel agents (and abroad), but totally brill for English resorts like Bognor or Scunthorpe (where it was very difficult to spend *more* than £50!).

He then slapped a massive increase on purchase tax (father of VAT) which meant that, just as more and more people had less and less money to spend, all the good things in life were going up as well. It's funny, but if a government starts to tax luxuries like fags and booze it tends to become a little less popular.

Nevertheless, these steps sort of worked and Wilson went on holiday to the Scilly Isles (with £50? You must be joking!) feeling relatively safe. By November, however, Britain was in a minus £162 million position and poor Harold was forced to look at the prospect of devaluing the pound. Everyone blamed everyone else, as always, but despite a desperate cabinet reshuffle, the Labour Party, once again, found themselves skating on the thinnest of ice.

Abroad?

Britain's position abroad continued to totter from one crisis to another but that was nothing compared to our old chums, the

Americans, who were happily digging the hugest pit for themselves in Vietnam. Although the Government claimed that they were right behind them, it became fairly obvious to all that if we British were actually ever required to take our jackets off and get our own noses bloody, things might well change.

Meanwhile three labour MPs traipsed over to Rhodesia to see if they could do any better with Mr Smith and his whities. All they got for their trouble was a severe heckling from an all white crowd who called them 'stupid nits, liars and communists'. Blimey, they were used to worse than this at home. But it was when the mob closed in and dowsed them in itching powder that the meeting was promptly scratched.

A Match Made in Heaven?

Over in Italy, the Pope and our Archbishop of Canterbury were caught kissing. Don't worry, it was the first time in 400 years that the Anglicans and the Catholics had been in each other's houses, and the ceremonial kiss was to cele-

brate the building of a bridge between the two churches. God proved to be fairly unimpressed by the event, though, as the bridge never seemed to carry much weight.

Murder Most Foul

On 6th May, two of the most horrendous murderers in the history of horrendous murderers were brought to book. Terence Brady, aged 27, and Myra Hindley, aged 23, were found guilty of torturing and killing at least three children, one with an axe. After a trial that made even the most unfeeling person's eyes water, they received three and two concurrent life sentences respectively and both are still languishing in their cells today.

What a Gas!

Talk about the luck of the British. Just as we were grovelling in the depths of an economic crisis something turned up to help. Phillips Petroleum, who were poking around the bottom of the sea off the East coast, noticed some bubbles from the sexily named Block 48/30 zone. With a little encouragement, the bubbles grew into a stream of 17 million cubic feet of gas a day (that's quite a lot of bubbles!), which was the equivalent of 3.5% of Britain's daily use. They reckoned that eventually they would be pulling enough gas out to supply all Britain's needs.

England on Top

England had taught footer to just about every country in the world – just so they could all beat us at it. Well, they didn't in 1966 – so there! Under the fab captaincy of, the now sadly deceased, Bobby Moore, England beat Germany in the final of the World Cup. Actually the celebration was nearly as big as when we beat the Krauts (with a little help from the Yankee squad) twenty odd years earlier.

London Tops the World

Despite the poxy economic situation, this really was the year that London became the centre of all things fab and fashionable. Mary Quant was now almost Establishment, but a bright new sensation, in the form of Barbara Hulanicki's clothes shop, Biba, blew away any doubt that if you wanted to be IN then London, and particularly the Kings Road, 'Kenny' High Street and Carnaby Street were the only places to be seen.

The clothes were often silly, always loud, mostly badly made, but unlike anything that had been seen before. Never, since Regency days, had men dared to be peacockish; and although pink, flared hipster trousers, huge 'kipper' ties and platform-soled, glittery boots were not exactly macho, girls seemed to lap them up. All this dovetailed in the late sixties into the new hippie movement. Now most ex-hippies will tell you that hippiedom represented a philosophy dedicated to loving one's fellow man and casting away

266

all aggression. Baloney! It was almost purely a fashion and drug club. American kids, of course, had a damn good reason for all this soppy peace and love mumbo-jumbo, as they were trying to find any excuse to forget about the crazy Vietnam war.

Even those Beatles, who really should have known better, abandoned their sharp little suits, grew out their silly hair cuts (into sillier ones), and trolled off to Wales to sit awe (or dumb)-struck in front of a 'guru' called Maharishi Mahesh Yogi who had a long white beard and a voice like Minnie Mouse.

The only musician who came out of the whole period with any real brownie points was gravelly Bob Dylan though – if we were to be totally honest – many of us didn't understand a single word of what he was droning on about.

Meanwhile

February: Britain's beer drinkers gulped in amazement when Watneys put the price of a pint up to 1s 8d. I bet they'd have choked if they could have foreseen that in 20 odd years they'd be paying a couple of quid.

March: The stolen World Cup that our football team had striven so hard to win was found by a dog named Pickle who dug it up in someone's front garden.

April: At least we only lost a priceless trophy. The American air force went one better, losing one of their very best H bombs when it fell off the back of a B52 bomber. Luckily they found it on the sea bed two months later – still ticking!

May: Graham Hill (Damon's daddy) won the Indianapolis Grand Prix in his Lotus Ford. He was also Formula 1 World Champion.

June: The BBC, in their infinite wisdom, showed a TV sitcom called 'Till Death Us Do Part' for the first time. Its hero, Alf Garnett, was fiercely nationalistic and totally racist. The Beeb thought they were being ever so modern by showing Alf up as the bigoted fool that he undoubtedly was. Some of us, however, realised they'd shot themselves well and truly in the foot, as it became fairly clear that loads of viewers quite liked old Alf, and that he was merely echoing what they'd been thinking all along.

October: Double agent George Blake (on the Ruskies side) escaped from Wormwood Scrubs using a home-made rope. There was little doubt that he'd had a little help from his old Commie chums.

December: Harold Wilson met his new enemy Ian Smith on a boat called HMS Tiger in the middle of the Mediterranean to try to sort out the Rhodesian mess. Presumably they didn't want to be overheard. Not that it made any difference – the talks were a flop.

1967

Cold Comfort

The wages freeze had now been going for over a year so little Harold Wilson, who was definitely no longer flavour of the month (or year), decided to call it something else. The aptly labelled 'period of severe restraint' seemed to correspond with an upturn in world trade and, for a while, everything seemed to look a little better. So much so that in July the 'wage freeze' or 'period of severe restraint' ended. Well, sort of ended – the Government reserved the right to delay increases for yet another year. Heads they win – tails you lose!

The poor old £ was still limping along like a three-legged tortoise and Wilson tried to blame the horrendous Six Day War between Israel and its Arab neighbours for its nosedive on the world money markets. This was highly dubious as the £ had begun on its slippery path downward at least six weeks before the Jews and the Arabs had even begun to get their guns, tanks or camels out.

Down We Go

The economy was plummeting in direct proportion to the Labour Government's popularity and, to cut a long, sad story short, hapless Harold was forced to chop the value of the £ by a massive 14.3% in November. It was the worst financial foul-up for over 20 years.

Then, in a desperate attempt to cheer everyone up (and hang on to his job), Wilson came into everyone's living room one night (on the telly) and told them in his honest, no nonsense, Yorkshire way: 'It does not mean, of course, that the £ here in Britain in your pocket or purse or in your bank has been devalued.' Not only was it dodgy grammar but daft logic. Maybe Harold should have mentioned that if anyone wanted to take their money *out* of their pocket, purse or bank to actually *buy* anything that remotely originated abroad (like the odd banana), it would cost them about 14.3% more.

Travel Trouble

Donald Campbell had this thing about fast motorboats just like his late, lamented dad. At his attempt to break the world water speed record on Lake Coniston, the 'boat' (really a floating plane with no wings) called *Bluebird* suddenly reared out of the water and flipped over backwards. All that was ever found of Donald was his helmet, his mask, his shoes and, strange as it might seem, his teddy bear. Obviously, if there was such a thing as a Loch Coniston monster, it didn't eat record-breaking cuddly toys.

Over in the States, three astronauts missed their trip around the planet when the blasted rocket caught fire before blasting off. Their deaths severely curtailed the Apollo mission to get men on the moon. Only a couple of months later, a Soviet astronaut was zapped when the brakes didn't work as he came back into orbit. The Ruskies claimed he should have used his ejector seat but anyone whose ever been in a Russian car would realise that they might well have forgotten to put one in. Astronauting obviously has its ups and downs.

Oil Abroad

Sadly 1967 turned out to be a very good year for very bad disasters. On 19th March, a ginormous oil tanker called the *Torrey Canyon* carelessly ran aground just off Land's End and instantly started spewing its load. It was described as 'The greatest peacetime threat to Britain' (after Harold Wilson). The only solution was to use incendiary bombs and napalm to break up and set fire to the oil in a vain attempt to avoid mucking up some of England's most beautiful beaches (before the English did).

America the Brave

Over in Vietnam, the Yanks were using their personal napalm slightly differently. On 16th February, 25,000 men attacked the

Viet Cong stronghold known as War Zone C. Their bombers dropped fireworks anywhere and everywhere, which disgusted the rest of the world. Strange logic to think it's okay to kill thousands of innocent people if you're defending their freedom.

Throughout the world, youngsters were losing patience with the war-mongering Americans, especially in America itself where, unfortunately, the peace and the hippie movements were becoming inseparable. Unfortunately, because about the only effect they had, was that new soldierlings spent most of the war wearing headbands and being stoned out of their boxes (before going into them).

Royal Meeting
All the Royals wore extremely thin smiles on 7th June at the unveiling of a small slate plaque (mean or what?) to commemorate our Queen's grandmother, Queen Mary. The reason for the tension was the appearance among the guests of that bad old Duke of Windsor (the one that preferred American chicks to ruling us) and the American lady herself. It was rumoured that the Queen Mum actually blamed the death of her husband on these two. Poor old King George IV (her hubby) had, apparently, never quite got over the shock of having to drop everything and rush out to hire a King kit.

Could you tell me of which country you will be becoming king, sir?

Concord or Concorde?

Was it really possible? Britain and France finally managed to do something together without it ending in tears. A staggeringly pretty supersonic airliner was unveiled on 12th December, designed to get you to the other side of the Atlantic exactly one hour before you set off. Did I say the project ended peacefully? Silly me! It must be recorded that as the plane rolled out for the first time, a huge scrap broke out over whether Concord or Concorde should or should not carry the French 'e'. After months of terse deliberations at the highest diplomatic level, they came up with a staggeringly inspired solution. The French one should carry the 'e' and the British one shouldn't. Mon Dieu!

Meanwhile

January: Plans to build the most boring city in the world were launched. Milton Keynes was to (and now does) ruin – whoops – occupy 22,000 acres of (once) beautiful Buckinghamshire.
• Jeremy hits the top. Old Etonian Jeremy Thorpe became the leader of the Liberal party on 18th January. Everybody seemed to like this handsome, slightly extrovert, rather top-drawer chap and few could have guessed the sticky end he was to come to.
• There used to be a paper for all those boys who did as their parents told them, helped old ladies across the street and brushed their hair in the morning. It was called the *Boy's Own Paper* and was about as exciting as a day out in . . . er . . . Milton Keynes. Thankfully it closed down owing to the severe decline of 'good' boys.

February: There also used to be a very silly teenybopper group in America called The Monkees (definitely an insult to apes). Heathrow airport became a war zone when their British fans went sub-human on their arrival.
• Talking of monkeys, the man in charge of them at London Zoo, Desmond Morris, wrote the first of his many quasi-scientific books called *The Naked Ape* and informed us, among other things, that

orang-utans are the sexiest primates alive. Was Mr Morris pulling our legs?

March: A strange (and rather silly) underground hippie magazine struggled up to street level in London. Run by a group of loony Australians, *OZ* used any writer or artist (including myself) prepared to take the mickey out of British society.

April: One would have been forgiven for wondering if the invention of the Ombudsman was some kind of April Fool's joke. It was, in fact, the name given to a chap whose new job was to help people stung by government departments. He'd have got home a lot earlier if he'd only dealt with those that weren't.

May: Those naughty Rolling Stones got stoned once too often and ended up in court. Mick and Keith both received prison sentences but in the end they got off. Rumour has it they offered the judge a joint . . .
• Never one to mince his words, Enoch Powell called Britain 'The sick man of Europe'. Isn't it about time we started feeling a little better?
• Elvis Presley married his childhood sweetheart. The cake had six tiers, and the female fans shed thousands.

August: Who says we live in a free country? The Marine Broadcasting Act fired a broadside and sunk 90% of the brilliant and popular new pirate radio ships by making them illegal.

October: Brian Jones of the Rolling Stones, not to be outdone, finally got himself jailed for drug offences.

December: South African surgeon, Christian Barnard, actually managed to find a new heart to install in a 53 year old grocer. Denise Darvall, a 25 year old bank clerk, found dying after a road accident, had contributed hers.

1968

Castle Strikes Out

Unofficial strikes by the unions were continuing to pull the Labour Government to its knees. Just as one crippling strike was killed off like weeds on a lawn, another couple would rear up. Barbara Castle (the Employment Secretary), in an effort to bring the unions to heel, introduced a bill called pretentiously 'In Place of Strife'. Senior government ministers, like Jim Callaghan, gulped at its cheek, being fully aware that if it wasn't for all that union loot ('donated' by its members), the Labour Party wouldn't have a pot to p... put water in. Not only that, but there was a General Election looming and the last thing the Government needed was to enter it with the Trade Union Congress tearing at their throats.

Basically, 'In Place of Strife' demanded that the TUC agree to compulsory legislation to deal with any industrial relations problems and recommended that unofficial strikes should be punished by cash fines, which was a bit like asking condemned murderers to help tie their nooses.

After a long drawn out (and terribly tedious) tug of war, both in the Commons and at the TUC, both Wilson and Castle realised they were massaging a dead duck and gave in the following year. The trade union leaders, hardly able to hide their honest, working-class grins, promised (with all their fingers crossed) that they would try to behave better in future.

I'm Backing Britain (Maybe!)
Talk about pathetic. Five typists from a two-bit heating firm deep in the Surbiton suburbs suddenly couldn't stand all the appalling news about their country's economy. They declared, with chins held high, 'We're Backing Britain' and, much to the delight of their bewildered boss, promised to work an extra half hour a day for nothing. The Government and the press (always game for a silly story) rushed round to sunny Suburbiton to slap the women on the back (and use up more hours of their working day). A huge press campaign followed, in those silly small papers, but the kiss of death came when Brucie Forsyth (yes, we've put up with him that long) made a record called – you've got it – 'I'm Backing Britain'. It became obvious that the crass campaign had just become a vehicle for flagging circulations, flagging governments ... and flagging show-biz careers.

Keep 'Em Out
Immigration was the other big buzz word of 1968. Thousands of Asians were pouring in from East Africa and Kenya carrying completely kosher British passports. The Government rushed out a quota system, in an effort to stem the flow, with Home Secretary 'honest' Jim Callaghan telling us that he had a responsibility to all those at home (hey folks, that meant us!).

On 21st April, old misery-guts, Enoch Powell, made a speech that was to make him famous (and seal his fate) for the rest of his career. He proclaimed, 'As I look ahead I am filled with foreboding. Like the Romans, I see the River Tiber (I think he meant The Thames) foaming with much blood.' He went on to say that we were mad, literally mad, to let 50,000 immigrants in every year. We were, he ranted 'heaping our own funeral pyre'. I wonder if he realised he was heaping his own.

275

Edward (I'll be PM at all costs) Heath immediately fired him from the Tory Shadow Cabinet labelling him an 'inflammatory racist'. Many other politicians buttoned their lips, realising that Enoch was merely saying what they and lots of Britons thought (remember 'Till Death Us Do Part'?). Politicians might be stupid, but they ain't daft!

Up, Up and Away

Just about the only thing booming in this country was the fashion industry. Mini skirts were reaching new heights and seemed to be turning into wide belts. Dry cleaners got so concerned that they started charging by the inch. Girls were all trying to look like half-girl, half-stick-insect Twiggy, the unbelievably pretty ex-shop assistant who had shot to modelling superstardom. Unfortunately, most had about as much luck as I would imitating Arnold Schwarzenegger.

Up America

Every time the Americans thought that the Vietnam War just couldn't get much worse . . . it did. President Lyndon Johnson was obviously feeling a little chilly around the feet area and announced to a shocked nation that, thank you, but no thank you, he wouldn't be running for President again. The dead John Kennedy's little brother Bobby, now a senator himself, obviously saw the ad in the Jobs Vacant section and decided to have a go himself. He did follow his brother, but not quite in the way he might have hoped. On 6th June, poor Bobby was fatally shot in the lobby of the Ambassador Hotel in Los Angeles. A young Palestinian Arab admitted the crime, claiming he did it for his country (which you may think sounds a bit like shooting the leader of India because you had a bad time in Spain. Oh well!).

The end of the year saw Richard Nixon (later known as Tricky Dicky) as the new President. Remarkably, Nixon looked like Pinocchio's psychotic uncle, and was later to share some other Pinocchio characteristics.

Meanwhile, the uncrowned king of America's blacks, the Reverend Dr Martin Luther King, was shot dead by a white man in Memphis. They sure know how to treat their leaders over there. This seemed to sum up the state of race relations in America, and riots suddenly exploded in major cities throughout the country.

Meanwhile

March: Road deaths fell by 23% as a direct result of the introduction of alcohol breath tests. No survey was done about how many people were getting rat-faced at home.

April: There's hard up and hard up but it really comes to something when an American oil millionaire can buy one of your capital city's major landmarks. Tycoon Robert McCullough bought our London Bridge for a mere £1,000,000 so he could put it in his backyard in Texas. I wonder how much he offered for the Royal Family?

• The fantabulous Jim Clark, twice World Champion Racing Driver, definitely saw the wood for the trees. Poor Jim spun off the road at 125 m.p.h. into a wood and was killed instantly.

• Chaos hit the streets when the first few decimal coins hit the purses and pockets of the British. Many people, including me, looked into their palms in total confusion when given change including the new 5p and 10p.

May: Ronan Point, a huge grotty tower block in East London, decided to save the demolition men a job by simply falling down like a pack of cards. Somebody on the eighteenth floor had unfortunately left the gas on. A major investigation began into shoddy building methods.

• What started as a little demonstration against American action in Vietnam, broke out into a major riot between French students and police in Paris. (NB French police are the sort that bludgeon you to death for bad breath.)

June: Black, black day for comedy lovers. Tony Hancock, just about the funniest man that ever lived (please debate!), killed himself in an Australian Hotel. C'mon Tony, even Australia's not that bad (also debate!). Apparently his totally despairing view of life on screen was little different off.

Tony Hancock

August: Those rotten Ruskies were at it again. This time it was Czechoslovakia that got the full treatment for trying to give socialism a 'human face'. Alexander Dubček, the Czech leader, was gobsmacked as the tanks rolled into Prague. He thought they were a bunch of rotters for stabbing him and his country in the back after years of cooperation.

September: Two members of the cast of the hit musical *Hair* appeared stark naked two days after the relaxation of theatre censorship was announced.

Hit of the Year: 'Those Were The Days', by the ever-so-prissy Mary Hopkin. Significant title or what?

1969

It's All Irish

It's always difficult to put one's finger on when the Irish started hating each other. Anyone who has stood outside a pub at closing time on a Friday night will gather that they're a pretty warlike race. As you probably know, this disharmony between the Catholics and Protestants started hundreds of years ago, but you'll have to read my last books to find out why (and that's called marketing, folks!). On 23rd January, violence reared its ugly head during a Catholic march in Londonderry demanding 'one man one vote' in the province. The Catholics trapped their arch-enemy, that priest with the voice and nature of a demented Rottweiler, the 'Reverend Dr' Ian Paisley but he, as always, managed to bark his way out of it. Several of his followers, however, were slightly injured.

Bottled Babies

For the first time ever, British scientists managed to fertilise human eggs outside the body (free range?). The method had first been tried out successfully with rabbits – the only hitch they  encountered was keeping the darn critters apart! One of the greatest problems scientists foresaw was the possibility of deformities in the foetus caused by this technique. (Who wants a nipper with long ears and a fluffy white tail?)

A Kray Day

Two of the nastiest villains that ever walked the streets of East London (and there's been a few) were sentenced to 30 years prison each. Ronald and Reginald Kray (who both looked a bit like

Jonathan Woss) had a nasty habit of murdering friend and foe willy-nilly in pursuit of their gangland activities. The terrible twosome are, thankfully, still in separate jails, though one is now said to be totally round the bend.

The Oil Fairies

You may remember a couple of years earlier when the gas fairy visited this country and waved her wand over our coast line (see page 102)? Well, she'd obviously told her mates that Britain was still in the sh . . . ambles (despite all that buckshee gas). On 30th June, high grade crude oil was discovered under the bottom of our bit of the North Sea. The oil companies weren't sure at the time whether it was commercially a goer, but I can tell you now, with the privilege of hindsight, that the find was to save our extremely vulnerable bacon.

The Men in the Moon

Anyone who was around in 1969 gets a slight shiver down the spine when they remember looking up at the man in the moon and realising that, almost unbelievably, there were earthlings walking on his face. Watched by trillions of awe-struck telly viewers throughout the world, American astronaut Neil Armstrong out-astronauted all the rest by stepping out of his little spaceship and taking 'one small step for man, and one giant leap for mankind.'

Predictably, the poor old moon was about as interesting as an empty car park in Slough but it didn't matter, it was just great to be somewhere that McDonald's hadn't got to first. Neil and his two mates brought back a few lumps of moon rock for the folks back home. These were instantly pounced on by brainy boffins who rushed them to the most sophisticated laboratories in the world, where they discovered, after months of painstaking study, using the most sophisticated of scientific equipment, that they would have been marginally more interesting if the moon had really been made of green cheese.

Ulster Explodes
On 15th August, British troops were actually *cheered* as they put barbed wire all the way round the Catholic Bogside district of Belfast. The troops had been *asked* in by the Ulster Government to try and put the tin lid on the furious fighting between the Catholics and Protestants. It didn't take long for the situation to erupt into violence though and five were killed and hundreds injured.

Royals Skint?
The Duke of Edinburgh, on an American TV programme, claimed that unless he and his Mrs got a pay rise, they'd have to give up Buck House and live somewhere cheaper (like one of their other fab homes). He then said they'd already sold off a small yacht (the *Queen Elizabeth*?) and that, unless something turned up pretty smartish, he'd have to give up polo. Now either Phil was telling Royal porkies or since then both of them have been doing paper rounds, as they sure seem to have made up for it since. Crikey! If you can't make ends meet when you're married to one of the richest women in the world, then what chance have we got?

Meanwhile

January: All bad things must come to an end. 'Mrs Dale's Diary', the Beeb's longest running radio soap, which made 'The Archers' seem like *Terminator II*, ended.

March: Oh what a lovely war! Britain invaded the postage stamp island of Anguilla in the Caribbean, to put down a revolution by the fearsome Republican Defence Force led by that infamous revolutionary Ronald (a revolutionary called Ronald?) Webster. The whole population of 6000 turned out to welcome the troops and the event turned into a bit of a party, televised by the BBC. There was no resistance, and 40 British bobbies were left to keep the peace. Watch out Russia, it could be your turn next!

April: Sikh bus conductors in Wolverhampton finally won their battle to carry on wearing their banned turbans at work.

July: Rolling Stones don't float (epsecially when stoned). Brian Jones drowned in his own swimming pool in Hatfield.
• Yet another Kennedy – Edward – hit the headlines. He failed to report an accident in which a girl, travelling in the passenger seat of his car, drowned when it plummeted over the side of a bridge in New England. It put the kibosh on any dreams he had of getting shot (like his brothers) as President. Nobody knows what really happened – except Teddy.
• Our Gracious Queen gave Charlie his very first crown to play with when she made him the Prince of Wales. If only the poor lad had known that he'd probably have to wait till his mum's dying breath to get his hands on hers.

September: ITV broadcast in colour for the first time, though it didn't seem to make 'Coronation Street' any less dreary.

• The super-trendy boutique Biba grew into a huge department store, only to prove that little ideas don't always grow into big ones successfully. It closed after a few years because the tourists, who flocked to see this hyper-trendy new phenomenon, mostly forgot to buy anything. Most of what wasn't bought was then nicked by the staff (allegedly).

October: The Divorce Reform Bill was passed, making the irretrievable breakdown of a marriage sole grounds for divorce. Can anyone think of a better reason? How about snoring?

• Just as mini skirts were reaching the point of no return, some bright spark invented the nearly-touching-the-ground maxi skirt. Cynics thought it had something to do with the imminent winter, the floundering textile industry and a preponderance of chubby legs.

November: A London woman, Mary Hanson, tried the new fertility drug gonadotrophine (from the Latin 'gonad'?). Good news, she became pregnant. Bad news, she had five!

December: While some people were desperate to have nippers, some were desperate to avoid them. A sterilisation clinic was opened in Birmingham, offering the 'cruellest cut of all' (vasectomy for men) for £16 (a mere snip).

Hurrah for Heath

Everyone was, finally, well fed up with Wilson and his not-so-merry men. Despite Harold's protestations that we were coming out of the economic mess (does this sound familiar?), nobody believed him. Even so, most of us were amazed when, at the General Election in May, Labour lost to the Conservatives, especially as the opinion polls had been telling us that it was going to be a walkover. The complacent (and lazy) Labour voters had obviously stayed at home thinking their little individual votes wouldn't be necessary.

After four years in opposition, Edward Heath, the jolly man with the plummy voice and the shaky shoulders, was clearly over the moon at being the Prime Minister, and vowed to undo all the Labour cock-ups (my words not his!). He told us he'd take us into Europe – which we liked – and he also told us he wouldn't make rash promises (like Wilson) just to catch the headlines – which we also liked. He then told us he'd tackle the unions – which we sort of liked, but dreaded the ensuing battle because, as far as industrial relations were concerned, the unions had had their foot on the Government's windpipe for as long as we could remember. In his new government, he gave the job of Minister of State to a grocer's daughter called Margaret, little knowing that she would eventually cause his downfall.

Votes for Youngsters

The year had opened with the news that the age of majority was to be changed from 21 to 18, which meant that teenagers could vote for the first time (if they could find anyone to vote for). Most young people thought this meant we might be in for a decade where the wrinklies would have to start taking account of what *they* thought, so bringing a period of fresh optimism. No way! The seventies were to be a period of pessimism, and worse, apathy. If Britain had ever been 'swingin'', it certainly wasn't any more, but (to be honest) nor was the rest of the world.

Hero rock stars like Jimi Hendrix and Janis Joplin were dropping like flies from drug overdoses; a new man on the world political stage, Colonel Gaddafi, introduced his new national sport, terrorism, to the world pitch; that funny (but insignificant) magazine *OZ* (see p.109) was prosecuted for depravity; and, worst news of all, The Bee Gees announced they were getting back together again. Perhaps the greatest indication that the sixties were over, however, was that The Beatles had fallen out of love and were now trying to divorce each other.

The Women's Movement

The early 70s saw the virgin birth of what came to be known as the 'women's movement'. Women had finally reached the end of their tether with regard to their subordinate role to men. Australian, Germaine Greer, led the cavalry with her analysis of how your 'women's-place-is-in-the-home' average man stereotyped the role of the opposite sex, in her book *The Female Eunuch*. Some believed, however, that the more extreme bra-burning, man-hating, over-the-top faction did the movement more harm than good.

Jumbo Journeys

On 23rd January, everyone looked up into the sky with amazement as a huge shadow passed over London. Was it a bird? Was it Superman? Was it pollution? No, it was a big fat plane from the States nicknamed Jumbo. The trouble with any kind of jumbo is that it won't fit into your average quarters, and this vast Boeing 747, carrying 352 passengers, had airport authorities tearing their hair out as they struggled with inadequate baggage and passenger handling facilities. They were also worried that the turbulence it caused would disrupt all the other littler planes as they went about their everyday business. As we now know, nothing of the kind occurred and before long, there were troupes of Jumbos – trunk to tail – in and out of London Heathrow.

Filthy Foreign Flu

But if the jumbo wasn't going to flatten us, a new strain of Hong Kong flu was. In one week alone 2850 people died. There's nothing like an epidemic to cause us to turn to the Lord, even though he often moves in mysterious ways. A new version of his old bestseller started selling like hot cakes. *The New English Bible* caused a great deal of fuss because, for the first time, it used language that people could almost understand (and, oh Lordie, the High Church didn't like it).

It wasn't all plain sailing for God, however, as on 22nd June, the Methodists announced that they were going to allow mere women to become priests. The Church of England giggled into its beard, safe in the knowledge that such a dreadful thing could never happen to them. Could it?

Terrorism Triumphs

In September, three airliners (one of them a young Jumbo) were hijacked by members of the 'Popular Front for the Liberation of Palestinian' (the PLO). The world watched nervously as the planes sat in the sweltering heat of an airstrip in Jordan, while officials tried to talk the terrorists out of it.

Meanwhile, on the same day, the crew of an El Al jet jumped two would-be hijackers, killing one of them. The surviving member, a rather pretty girl (for a terrorist) called Leila Khaled, was handed over to British police when the plane landed in London. The PLO, (who'd by now evacuated the first three planes and blown them up) then had the damn cheek to ask for the release of

Leila as swapsies for the passengers that they were still holding in the other hijacking. There was one hell of a fuss when the British wimped out and gave them their girl back.

De Gaulle De-Dead
Stroppy old General de Gaulle always had to have the last word – even when dead. He'd insisted (when not dead) that none of his government colleagues should be allowed to attend his funeral. Instead he invited everyone else, and his graveside was besieged by tens of thousands of weeping French. Our dear old Harold Macmillan was there with all the world's leaders, though one suspected that he might be one of many glad to see the cantankerous old f...rog safely underground.

Flying Circus
Just about the best thing to happen in Britain in 1970 (which wasn't difficult) was the start of a new TV comedy called 'Monty Python's Flying Circus' which was the nearest thing to the old radio 'Goon Show' from years ago. Some of the sketches, including the one with the dead parrot, have gone down in comedy history.

Meanwhile

January: The Football Association, who always knew best, suspended George Best, Britain's most famous soccer player, for disreputable behaviour.

March: Most people were slightly surprised (and his mum and dad relieved) when David Bowie married a girl. Nobody had been quite sure (including Bowie) on whose side this somewhat androgenous pop star batted.

April: It was announced that the Morris Minor, the longest ever car in production (in time – not length!), and now a minor dinosaur (or minosaur), was to cease production the following year.

July: A 50 year old woman was given the first heart pacemaker powered by nuclear energy. It was a great success (and nobody seemed to mind that she glowed in the dark).

August: George Brown, who'd always resembled an inebriated owl, was made a peer, so that he could join all the other doddery oldsters in the House of Lords.

November: Pope Paul IV banned all Cardinals over 80 from voting in Papal elections. Five days later, he was attacked by a man carrying a dagger in Manila. I reckon the guy must have escaped from a Catholic old people's home.

December: MPs rejected a move to keep British Summer Time through the winter. Heaven knows why – there's no difference anyway.

1971

More of the Same

Heath's brave attempts to give the British economy a kick up the backside were sadly to no avail, and the Government, with their coat-tails firmly between their legs, skulked back to a lot of the economic policies they'd ridiculed Labour for. Not only that but, as might have been expected, the Tories' new policy of confrontation with the unions made the Labour/union relationship look like a teddy-bears' picnic. In the first quarter of 1971, the days lost by strikes were four times that of the same quarter the year before. Even our dear old postpersons went on strike on 20th January causing total mayhem. Heath, determined to be the hard man, refused to budge and even allowed private entrepreneurs and wide boys to set up alternative services (Postman Prat Ltd), which gave the British an eerie premonition of the major flogging-off of utilities that became such a feature of the eighties.

Holy Rollers

Another shock came on 4th February when Rolls Royce, that very British symbol of engineering excellence, went bottom up. The Tories, in a complete about-turn, decided to nationalise the aero-engine and aerospace activities and let the poor car bit fend for itself. The Rolls Royce company had been brought to its immaculate knees by a disastrous contract with the US company, Lockheed, who'd screwed them (in more ways than one) down to an almost ridiculous price and time restriction.

Happy Heath

The only thing that did cheer Heath up was when the EEC (with de Gaulle safely out of the way) decided that the terms were now right for Britain to join. To be truthful, everyone was now bored to death with the endless yapping so, although the faithless French whinged that things would never be la même if we joined, most of the other members thought we'd stayed out in the cold long enough.

Death in Ulster

Things were hotting up over in Northern Ireland and on 9th February the first British soldier was killed during rioting. Up to this time, the Protestants and Catholics had seemed perfectly happy just slaughtering each other. On 11th August, occurred the most controversial development so far when 300 IRA suspects were arrested and banged up in prison without any trial. This practice was called 'internment' and the IRA went crazy (or should I say crazier), embarking on an orgy of killing within hours of the announcement. The British Government then banned all marches and demonstrations, but it was like trying to hold back a pack of rabid dogs. Four days later, 5000 Catholic houses and 2000 Protestant houses were burned to the ground. Ireland was now at war with itself, with the poor British soldiers getting it in the neck from both sides.

Up to this time, the Great British Public had looked over to Ireland with only a little more than a vague casual interest. If they want to wipe themselves out, let them, we thought. It really wasn't anything at all to do with us. It all became very different when we heard that the IRA had decided to bring their bombs over the water.

New Money for Old

On 14th February, everyone was thrown into complete and utter turmoil when complete decimalisation became official. Our dear old pennies, threepences, shillings and half-crowns were finally kicked into history.

Cold War

Meanwhile, back at the Cold War with Russia, a KGB defector had spilled the beans on all his mates working in Britain. We reacted by kicking out 90 of their diplomats and officials which really cheesed off their bosses back home. The USSR responded by sending only five of our chaps home and so we got off relatively lightly.

Hot Pants

On a lighter note, the British (particularly men) were getting bored with maxi skirts, and so were girls with good legs. The solution was 'hot pants', which were tiny shorts that should have been locked up for their brevity.

Foreign Parts

On 24th November, six years after that nasty Ian Smith had proclaimed Rhodesia's independence and told us to go forth and multiply, an agreement was signed with Alec Douglas-Home (now our Foreign Secretary) to legalise their independence and to open up all the links that had been lost with Britain (well, surprise,

surprise!). The Labour Party didn't waste any time pointing out that nothing had changed for the blacks, and that they were further from being in charge of *their* country than they'd ever been. Silly Billies! Didn't they realise that international affairs have nothing to do with ethics or morality – at least not when there's hard cash involved.

Meanwhile

February: Still on the war path, Enoch Powell went one further and suggested that we should start sending immigrants 'home' as he foresaw an 'explosion' of not-quite-white people. On 24th February, the Immigration Bill was passed ending the right of Commonwealthers to settle here.

March: The *Daily Sketch*, which was a more awful paper than the *Daily Mail*, or the *Daily Express*, closed after 62 years. It was sadly (not) missed.
• A very weird guy called Charles Manson who, with his 'family' of hippies, chopped up the gorgeous film actress Sharon Tate and a few of her glam chums, featured in the most bizarre murder trial that the States had ever seen (and that sure is bizarre). Charlie, who was barking mad, was eventually sentenced to life on death row.

June: Just to prove that the British public have always enjoyed their fair share of junk on TV, 'Opportunity Knocks', a 'talent' show, was top of the ratings. Hughie Green, its slimy presenter, displayed about the same amount of talent as the contestants.

August: Edward Heath led his crew of jolly sailor boys to win the Admiral's Cup on his own boat *Morning Cloud*. Many people accused him, however, of sailing while Ireland burned.

October: When the diminutive Emperor Hirohito of Japan drove through London on a state visit, he was a little surprised when the commoners, who could normally be guaranteed to cheer or wave flags at anything in a state coach, remained silent. The Queen told him 'We cannot pretend the past did not exist. We cannot pretend that relations between our two peoples have always been peaceful and friendly.' This was really a polite way of saying 'Look you little creep, don't go thinking we've forgotten what you did to our boys in the war. The only reason you're here is because we want your loot.' Or words to that effect.

November: Princess Anne was not just a pretty horse – sorry – face! She was also good at riding. The British Sportswriters Association made her Sportswoman of the Year.

The BBC was flooded with complaints after a boy used a four letter word on 'Woman's Hour'.

December: I bet the Queen was secretly delighted with her husband's claim that the Windsors were going broke. Anyway, her allowance was doubled to near on £1,000,000. I bet that kept her in horsy headscarfs for a bit longer.

1972

EEC at Last

The only possible chink of light at the end of our economic tunnel of doom seemed to be the European Economic Community which we finally joined, much to the disgust of the French, in January. We were now part of a population that was even bigger than that of the United States.

But, for a veteran yachtsman, poor old Heath never seemed to

enjoy any plain sailing. As he was entering the Egmont Palace to sign for Britain, a woman jumped out of the throng and chucked a bag full of black printing ink all over him. Strangely enough, it had nothing to do with the EEC but turned out to be a rather misplaced protest over Government plans to redevelop London's Covent Garden. It was obviously to no avail, as the dear old fruit and veg market was soon to turn into the yuppie fairground it is to this day.

Ireland Hots Up
At least it was only ink that flowed over Ted. Eight days later, British paratroopers opened fire on what was soon to be known as 'Bloody Sunday', killing 13 civil-rights-marchers-turned-rioters and injuring a further 17. The IRA then announced, charmingly, that they planned to kill as many British soldiers as possible. The 'troubles' in Northern Ireland had so far only been sauntering along in the slow lane – now it was all-out war.

Heath, realising the nightmare ahead, announced that Northern Ireland would henceforth be run from England. (Oh boy, did the IRA like that!)

Heath S(t)inks!
During 1971, the Heath Government had done everything they could think of to bludgeon some life into the economy and get unemployment down. All to no avail. By January 1972, nearly

1,000,000 were on the dole (these days that sounds pretty good) and the value of the £ abroad was sinking faster than a Page 3 girl's suntan. Industrial relations couldn't have been worse (they thought) and Heath's blood pressure went through the roof when 280,000 ungrateful miners rejected his £31 million pay offer. Their president, Joe Gormley, called on all the other unions to add muscle to the first total pit shutdown since 1926. Gormley was assisted by a guy who was to become famous for his terrier-like tactics. Arthur Scargill, a funny little rodent of a man who seemed to be wearing someone else's hair, was one of the first to lead 'flying pickets' – groups of men who travelled round the country effectively shutting off any pit they felt like.

Just to make Heath squirm even more, the Wilberforce Commission, set up to look into the deadlock, awarded them a 20% pay increase, which they grabbed with open arms.

Prices Soar

To make things worse, all the world's commodities like copper, cotton and cocoa (not just for the drinking of) started going through the roof price-wise owing to the success of those countries like Germany and Japan who'd (thank God) lost the war, but were (no thanks to God) whipping us in the peace. By November, things were so dreary that the Government was forced to do a complete U-turn and, instead of trying to inflate the economy, set about squeezing it down with a 90 day price and pay standstill to try to stop wages going crazy. The TUC giggled behind their horny hands, flushed with the knowledge that they had finally got the Government by the short and curlies.

Strangely enough, the electorate were becoming well hacked off with the union's bully-boy techniques and starting to let it be known that they might well back Heath if he took off his kid gloves and had a proper no-holds-barred fight.

It was time to shuffle Heath's bratpack again, so all the Cabinet changed seats when the music finally stopped. All that is, except poor Reggie Maudling, the Home Secretary, who was left without one. He'd been found, not exactly with his fingers in someone else's till, but at least 'involved' with the newly infamous John Poulson. Poulson was the rich, successful and extremely dodgy architect at the centre of a huge scandal in which it was proved that he had been bribing bent officials with fat backhanders to gain lucrative Government contracts. Funny, ministers are usually such good judges of character!

Scandal in Washington

In the USA, five men were arrested for trespass in the offices of the Democratic National Committee (the opposition party). No big deal. When, however, it turned out the men were trying to bug the Democrats, the whole business became a lot more sinister. Bug-eyed Senator Hubert Humphrey, the Democratic candidate, demanded an explanation from President Nixon. Nixon denied all knowledge but his Pinocchio-esque nose grew another inch. (This was the beginning of the Watergate Scandal (see p.138).) Later in the year, he obliterated the challenge from Democrat George McGovern with an overwhelming vote of confidence from the American people (if only they'd known what was about to break). I suppose by then he'd found out all there was to know about their election strategy from his spies.

Trouble in Uganda

The party was over in newly independent Uganda. Suddenly General Idi Amin who had seemed 'such a decent chap' to the British Home Office, was turning out to be a dictator just like his hero, Mr A Hitler. He claimed that the Asians (who were carrying British passports) were sabotaging his economy and said he was kicking them out in three months. Some of these Asians thought the whole thing rather brilliant as it meant they could bypass the quota system controlling their entry to Britain ... until Amin's soldiers nicked all their money at the airport.

Meanwhile

February: Psst! Wanna buy some lions? Billy Smart's Circus, the

biggest and best in Europe, closed due to rising costs.

• Bernadette Devlin, the Ulster MP, flew at poor Reggie Maudling, in the House of Commons, pulling his hair and scratching and punching his face, like a demented witch. All he'd said was that he was launching an enquiry into the 'Bloody Sunday' massacre. I wonder what she'd have done if he'd said he wasn't? He was probably relieved to resign later in the year.

April: Cambridge scientists claimed that putting salt on your food led to heart disease. So what? Just about every sort of food you could sprinkle it on was apparently bad for you anyway.

June: Thousands of people turned up to say a last bye-bye to the Duke of Windsor, the uncrowned Edward VIII who was buried on 5th June.

July: Brilliant news! Women were to have a bigger role in TV current affairs programmes. Not so good news, the women in question included Esther Rantzen.

August: The Bishop of Kingston claimed that London was on the brink of collapse because of a sickness that was affecting the whole world. He was referring to the lack of community brought about by hideous tower blocks and the pressures from urban and industrial life. 18 years on we're still waiting.

September: Auntie BBC still had some taste. The powers-that-be asked the slippery smooth Jimmy Young to stop singing on his morning radio programme. He had to content himself in future to crooning and crawling to senior politicians. Bring back the singing I say.

November: American firmly believed, in their inimitable way, that they'd done so much damage to North Vietnam that the enemy would be forced to agree to a ceasefire. The Commies replied by shooting down the first American B52 bomber.

December: I've heard of aircraft food being revolting but this was ridiculous. A plane carrying 45 passengers crashed in the Andean mountains. The sixteen that were left, a rugby team called the Old Christians, having eaten all the peanuts, survived their long wait for rescue by eating the others. That's old Christians for you.

Oh no, not the scrum-half again

Hit of the Year: 'Amazing Grace'!

1973

Inflation Inflates

Basic Economics: Lesson 1
If you happen to be a country and you want to trade with other countries, it's rather important that you try to sell them as much as they sell you. Otherwise you have what is known as a balance of payments deficit. Britain in 1973 was really good at buying loads of gear from abroad, but really lousy at shifting any of our stuff over there, which resulted in a deficit of over a £1,000,000,000,000 (and a very embarrassed government).

Basic Economics: Lesson 2
If you happen to be a country that is manufacturing less and less (for whatever reason), it's rather important that you don't pay the workforce – who is making less and less – more and more. Between 1963 and 1973, despite a weedy increase in production, average weekly earnings soared by 249%. All this, with added problems like stroppy unions threatening strikes, go-slows and work-to-rules at the drop of a cloth cap, indicated a country in big, big trouble. This was Britain at the beginning of 1973.

The only glimmer of hope lay in Europe. On 5th January, we finally became (theoretically) working members of the EEC, much to the disgust of the Labour Party, the trade unions and, true to form, Enoch Powell. It could never be said that dear old Enoch's racism was based solely on colour; he just seemed to loath the idea of *any* foreigner setting foot on our shores. EEC entry must have been a real blow to him as, no sooner had his party managed to curb the flow of Commonwealth immigrants into the country, than the floodgates were opened to a whole load of Europeans. He really shouldn't have worried, however, as no European with half a brain would have wanted to come here anyway.

Three Day Week
By the end of the year, the economic situation was said to be the worst since the war (again) and Edward Heath was no longer the jolly red sailor we knew and sometimes loved. The Government was at total loggerheads with the unions and industry was flattened by the industrial action of the miners, power and railway workers. 'Who rules the country?' everyone cried, and the Conservatives sussed that, if they couldn't squash the unions, they would soon be forced into a General Election. Talk about stalemate! It was just like two kids' gangs facing up to each other in the playground. Edward Heath's lot refused to give in to the workers, and the workers refused to be pushed around by them. On the 13th November, he called another State of Emergency which put the wind up the whole country. No one was allowed to heat their home by electricity; no advertising signs could be lit up; drivers couldn't go more than 50 m.p.h. (apart from in aeroplanes); heating was restricted in factories; and horror of horrors, telly had to finish at 10.30 p.m. – and still neither side would budge! Worst of all, businesses – be they big or small – were only allowed to work for three days a week. This, obviously, became totally ridiculous and so it became commonplace to black out windows (like wartime) and work illegally (er – so I'm told!!). It was a cold and miserable Christmas with only turkeys managing to keep warm for just a few hours.

In January, Heath, in typical nautical manner, tried another tack and told the nation that things weren't as bad as the Government had at first expected and that the country might well go back to a four, or even five, day week. This scared the pants off the miners' leaders who then, in desperation (and seeing the writing on the wall) threatened an all-out strike.

Keeping the Punters Quiet

What do our betters do to divert the attention of their worsers when at the point of rebellion? Right first time. They either start a war or give us a royal wedding. This time it was the latter. The day after the announcement of the State of Emergency, Princess Anne got herself hitched, and everyone forgot the lousy situation, went soppy and waved Union Jacks. The subject of her affection was a right Hooray Henry called Captain Mark Phillips who, like Anne, was a world class rider (and twit). The day after the wedding the happy couple scarpered off to the sunny Caribbean to escape the misery that all us commonfolk had to endure.

Distillers Lose Spirit

The huge group of companies under the Distillers umbrella suffered a blow when a leading supermarket chain decided to boycott their products, owing to their tardiness in settling the compensation claims for the poor little mites disfigured by their mums' use of the drug thalidomide during pregnancy. Their biggest loss was in the booze market, as Distillers produced many leading brands of whisky, gin, vodka and brandy.

IRA Targets London

Well, we might have guessed that the IRA wouldn't like the idea of Northern Ireland being run by the British Government, and they showed their wrath by blasting the Old Bailey in central London. They managed to kill one person and injure 250. From then on, nowhere was safe. Still, we all felt better when we found out that they weren't using their own pocket money to make bombs. No; that nice Mr Moamar Gaddafi of Libya was footing most of the bill, saying that he 'must support any little country which has taken up arms to defend its rights and freedom.' Ah yes, freedom to go into a shopping centre in another country and blow up innocent kids and their mummies. Nice one Moamar!

Dickie's So Tricky!

Just so that you know that Heath wasn't the only leader in a deep mire, Richard Nixon was revealed to be far more deeply involved in the Watergate bugging scandal than was ever imagined, and had gone to great lengths to hide his tracks (even though his nose was now two feet long). The world's press were after him like a pack of hyenas, and it seemed to all that watched him squirming on telly (before 10.30!) that even he couldn't survive this one.

Then unbelievably, some tapes were discovered which were said to put the finishing touches to proof of Nixon's involvement but, at the last minute, his loyal secretary said that she was ever so sorry, but she appeared to have accidentally erased 18 minutes of the most important tape. And this, dear readers, was the secretary to the President of the United States of America. Read on.

Meanwhile

January: Jim didn't fix it this time! Smarmy Jimmy (good works for maximum self-publicity) Savile made a bundle promoting the silly 'Klunk-Klik' TV commercials to enforce the new seat-belt laws. It was then noticed that his own flashy new motor caravan wasn't fitted with them. Ow's about that then, guys and gals?

March: Teeny-bopper band The Osmonds arrived on our shores for the first time. The squeaky-clean Mormonlings came from Salt Lake City in the US. Five sixths of the singing troop were pretty awful, but the sixth, 9 year old Jimmy ('I'm your Long-Haired Lover from Liverpool'), was just about the worst thing to land on Britain since the horrible Hun's flying bombs.

April: Pablo Picasso died. Whether or not one thought that he was the world's greatest twentieth century artist or an overrated self-publicist, nobody could deny he made the most loot.

May: Wanna buy a bit of Rolls Royce? When nobody came up with a decent offer for the whole company, they decided to sell off the £38,400,000's worth of shares to anyone who wanted them.

July: David Bowie announced at a London concert that he would never perform live again. It turned out to be like a fish saying it was going to give up water.

October: President Nixon, who'd been withholding some significant tapes, gave in to a court order to give them up.

December: St Michael, the patron saint of underwear (and millionaires), sure had his protective eye on Marks and Sparks boss Joseph Sieff, who was gunned down by an assassin in his own home. Mr Sieff, a top Jewish figure, had always been a major target for Arab terrorist groups. The bullet, fired at close range, failed to kill him.

1974

Welcome Back Wilson

Edward Heath was smarter than he looked. He managed to turn the 'Who runs Britain?' question to his own advantage when he asked the British people whether they wanted the Government or the miners to call the shots. Unfortunately, poor old Ted, battered and bruised from probably the worst year of his life, was committed to putting his head on the block at the General Election in March, even though the country was still in a State of Emergency and collapsing under a three day week. On top of those little confidence boosters, the miners, never known to miss a trick, threatened to strike for the whole duration of the campaign. If all this wasn't bad enough, on the final Monday of the campaign, trade figures were published that made anything that had gone on before in our country's history look like a cocktail party.

With the timing of a fine strip-tease dancer, Enoch Powell (the famous Tory rebel), removed the final garment covering Heath's humiliation, and said he was going to vote – can you believe it – Labour.

Labour Knows Best

The Labour Party's strategy was, of course, to try to show us all that they could get us out of the fine mess the Conservatives had put us in (the same Conservatives who'd once tried to get us out of the fine mess that Labour had put us in).

The voters, however, were so punch-drunk by the messy affair that most of them really didn't give a monkey's either way, and this showed in the results. The Tories and the Socialists all lost hod-loads of votes, mostly to the lacklustre Liberals and Scottish Nationalists. Neither Heath nor Wilson had a majority and despite Heath's fruitless attempt to snuggle up to Jeremy Thorpe (the leader of the Liberals) in order to form some sort of pact, Wilson became the first Prime Minister since 1929 to lead a government without a majority in the House of Commons.

Wilson's first action was to make Heath's head-on fight with the miners count for nothing by chickening out and giving in to all their demands. The unions had won – grubby hands down.

Another Election
Talk about boring. No sooner was that election over than the politicians started creeping round their electorate again. There had to be yet another election as soon as possible because even cocky Harold Wilson found it impossible to run a country with a minority government. This time Labour got a small majority (if you call just three seats small), but it was enough for clever little Harold to do what he wanted. Unlike Heath, who had gatecrashed other parties like a cut-price tart, trying to get them into bed with his Conservatives, Wilson had decided to go it alone.

Anne Nearly Gets the Bullet
It was a good job that Princess Anne's and Captain Mark Phillip's relationship was already cooling down, for if they'd been cuddling in the back of the Royal limo on 20th March, one of them would almost certainly have been hit by the assassin's bullet that went straight between them. A car slewed round in front of theirs, only yards from their front garden at Buck House, and a guy jumped in and dragged our Anne out in order, as we all found out later, to

It's OK Anne, I think he only wants our autographs

ransom her for £1,000,000 (a lot more than he'd have got for poor old Mark). As might be expected, everyone around got hurt apart from the royal couple and, when eventually arrested, the chap (called Ian Ball) claimed he was doing it to bring attention to the lack of mental health facilities. I suppose it *did* make us all realise that there are still a lot of nutters on the loose!

Counties on the Move

Just to show how powerful they were over those who couldn't answer back, the Government (who always knew best) decided to muck around with names and borders of towns and counties going back to the *Domesday Book*. Only 10 of the 45 English counties and one of the 13 Welsh counties remained unscathed and some, like Rutland, Cumberland, Huntingdonshire and Westmorland, went altogether.

Nixon Hands Over

Over in America, the Watergate scandal was hotting up nicely. Tricky Dicky Nixon had handed over the infamous tapes to avoid impeachment from the Congressional Committee (see page 138). On one of the tapes, he could be heard telling his counsel, John Dean, that he reckoned he could get hold of the odd $1,000,000 required to stifle any blackmail attempts from a conspirator called Howard Hunt. No wonder he'd tried to 'lose' the tapes. On 8th August, he could hang on no longer and chucked in the Presidency. He had now become famous for being the first American President ever to resign.

Nixon was replaced by the one President that everyone forgets when listing presidents – Gerald Ford. He'd got to the top, not particularly for his own merits, but simply because all the others seemed so bent.

Meanwhile

January: Brilliant schemes (and wide boys) were emerging to beat the restrictions of the three day week. One enterprising hairdresser

306

in Dagenham thought up a great wheeze. As food shops were exempt from the three day week, he offered baked beans for 75 p a tin with a 'free' shampoo and set thrown in.

February: Dr Spock, the world famous millionaire American doctor whose book on child-rearing had been a bible for millions of young parents, was suddenly blamed for the rise in hooliganism in later life. When challenged, he simply turned round and said sorry he'd got it all wrong. Fair enough Doc!
• Too healthy for his own good, a fitness freak called Basil Brown drank eight pints of carrot juice a day and died, bright yellow, of an excess of vitamin A. His condition was indistinguishable from alcohol poisoning. Moral: if you're going to die from drink, you might as well enjoy yourself on the way.

March: Abba, the dreadful Swedish band, who looked as if they'd just raided a pantomime dressing-up box, won the excruciatingly embarrassing Eurovision Song Contest.

April: Chinese Take-Aways had taken over from good old fish and chips in the affections of the British. All velly deplessing.

May: The term Ms (pronounced Miz) was introduced at the passport office to placate all those women who found it embarrassing to be either Mrs or Miss.

July: The perfect actress and bishop scandal. Jess 'the bishop' Yates presented the most yucky religion-cum-showbiz programme called 'Stars on Sunday' on the weekly God slot. This tubby, balding, slippery-smooth example to us all, turned out to be having an affair with a blond 'actress' who'd recently appeared topless in the *Daily Mirror*. No wonder poor daughter Paula turned out the way she has.

August: Would you believe it? A Tory MP called Jeffrey Archer had to stand down because of severe financial problems. To be fair, the rise in the fame and fortunes of the now Lord Archer should be a lesson to us all. Quite what the lesson is, I'll leave up to you.

September: Discrimination against women was finally outlawed in a new White Paper by Woy Jenkins. Anyone who refused a woman anything from a job to a pint of bitter because of her sex became liable to prosecution. (Nice try, Woy, but many would argue that things aren't much better now.)

October: The IRA had different ways of dealing with women. They blew up, in their cowardly manner, two pubs in Guildford known to be frequented by members of the WRACS (Woman's Royal Army Corps).

November: Nobody realised that when the dashing Lord 'Lucky' Lucan disappeared, having allegedly murdered the family nanny and nearly his wife, that he would still be missing to this day. If you had a £ for the number of alleged sightings, you would be nearly as rich as the errant Earl. C'mon Lucky, where are you? I won't tell.

December: Everyone was slightly amused when Margaret Thatcher told us that she was entering the ring to fight for Edward Heath's job. Equal opportunities fine, but a woman (and a bossy one at that) as head of the Tory party? No chance!

1975

Thatcher Hatches

It had to happen. On 11th February, Margaret Thatcher, a 49 year old mother of twins, finally became the first woman to become leader of a political party, despite frantic efforts from her chauvinist colleagues to block her passage. Willie Whitelaw, who looked like a sycophantic toad, and was soon to act like one, nearly blubbed, as he, and most public opinion, had thought he had the job in the bag.

Maggie's timing was brilliant as always. Wilson was scrabbling around for hide-saving ideas and longed to get back to the homely, pipe-smoking, confidence-inspiring leader of a few years ago. He showed what a wily old fox he was, however, when, on 18th March, nearly half his cabinet, totally fed up with the Common Market, rebelled. Nothing like it had been seen for over 40 years. Wilson neatly side-stepped his personal dilemma by stating that he was not that bothered either way and certainly wouldn't resign over the final decision. Cabinet members were left free to campaign according to what they truly believed (for nearly the first time before or since) as opposed to having to toe the party line. Any fool could see that this was just a sign of a desperate government that couldn't even make up its own mind, let alone persuade anyone else.

Drooping Pound

On 16th March, the £ took a nose-dive to only 75% of its value four years earlier. At the same time, prices were rising by 22%, and unemployment hit the 1,000,000 mark for the first time ever. You don't have to have a first-class degree in economics to realise that the Labour Government had lost it, and even they knew it.

In June, there was a referendum to find out, once and for all, whether we British were still into being European. The vote was a surprisingly overwhelming 'Yes please', which put the tin lid, once and for all, on any arguments. We were *in* the EEC now and we could like it or lump it.

Uneasy Education
This was the time when the Labour Government, in its infinite wisdom, was trashing the grammar schools (much loved by middle-class Britain) and replacing them with comprehensive schools (much loved by er . . . ?). Many of the finer grammar schools, like Manchester, refused to play ball when their funding was whipped away, and went totally independent, relying on a payment-according-to-means fee structure. The joke was that this method was really more socialist in practice than the smart new comprehensive system which still failed to give the poor kid from the working class background the same chance of a good education as those better off.

Of course, all this played into the hands of the posher public schools whose administrators were bowled over by the rush of applications from 'nice' mummies and daddies, who didn't want their little treasures going to school with (let alone talking to) those awful little oiks from the poorer areas.

Fashion

It certainly wasn't a bright idea to go into gent's hairdressing in the mid 70s. The only young men that didn't wear their hair long were soldiers, prisoners or the follicly-challenged (bald to you!). The hippie movement, now (thankfully) on the way out, had left funny little reminders that had crept into everyday fashion. Trousers still flared below the knee; shoes made you at least an inch taller, and big moustaches (on men) were politically correct. T-shirts, which had once been called vests and worn under the shirt to keep you warm, had now become a major fashion garment. Kids exhibited controversial, or really rude, one-liners on their chests and advertisers saw them as an excellent way to promote their products and, for some totally obscure reason, punters of all ages seemed to love to be seen advertising God-knows-what for no money. Beats me!

The mid 70s were a kind of fashion no-man's-land for women. Bits of ageing Biba gear were worn with hot pants or maxi skirts. Clumpy platform shoes were coupled with floaty flower power frocks and hair couldn't decide whether to be long and wispy or short and permy.

And Music?

Musically it was similar. Strong diving forces like rock and roll, rhythm and blues and soul were still alive, but fighting against a very unpleasant, 'easy listening' virus. People like Barry Manilow, The Carpenters, Englebert Humperdinck (his singing matched his name), or Paul McCartney's rather weedy Wings were increasingly popular. Hit of the year was 'Sailing' which was about the blandest song Rod Stewart (by then nearing his sell-by date) ever sung.

Hip kids of the time were listening to some brilliant bands from the States like Steely Dan, Bruce Springsteen and Velvet Underground. In Britain, we had The Average White Band, David Bowie, the now great Eric Clapton, and a much more jazzy Van ('the man') Morrison; but the really good sounds seldom made the singles chart.

Meanwhile

January: Having spent a cool £40 million buying buckets and spades to dig the Channel Tunnel, the whole thing was put on ice yet again by the Government. A lot of non-Francophiles heaved a hugh sigh of relief.

March: What a comedown. The once highly regarded Shadows led by Hank (dorky-looking) Marvin actually entered the Eurovision Song Contest and came in second behind a Dutch group who sang a song called 'Ding-a-Dong' (which is what all those songs seem to be called).

April: Another comedown. Aston Martin-Lagonda, perhaps the finest British car firm ever, was sold to the International Semi-Conductor Company of America. Good job they didn't call the car that. (Hey! Wanna lift in my International Semi-Conductor!?)
• On 1st April, the wholly disgusting Vietnam War officially ended when North Vietnamese tanks rolled into Saigon, the capital. The Americans had already pulled out of a 15 year war which had achieved nothing but the deaths of thousands of young men, women and children and the end of America's belief that it could do and go anywhere, whenever it damn well wanted.

June: A brilliant new TV series called 'Fawlty Towers' was launched on British TV. Starring John Cleese (ex-Monty Python) and Prunella Scales, it proved conclusively that British comedy was the very best in the world (unless you're foreign).

July: Fact meets fiction. Police discovered that Carlos Martinez, otherwise known as the 'Jackal' the most famous international assassin ever, had been living in London, when his heavily weapon-stocked lair was found. He is still on the run.

August: A Japanese ex-army mechanic offered Britain a dream. The Honda Dream became the first of a flood of Jap. motorbikes that completely destroyed Britain's stick-in-the-mud industry. Served 'em right I say.

October: Trust the British to catch something horrible from the Dutch. Over 6.5 million elm trees died from the cleverly named Dutch Elm Disease.

November: He should have stuck to cars. Graham Hill (Damon's dad) became an ex-racing driver when he ploughed his plane into a field near Elstree and died.

1976

Room at the Top
On 5th April, James Callaghan became the new Labour Prime Minister following the shock resignation of worn-out Harold Wilson. As when Heath replaced Douglas-Home, if you'd looked for anyone more different, you'd have found it difficult. For a start, everyone seemed to like Callaghan. For a second, unlike Wilson, who'd been dead clever at school and later Oxford, Jim

Callaghan (who was no spring chicken at 64) had come from a dead ordinary elementary, and then secondary school, education. For a third, he was a non-smoker, non-drinker, regular church-goer and about as straightforward as you could get (for a politician!).

Callaghan came from the right of centre, but was well clued up as to the growing power of the left. His great intention was to unite the party and he was therefore hellbent on swatting the leftie minority groups, who were multiplying like flies while trying to hoist their views on to party policy. In a way, he came into the job with one hand firmly tied behind his back, as Wilson had made himself and the Labour Party extremely unpopular and his government had been losing loads of by-elections to the Liberals.

Jobs for the Boys

Wilson had gone out under a hail of bricks owing to his resignation honours list, which had been drawn up in conjunction with his very personal secretary Lady Falkender and published in May. Amongst the group of extremely dubious 'friends' he'd showered with knighthoods and lordships was one Joe Kagan. Kagan was an extremely dodgy, self-made millionaire northerner who, amongst other things, manufactured the hideous raincoat (called a Gannex), that looked as if it was made out of reconstituted chewed-up cardboard, and was much favoured by Wilson. The lengths some people will go to for a free mac! A few years later, Kagan was 'de-lorded' when charged with cheating and defrauding the Inland Revenue.

And Another

MP John Stonehouse had arranged a 'disappearance' by leaving his clothes on a Miami beach before heading off to Australia under a forged passport. He then turned out to be a forger, a cheat, a fraudster, a liar (as well as a politician). This brilliant man, who'd been tipped to be the future leader of the Labour Party, was found guilty on 6th August of a whole series of naughtinesses and sentenced to seven years hard 'labour'. I would have thought that his ingenuity was just what the Labour Government needed. Stonehouse for PM I say.

Thorpe Backs Out
Probably one of the greatest and most fascinating scandals began in May when Jeremy Thorpe, the ultra-posh leader of the Liberal party, suddenly resigned after allegations of sexual relations with a model. Not any old model, either, as this one was called Norman. If you think I'm going to descend into all the sordid details of this business, I'm afraid you're absolutely . . . right, but you'll have to be patient and wait until 1978 for the next bit.

Snowdon Slides Out
Just as the Royal Family are never seen visiting the toilet, they never discuss personal problems either. It was, therefore, quite a shock when it was announced that Princess Margaret and her hubby, Lord Snowdon, were splitting. At the press conference, Lord Snowdon, who'd looked miserable for years, seemed positively ecstatic. The only problem the Royals had was who would now take the family snaps (and whether it would cost 'em).

Phew, Wot a Scorcher!
What do we British moan about more than anything else? You've got it – the English summer. Why is the weather so unpredictable?

Why can't we have barbecues without the fear of wet sausages? Why do we sometimes have to wear overcoats on the beach? And so on, and so on. The summer of 1976 was the driest, hottest and longest this century. So were the British people, at long last, happy? . . . Don't be silly!

You just can't remove the British pastime of complaining at the drop of an umbrella. Before long, sunburnt people were happily moaning about everything from the state of their lawns, the queues for ice cream, the water rationing, the forest fires, the hole in the ozone layer or the Government's inability to make it rain. A Minister for Drought (can you believe) was appointed who, after weeks of careful scientific analysis by his brilliant hand-picked staff, using the latest, state-of-the-art instrumentation, came out with the inspired statement that unless we all cut our water consumption there would have to be rationing. Eventually the rains came again . . . and everyone complained. Wretched weather!!

Peanuts for All

The big news from abroad this year was the death of that old tyrant Chairman Mao, and the election of a peanut farmer from Georgia as the new President of the United States (and why ever not?). Rhodesia was struggling to keep its boot firmly on the reluctant black rebels, while further down in South Africa the pot was boiling over with rioting and looting throughout the black townships (and we had our own race riot at the Notting Hill Carnival). Everyone seemed to be fighting everyone else (as usual) in the Middle East, while Isabel Peron, President of Argentina, was chucked out, giving the dreadfully overrated Lloyd-Webber and Rice yet another plot for a dreadfully overrated musical (*Evita*).

Meanwhile

January: One of the few millionaires not to lose their shirts in the worst year ever for bankruptcy was the crime writer Agatha Christie. She just died (aged 85).

February: Balletic ice-skater John Currie won the Olympic Gold Medal at Innsbruck. He managed, for the first time in history, to make skating into almost an art form (but not quite).

March: Arthur, the fab feline star of the Kattomeat (inspired name!) commercials, died. He had been scooping his supper straight from the tin, with his paw, for over ten years (who can't do that?). The poor pussy didn't make a penny, however, as he was owned lock, stock and whiskers by Spillers Pet Foods.

• More death. L. S. Lowry, the famous and much-acclaimed artist (and former rent collector), who couldn't paint to save his life – died.

May: All over London one could see graffiti proclaiming the innocence of George Davis, a taxi driver, jailed for armed robbery. Eventually the courts gave in under the enormous public pressure and released him. A couple of years later George was back inside again . . . for armed robbery. Egg on face? Not much!

June: A milestone in the culinary history of our fine country. McDonalds, the only meal you can eat without teeth (I should be in advertising), arrived (uninvited) from the States.

July: Obsequious little David Steel, son of a Presbyterian minister, leapt into poor Jeremy Thorpe's trousers (figuratively speaking), to lead the Liberal Party.
• Those horrid, blue three-wheeler invalid cars, that acted like huge fingers pointing out the disabled, were phased out. They were

apparently so dangerous that there was a good chance that if you were given one you'd like as not end up in a worse state than before.

September: Percy Shaw, the man who'd invented cat's eyes, closed his own for the last time. Apparently he'd had the idea when he'd seen a cat's eyes light up as he pedalled home from the pub on his bike (no! not the cat!). Most people just see pink elephants.

October: If it wasn't bad enough losing your husband, poor Mrs Mao was compared to 'dog dung' (Pekinese no doubt) and jailed, with her Gang of Four, for allegedly trying to overthrow the Chinese Government. It really hadn't been her year.

November: All the girls at Girton, the female Cambridge college, were found to be 'expecting' . . . men. The decision was taken to open its doors to the unfairer sex the following year.

December: The first of the punk bands, The Sex Pistols, invented by the great Malcolm McLaren, ran riot on a TV news review programme. Bill Grundy, the presenter, obviously trying to be hip, challenged them to repeat the 'F' word. This opened a tirade that the poor old 'viewers at home' had never before experienced. God knows what poor Bill expected.

1977

Jubilee Fever

Time to jolly up the British people's flagging self-esteem. Good Queen Elizabeth II had now held down the top job (albeit damn well paid) for 20 years, and her Silver Jubilee parade proved that there was still a forelock-tugging nation lurking behind their front doors, dying to wave a flag at something. No one could deny that those shiny old gilded coaches, driven by men in dreadful second-hand outfits, and pulled by big white royal horses, could still give the British punter a sense (misguided or not) of loyalty and patriotism that no politician could even dream of.

Lucky Jim Has An Idea

Jim Callaghan, the Prime Minister, must have dreamed he could do the same for himself. His nightmare term of Labour Government was still going down the electoral plug-hole, losing loads of by-elections, including two at the heart of cloth-cap-land – Walsall and Workington. The Government was back walking the tight-rope, with a majority of only one, and even that was looking a bit precarious. It was time for them to sweet-talk the Liberal Party as Ted Heath had tried some years ago to save his own (considerable) bacon. Remember? He, though, had got his face slapped for his trouble (see page 140).

This time David Steel was top Liberal and, luckily for Jim, young McDave would have sold his grandmother just to sniff even a tiny bit of power. The Lib/Lab pact was the first deal of its kind ever seen and Steel, no doubt, saw it as a way of eventually getting through the electoral reforms that would bring him and his Liberal lads and lassies in with a fighting chance.

Unfortunately (tee hee) it had exactly the opposite effect, as ardent Liberal supporters thought that sneaky Steel had sold out everything they stood for. So, at the next by-election, they let him know just what a tacky thing they thought he'd done by voting elsewhere. Callaghan, of course, didn't give a damn; he'd bought himself just enough time for the economy to come round, wiping out a Tory 'No Confidence' motion which, sure as hell, would have seen him and his party back down at the Job Centre.

Oil Aboard

The economy, which had really hit the deck in 1976, was just beginning to twitch again, thanks largely to all that lovely, black North Sea Oil. But the situation still looked impossible, with nearly 1.5 million on the dole and production practically static.

Luckily the $ was in a worse state than the punch drunk £, which was looking, believe it or not, a lot less peaky than usual.

Work or Walk

Those perishing strikes had become a ball and chain round any real chance of Britain's economic recovery. On 15th March, the exasperated bosses of British Leyland, the mammoth state car and truck firm, finally flipped their lids (or bonnets) and told three thousand striking toolmakers that if they didn't get their idle backsides right back to work that instant they'd be sacked – no ifs or butts. Jim Callaghan backed them all the way, telling the strikers that there would be no more state cash to paper over the damage they were doing. By now, we had all fully realised that foreign car makers were champing at the bit to flood the country with their motors, and that these strikers were playing right into their hands. I wonder what they'd have said if they'd known that eighteen years later the whole company would be flogged to the Krauts (BMW).

Echoes of Adolph

One of the nastiest things to come out of the mid 70s was the rise of the National Front Party – a bunch of racist morons who, for some inexplicable reason, thought that they alone were the race chosen to inhabit Britain (shaved heads, lager bellies and covered in spots and tattoos). A pitched battle against the police occurred in Lewisham (home of pitched battles) who used their cosy new

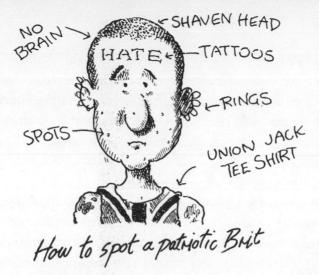

NO BRAIN

SHAVEN HEAD

HATE

TATTOOS

RINGS

SPOTS

UNION JACK TEE SHIRT

How to spot a patriotic Brit

Ulster-tested riot shields for the first time.

School for Skivers
Scruffy Shirley Williams, the leftie Labour Education Secretary who made even her fellow politicians look stylish, had been largely responsible for the death of the grammar schools. She now had to eat humble pie and admit the failure of her latest wheeze to imprison kids, desperate to quit her new comprehensive schools, for an extra year after the age of fifteen.

Skateboard Summer
So what could all those kids do on leaving school? Simple – they went on the dole – and then on the skateboard. This was the year that every pavement, pathway, or drive was jam-packed with kids riding (or falling off) those funny little, American inspired, plywood planks-with-wheels-on.

Cricket-a-Go-Go
A loud, disagreeable Australian, who resembled a robber with a stocking over his face, Kerry Packer, came over to our country, like the devil incarnate, to buy the very souls of our best cricketers. He wanted them to play exhibition tests on telly wearing the most gaudy outfits, advertising everything from cars (foreign) to cat food. Like the sport or not, this simply wasn't cricket. The gentle sport of gentlemen was turned into showbiz overnight.

Punk Gets Pop

For years kids had searched for something that would be *really* guaranteed to drive their nearest and dearest to the therapist. The punk movement was perfect. Looks-wise, it had started on the streets (like all crazes) but, like day follows night, eventually it became a kind of half-baked fashion movement adapted by the clever(ish) designer Vivienne Westwood.

Fashion-wise, true punks were a dirty, delicious disaster area: ripped bondage clothing; spiky, greasy, parrot-coloured hair; studs and rings through the most unimaginable (and painful) parts of the body (yes – there too!!); and tattoos proclaiming obscenities across their foreheads or necks. Punks simply didn't give a monkey's what anybody thought and even competed with each other to see who could look the most hideous. Punkism only began to wither when certain smartened up and diluted items of their dress (like tartan bondage trousers) started to appear in high street gentlemen's outfitters in places like Tunbridge Wells and Bath.

Music-wise (if you can use that word), the 'credit' for the birth of the totally anarchic punk rock must really go to The Sex Pistols and their manager/guru Malcolm MacLaren. This horribly brilliant band started to crop up, like a contagious disease, around some of the seedier London clubs. 'We're not into music, we're into chaos' they proclaimed.

The most interesting aspect of punk was that it came from the kids, was for the kids and was largely controlled by the kids. It was a way of showing two filthy fingers to an establishment that had let them down so badly.

Meanwhile

January: No wonder Woy Jenkins resigned from the Cabinet. He'd obviously had the nod that he was to become the much higher paid President of the EEC in Brussels.

February: We might have guessed that the nice Mr Amin, head of Uganda, would turn into a despotic murderer. His most outrageous act was to have the Archbishop of Uganda murdered. Even his long-gone hero, Adolf, never tried things like that.

May: Nigel Short, who now looks like an ad for 'Man at C&A', was once a normal child. Well, if you call being, at eleven, the youngest ever competitor in a national chess championship normal.

August: The undisputed King of Rock and Roll, Elvis Presley, died from a drugs overdose at his deliciously tasteless home, Gracelands, in Memphis. If anyone still believes that money and fame automatically brings happiness, take a look at the state of 'Elvis the Pelvis' just before he went to rock and roll heaven.

Footnote: His 9 year old daughter Lisa Marie seemed relatively unmoved when told she was now a billionaire.

I'm all shook up!

September: Freddie Laker astounded the world (and the other airlines) by offering cut-price flights to New York for £59 – and he even managed to make a profit.

Hit of the Year: 'Don't Cry For Me, Argentina' (ominous or what?)

Bring Back Hadrian

So far, I haven't mentioned the fact that the Scots and Welsh, noticing that Britain was rapidly becoming the 'sick man of Europe', were revolting, claiming they were fed up with being simply an English colony. The clamour for devolution (self-government) was becoming deafening. If England wanted, as some bright political commentator put it, 'to embark on a journey from being a developed to an undeveloped country' then bully for them, but why should Scotland and Wales be dragged down with 'em?

Actually, much more to the point, the canny (and tight) Scots were miffed that the black gold (North Sea oil), was not pouring into *their* country from *their* sea-bed. Why, for Robbie Burns' sake, should they have to share it with the rest of us? Had the Scottish Nationalists read their history books, however, they'd have realised that they'd actually been given their precious home rule way back in 1913. Why else did they have their own McLaw system, own McChurch, own McNewspapers and even their own McTelly. McStrewth!

The Welsh were slightly different. Nobody could see Wales operating on its own economically (what if the bottom fell out of the leek and harp businesses?), so there had to be another reason for their wanting devolution. It seems, in retrospect, that they were more concerned about the loss of their language (I'd have thought that having places called Llanfairpwllgwyngyllgogerychwyrndrobwllllantysiliogogogoch was something to be well avoided); and also the occupation of dinky little cottages by the English as weekend homes.

The Welsh pre-devolution solution to these problems was:

a. As soon as any foreign visitor (particularly English) were to ask them anything, they would suddenly not understand a word and switch to speaking their own, totally unintelligible, lingo.

b. To burn all the holiday cottages down (which seems more of an Irish solution). As their objection was the fact that the poor locals could no longer afford the inflated prices, then their actions simply meant there was nothing left to buy anyway.

Very nice Dai, shame it's my parent's new house!

This whole devolution business came to a well-silly head when Cornwall suddenly jumped up and said that it also wanted to free itself from the rest of Britain (and nationalise the pasty industry, no doubt). Anyway, how's about home rule for Wandsworth, where I live? What happened? Read on.

Poor Old Jim

Though just about everyone liked Jim Callaghan, his go at prime ministering was turning out to be fairly depressing. If Wilson had been a failure, then poor Jim seemed to be making matters worse. It has been said that every decision he made, either before or since becoming PM, had, in retrospect, turned out to be wrong – failing to devalue the £ in 1964, letting all the Asians in from Kenya in 1969, and trying to hang on to power too long in the vain hope of doing some pay deal with the unions who, thanks to crawly Wilson, had the Labour Government well and truly tucked up.

Although it was not as bad as the situation in 30s Germany (when Hitler took over), the time was ripe for a complete change and a real macho leader. David Steel, who was anything but stupid (or macho) realised that the Lib/Lab pact had no chance (and more to the point nor had he) so promptly yanked his Liberals out. So who on earth would this new leader be? No prizes for guessing . . . please read on.

Abroad

Time for a look across the waters. Who was doing what to whom in 1978?

1. The Ugandans were fighting the Tanzanians.
2. The Israelis were fighting the Palestinians (as usual).
3. Rhodesian rebels were fighting Ian Smith.
4. The Ethiopians were fighting the Somalians.
5. The Russians were helping the Ethiopian army to fight the Ethiopian Government.
6. The Iranians (ex-Persians) were getting ready to fight their leader, the Shah.
7. The Argentinians were fighting The Dutch . . . in the World Cup Final.

The Royals?

Following all the fabulous fun of the Royal Jubilee, and the birth of the first of a new generation of kids for us all to support (Princess Anne's nipper – Pete), our Royal Family began to settle down. The Queen, now a granny, only really had *that* sister to worry about. Princess Margaret now alarmed everyone by lurching perilously close to marrying Roddy Llewellyn, a sort of up-market playboy like his brother Dai – the sort always seen outside London nightclubs or with debby bimbos (dimbos?) called Henrietta, Camilla or Lucinda. Luckily, Roddy thought better of the match, so poor Margaret went back to her booze and fags.

Medical Madness

British doctors, scientists and quacks stunned the world. A gynaecologist from Oldham successfully planted the very first 'test tube babies' into their grateful mums; while at St Bartholomew's in London, doctors started using leeches again (in 1837 the hospital got through 96,300) to suck blood out of unsightly bruises. Yukk!!

Even weirder, Ivor Rice from St Austell, resigned to going blind, took the advice of 70 year old Julie Owen of Kent, who claimed that regular bee stings (from her regular bees) would bring back his sight. He was so impressed with the result that he soon got up to ten stings a day. Pass the bees, honey.

Weirder Still! Embryonic mice, frozen over five years before, were scuttling around their cages after a nice warm bath. Scientists now reckoned it was totally possible to conceive a human nipper, freeze the poor little foetus, then actually have it whenever you wanted.

Meanwhile

January: Margaret Thatcher stated the obvious, in a slimy statement to gain popularity, when she said that many Britons 'fear being "swamped" by people with a different culture.' I wonder if she really meant that last word.

March: Foley Boxing Club were looking for someone to have a scrap with their new heavyweight star, Paul McDonald. All they came up with was a young 16 year old who was just leaving approved school. Unfortunately, the boy – a certain Frank Bruno – didn't have the right ABA (Amateur Boxing Association) cards so could only spar. Fortunately for Paul McDonald though. Know what I mean, 'Arry?

April: Our politicians' egos certainly got the better of them when they allowed proceedings in the House of Commons to be broadcast on the radio. Britain was shocked when it heard the behaviour and often sad level of debate of those it had elected.

May: Silent comedy? The hardly-cold corpse of Charlie Chaplin, which had two months earlier been nicked from his Swiss grave, was now found buried ten miles away. Perhaps old Charlie might have got the joke. Nobody else could.

June: Guy the gorilla, London Zoo's biggest attraction, had a bad time at the dentist. The 32 year old, 27 stone ape never woke up from the anaesthetic. I bet he would have done if he'd known they were going to stuff him.
• Absolutely no connection, but Jeremy Thorpe, the ex-Liberal leader, was interviewed by detectives investigating a plot to kill gay model Norman Scott. He was later charged in December.

August: Job vacant . . . Pope. Good news – after only four ballots, albino Cardinal Luciani was elected Pope Jean-Paul I.

September: Who said God looked after his own? After only 33 days of poping, Jean-Paul I, was found dead. (Yet another ad in the *Vatican Times*.) His replacement, Karil Wojtyla (a Pole) was named, rather unoriginally, Jean-Paul II (I think I'd have wanted something completely different). Still, at least you could get your tongue round it.
• Be careful when waiting for buses at Waterloo Bridge! Mr Georgi Markov, a Bulgarian defector, was jabbed in the leg by a poisoned umbrella. He died four days later. I suppose he'd have been all right if it had been raining. Murderers hate getting wet.

November: One of the problems with being a member of Reverend Jim Jones' religious sect, The People's Temple, was that you had to kill yourself. 913 devotees drank Kool Aid with just a little hint of cyanide (to give it that extra kick) and were found piled up at their hideaway in Guyana. Anyone could have told them soft drinks (and crack-pot religions) were bad for them.

1979

Winter of Discontent
The few long, miserable months which spanned 1978 and 1979 became known as the 'Winter of Discontent'. The on-going scrap between the Government and the unions had finally descended to an out-and-out brawl, with the unions doing everything in their power to beat the pay ceilings put on them by poor 'now-not-so-lucky' Jim Callaghan and his boys. Food and petrol supplies were up the creek owing to lorry drivers' go-slows, huge mounds of rubbish lay piled up in the streets and, in Liverpool, dead people lay piled up in the mortuaries impatiently waiting to be dug in. The pesky pickets didn't even stop at harassing hospitals and practically decided who they'd let in to get better.

This could well have been the most unpopular that any Government had ever become and, as Labour plummeted down in public opinion, in true see-saw fashion, the Tories rocketed up.

Devolution Dives
Remember all that fuss about self-government last year? After numerous debates in the Commons, loads of demonstrations and protests, both the Welsh and the Scots peoples were asked what

they thought in a referendum. The Welsh, bless 'em, turned it down overwhelmingly, while the Scots who, we'd all been led to believe, hated being ruled by Sassenachs, hardly turned out to vote, so no conclusion could be come to.

Here Comes Margaret

At the back end of March, poor old Jim Callaghan lost the first vote of confidence for 55 years which meant there had to be an election as soon as possible. There was, and in early May, after the greatest political swing since the war, a certain Mrs Margaret Thatcher, wife, mother and superstar, became queen of all she surveyed – the first British Prime Ministress ever.

The Labour Party was completely shattered and, in order to get some kind of opposition together, the poor losers were forced to dip into the bran tub and have a re-selection of MPs. Britain had a new government, a new PM and, best of all, a new target of fun – Mr Denis Thatcher – who took on the role (in the silly papers) of the poor little red-nosed husband dominated by the big fat lady in the seaside postcards.

The biggest joke of all came when the unions, realising they'd slain the rather shabby goose (the Labour Government) that had laid, for so long, the golden eggs, agreed to a sleazy pact with the new Tory Government. Maybe they'd spotted the steely, I'm taking no nonsense, glint in the eye of 'her that must be obeyed'!

Blown To Bits

It certainly didn't pay to be a hardliner regarding Northern Ireland (or a close friend of Margaret Thatcher). The man with the daftest name in politics, Conservative Airey Neave, was blown up in the House of Commons car park. Later in the year, we were all once more shocked to the core when dear old Earl Mountbatten (Prince Philip's uncle) caught more than he bargained for when his fishing boat was ripped to smithereens by an IRA bomb off the Irish coast.

Irate Iran

Just as the situation in Iran had got to bursting point, on 16th January, the Shah, realising the natives weren't joking, hightailed it off to Egypt. His downfall had been engineered by the Ayatollah Khomeini who was himself in exile in Paris. Elated Iranians jumped up and down (as only they can) with joy, while women stuck flowers down the barrel of tanks which only the day before were trying to crush the demonstrations.

Someone asked the Shah, as he was leaving, how long he reckoned he was going to be away. The Shah said he wasn't sure, but one look round at the extremely cross, fanatical and screaming Iranians would have told him to take at least a toothbrush and a change of clothes.

Later in the year, the masses took the unprecedented action of storming the American Embassy in Teheran (see Things You Simply Don't Do). Screaming anti-American slogans, the mob took nearly 100 embassy staff hostage. America had always supported the ex-Shah so this action seemed to them like serious fighting talk.

Meanwhile

February: Sid Vicious, the member of the Sex Pistols who made the other punks seem like Cliff Richard, went most certainly down to the hot place when he died of a heroin overdose in New York.

331

April: Pictures taken from the US spacecraft, Voyager 1, revealed that the planet Jupiter has rings round it like Saturn. At the same time, earthbound astronomers discovered rings round Uranus too.
• Totally unconnected, Norman Scott, the male model 'linked' with ex-liberal leader Jeremy Thorpe, claimed in court that he'd been seduced twice by the politician at his mum's home. I've heard of liberal behaviour, but this was ridiculous. A month later poor Jeremy was found innocent of plotting murder and acquitted.

June: John Wayne (the Duke), the most famous film cowboy of all time, went to ride the great range in the sky when he died on the 11th. Outside his film career, Wayne was as right wing and red-necked as Genghis Khan, seeing the Vietnam War as the last great exhibition of American might.

August: Sebastian Coe became the very first athlete to hold three world records – the mile, the 800 and 1500 metres – at the same time. His ability to move fast, and keep looking behind him, could well be useful for his current job – Sebastian is now a Tory MP.

September: A very horrid murderer, nicknamed the 'Yorkshire Ripper', claimed his round dozen when he killed 20 year old Barbara Leach. Unlike most of his other victims (who were prostitutes) young Barbara was at Bradford University.
• Pope John Paul II flew to Ireland to beg all his Catholic fans to stop killing the other lot. As his plane flew over, many devout Irishmen stopped fighting and dropped to their knees in worship. When he'd gone, the 250,000 people who'd gone to see him went home and carried on exactly as they had before.

October: A new report from the Church of England proved that they were still split over whether to treat homosexuals as normal Christians or unreformed sinners. Their woolly thinking really came to light when they pronounced that gay sex was only all right if the partners *really* loved each other (and didn't do *it* with anyone else). Did this mean that 'straight' people could do whatever, to whoever, whenever they liked, as long as it was with someone of the opposite sex?

December: We all had a giggle when it was disclosed to a shocked House of Commons that the Queen's personal aristocratic art advisor had been, on his days off, a spy for the Russians. Sir Anthony Blunt turned out to be the infamous 'fourth man' in the Burgess, Maclean and Philby affair (see page 32). Naughty old Anthony had his not-very-hard-earned knighthood taken away. Apparently the Government had known about him since 1964 but they'd given him immunity in exchange for not spilling the beans. Nobody seems to know why Mrs Thatcher decided to shop him now.

Gosh Mr. Blunt, you know so much about Russian Art.

Russian Revelations

A couple of days before the end of 1979, just as Mrs Thatcher was putting up the blue curtains in Number Ten, a shiver went up the spine of anyone who wasn't Russian. The news had broken that the Soviet Union, who had been far too quiet for far too long, had invaded Afghanistan. They certainly don't do things by half, those Ruskies; in only a few days they had 80,000 remarkably old-fashioned looking troops, armed to the teeth, pushing their considerable weight around. Afghanistan's President Hafizullah Amin (what is it about that name?) and his family were promptly executed by the KGB 'for crimes against the Afghan people'. You'd have thought the poor blighter, being a Communist, would have at least been politically correct as far as the Russians were concerned, but he obviously wasn't the right sort of communist, and the Kremlin claimed that its forces were 'requested to render urgent political, moral, military and economic assistance'. That's the Ruskies for you – all heart!

Poland Next?

The free world then waited with freshly baited breath when, after months of demos and strikes, Polish workers were, surprisingly, given loads of concessions by their Russian overlords. Most people assumed that just as they'd done in Hungary, Czechoslovakia and most recently Afghanistan, the Soviets would soon uncross their fingers, get the tanks out and crush the living daylights out of them. This might have happened if they hadn't been so stretched, soldier-wise, in Afghanistan, or weren't seriously running out of brownie points, public opinion-wise, with the rest of the world. But, wait as we all did, the iron fist hovered. Polish workers were allowed free trade unions and a central organisation called Solidarity, 'designer' stickers for which (for some bizarre reason) started to appear in the rear windows of British cars whose owners thought they were being frightfully 'right on'. The hero of the strikers, a shipyard worker called Lech Walesa, became their leader and much, much later the President of Poland.

Last Colony Disappears

Ian Smith displayed a wobbly smile when the Union Jack was finally lowered in Rhodesia, Britain's last remaining colony. The gentle Robert Mugabe came back from detention (for opposing Smith) to become the first black Prime Minister of the freshly named state of Zimbabwe. At long last, the seats in parliament were 80 to 20 in favour of the blacks.

Carter Boobs in the Desert

President Carter of the USA, meanwhile, sent his extra-special, super-dooper Delta Force to rescue those US hostages taken by the Iranians (see page 167). It was a monumental, gold-plated, impossible-to-repeat cock-up. For a start they didn't even get there!

On arrival in the Iranian desert, where they'd stopped for coffee and sandwiches, the mighty American Air Force realised it didn't actually have enough helicopters working properly. Just as they were all turning their planes and choppers round to come home, one of the few helicopters which *was* working crashed into the fuel supply aircraft and the whole lot went up in a fireball. Eight men died in the wreckage caused by the explosion. The Ayatollah Khomeini, hardly suppressing his glee, said that if the Yanks tried anything like that again he'd do horrible things to their precious hostages.

The late John Wayne must have turned in his grave to see his mighty country wearing a bright red face, and poor President Carter, sensing the worst, probably rang home to order his staff to get the old peanut farm ready for his unavoidable return from political life.

Sure enough, in November, a soon-to-be-doddery, old, ex-cowboy-film star, Ronald Reagan, Governor of California (where else?), beat him easily to the draw in the presidential elections.

Meanwhile Back in Britain

Poor Margaret Thatcher wasn't having that easy a ride in the top job. Unemployment had reached 2 million (the highest since 1936) and inflation was running at an unheard of 20%. Industry reported that orders were down anything between 10-40% and that it was now costing us 22% more to produce 4% less.

After my brilliant and incisive economics lecture (see page 135), you will realise that this situation could not be described as good and, true to form, the unions, bless their cotton socks, blamed the Government and, vice versa, the Government blamed them.

Jim Goes

Towards the end of the year, dear old Jim Callaghan resigned as Leader of the Opposition in favour of Michael Foot, a funny, old-fashioned, left-wing intellectual, who looked as if he'd bought his clothes from a Labour Party fund-raising jumble sale. The Tories could hardly hide their joy at Labour's choice, as they saw Foot as someone they could easily tread on. Foot, aged 67, who'd been one of the Ban the Bomb's leaders (he practically invented the dress code), instantly threw his somewhat light weight behind the protest against the installation of American Cruise Missiles at Greenham Common in Berkshire.

Meanwhile

February: A new survey revealed that over 50% of British married women now worked – higher than any other European Country.

Now this could have meant that we're more liberated in this country or, more likely, that the British were falling so far behind in the pay league that women had no blinking choice.

March: The 'New Wave of British Heavy Metal' was beginning to fill all the rock clubs. One must admit it looked, to us old timers, exactly the same as everything we'd seen before. A bunch of skinny geezers with hair over their faces, wrestling with guitars (in pretend anguish), playing the same chords and riffs at a volume that made your ears bleed.
• One of the foremost bands, Def Leppard, didn't appear to suffer at all when their drummer lost one of his arms. Actually, I reckon his style of drumming could have been equally as effective with no arms at all.

May: Alfred Hitchcock, the best suspense film director ever, died on the 29th. His trade mark had been to appear fleetingly in all his films looking like a cross between Winston Churchill and a pink football.

June: Police discovered, in a crate bound for the Moroccan Embassy in London, 650 lbs of cannabis. Talk about taking coals to Newcastle.
• Sir Billy Butlin, the king of holiday camps, died on the 12th. The idea of offering indoor and outdoor facilities for inmates –

sorry – holidaymakers, on a tight budget, had come to him after spending a miserable, rainy holiday in Skegness (what other kinds are there?). As if it wasn't bad enough being hard up, the poor working class British had to suffer Butlin's Holiday Camps as well.
● Excuse me, can we have our boat back? The wreck of the *Titanic* was found 12,000 feet below the surface of the Atlantic.

July: Britain invented a brand new sport with a great international flavour. The game was called 'Hooliganism' and the beauty of it was that there were no rules. The players would simply follow their favourite football team to foreign matches, and act like animals (sorry that's animalist) on arrival. In Turin, tear gas was useful on British fans (the finest hooligans in the world) but, unfortunately, the authorities scored an own goal when the wind changed direction and knocked out the players instead.

August: Good news! John Lennon's long awaited comeback lurched a step closer when Geffen Records signed him and Elton John.

December: Bad news! John Lennon's long-awaited comeback took an irreversible step backwards when a guy came up to him outside his hotel in New York and shot him dead.

Hit of the Year: 'Don't Stand So Close To Me' by the Police (should have been John Lennon!).

My, My, It's Lady Di

Britain had another new game to rival football hooliganism and Monopoly. It was called 'Guess who Prince Charles is going to Marry'. It seemed that every day a new aristocratic young wench would be dragged through the gutter press as a potential Queen of England. Poor old Charlie, it must be said, would have had to have been a super-stud to have got through all that lot and, actually, if the truth be told, might have been happier remaining a bachelor. It

I hear he only likes virgins

ROYAL AUDITIONS — QUEUE HERE.

was, therefore, with some considerable relief that it was announced on the 24th February that he was going to marry a pretty, butter-wouldn't-melt-in-her-mouth, super-posh 19 year old called Lady Diana Spencer, daughter of Earl Spencer (who'd once been his mum's equerry). As A N Wilson rather cruelly put it, in his brilliant and illuminating *Rise and Fall of the House of Windsor*, Prince Charles, just about the most eligible bachelor in the world, had chosen a bride, in the same way as the guy who leaves buying his presents to the last minute and rushes round on Christmas Eve picking up what's left. Little did he, she or we know that in a few years' time, shy Di would become more famous and press-worthy than all the other Royals put together.

Needless to say, all those old coaches were dragged out and dusted down, the big grey horses were tied to the fronts of them, the men in the silly hats sat on them, and the flagging Union Jack industry went into overtime so that the long-suffering British public would again have something to wave.

Brixton Blows Up

There was, however, one group of the community that, given half a chance, would have waved far more than flags at the royal pair. On 4th April, Brixton, a South London suburb, exploded in an orgy of burning, looting and violence the like of which had never before been seen in this country. Before you could say 'Bob Marley', every black teenager had exploded and set off on a terrifying rampage 'as a protest against police harassment'.

Rioting soon became craze of the month throughout most major towns in Britain. Everyone blamed everyone else, but it soon became obvious that the whole thing no longer had anything to do with blacks, police methods, lack of teenage prospects, or the terribly high price of drugs. It was just an excuse for young, bored kids to go berserk and do all the things that they'd longed to do while standing around, bored out of their wits on street corners. The riots, therefore, were a phenomenon which disappeared, like ice lollies in a sauna, as quickly as they had arrived.

Gang of Four

On the British political scene something occurred that made people who thought the two major parties were as useless and predictable as each other, sit up and pay attention. A 'gang' of four senior members of the Labour Party were given the elbow for forming a 'Council for Social Democracy', which was a posh name for a new clique fed up with the party's silly extremism. The four – Shirley Williams, Dr David Owen, 'Woy' Jenkins and William Rodgers – formed their own little party called the Social

Democrats, and all of the 'middle of the roaders', after the initial excitement had died down, waited (and waited, and w . . a . . i . . t . . e . . d), to hear their policies.

Thatcher Digs In
Just as the Labour Party were going further left, Maggie (now totally in charge) was definitely going further right. For a start, she had announced plants to sell off all the nationalised industries starting with British Aerospace. This was like a slap in the face with a wet kipper to the poor old Labour chaps for whom nationalisation was central to their beliefs. They also knew that once she'd done it, it would be practically impossible to reverse the process if they ever got back. In other words . . . they were about to be well and truly shafted.

Ripper Found
The now famous Yorkshire Ripper – a lorry driver called Peter Sutcliffe – confessed to killing and mutilating 13 women. He claimed he'd done them in because he was round the bend but the jury didn't think so (can carving up women who you've never seen before be perfectly natural behaviour?). When sentenced to life, Sutcliffe (who looked as normal as you or me) was totally impassive, though his poor wife, Sonia, seemed a little put out when she realised what he'd been up to on his nights out.

A Pop at a Pope
Why is it that only the nice people get shot at? On 15th May, an armed Turkish nutter leapt out of the crowd and shot the Pope four times (bad move if you want to get to heaven) as he was on multitude-blessing duty. I don't know if John Paul II was wearing his papal bullet-proof robe (well – he mit're been!) but either way, he survived the attack. It later turned out that the very undelightful Turkish gentleman who was known as 'Grey Wolf' was part of a much larger communist plot.

A month earlier, a disc jockey had tried to assassinate dear old President Reagan outside the O K Corral (sorry, it was really a hotel in Washington). Ex-film gunslinger Reagan was lucky to be heading for hospital rather than Boot Hill, but when the surgeons were preparing to dig the bullet out, he was still able to quip 'I hope you guys are Republicans', which really ain't bad for a decrepit old world leader.

On 30th June, the Queen fell off her horse when six shots were fired during the Trooping of the Colour. The shots turned out to be only blanks, but I don't suppose the horse (or the Queen) knew that.

Off with his head

They're not paying me enough for this.

Poles Poleaxed

It had to happen. Like day follows night, the long-awaited clampdown on Solidarity, the free trade union movement in Poland, by the Soviet-led authorities, ended in the arrest of 14,000 trade unionists including their hero leader Lech Walesa. A Military Council of National Salvation was set up, which was just a neat name for an organisation designed to put all the unionists and dissidents back in their boxes.

Meanwhile

January: A shudder went through the readers of *The Times* and *The Sunday Times* when it was bought by the owner of *The Sun* –

Australian Rupert Murdoch. Still, it could have been worse. At least he hasn't made us gawp at up-market, half-naked ladies on page 3 (yet).

February: Torvill and Dean, the squeaky-clean young ice dancers from Nottingham, won the European Ice Skating Championship. The best thing about it was that the championship had been in Russian hands for 12 years. The worst thing was that they were to make this naff 'ballroom-dancing-on-ice' even *more* popular.

March: The Sony Walkman, the first portable tape player, had taken the world by storm. At last kids could ruin their hearing without mum and dad knowing anything about it. Now a new band called Heaven 17 produced an album called *Music for Stowaways* specially for it.

April: Steve Davis, the red-headed snooker player, who looks like one of those faded plaster dummies in old-fashioned gentlemen's outfitters, won the World Championship at the age of 23. Later a production company tried to make him into a TV chat show host, but poor Steve snookered them well and truly by turning out to be even more boring than he looked.

May: Ken Livingstone – the man who sounds as if he's got a couple of the newts he breeds stuck up his nose – became the new leader of the Greater London Council. Despite being criticised for giving grants to organisations like 'Gay, Elderly, Ethnic Minorities Against Cruelty To Deaf, Incontinent Whales', he did become a firm favourite amongst Londoners.

July: Trouble broke out in Southall (now a suburb of Delhi) when a delightfully named skinhead band, The 4 Skins, were booked to appear in this predominantly Asian community. The skinhead supporters, who shared one brain cell (sometimes) and were known to be right of Margaret Thatcher (and racist with it) set fire to the hall that their band was playing in. Now that's what I call bright!

August: Moira Stewart, bless her, became Britain's first black newsreader.

September: Marcus Serjeant, the 17 year old lad who'd shot blanks at the Queen in June, got five years in prison. Daft really, if he'd done it to anyone else he probably wouldn't have been arrested. I wonder what he'd have got if he'd used real ammo. Probably a bedsitter in the tower!

October: A report came out stating that one in eight children lived in a one parent family. I wonder where the other poor little perishers lived. Out in the shed maybe.

November: British Leyland announced that they were to develop a new car with the Japanese motorcycle company, Honda. The scheme was called Project X and the car, I believe, ended up with only two wheels.

December: Two extremely nice Iranians were blown up when a bomb they were carrying through Marble Arch in London unsportingly went off.

Album of the Year: *Flesh and Blood* by Roxy Music.

1982

Thatcher V The Unions

There was simply no doubt in Maggie's mind that she'd been chosen by God (a family friend) to head the Tory Party and, therefore, the country, because she was the only politician ballsy enough to tell the unions where to get off. There would be no 'beer and sandwiches' meetings round at Number Ten, like the old Labour days; and there would certainly be no attempt to sweet-talk the union barons.

Maggie was not intimidated by the unions and to show she meant business she employed Norman Tebbit (a known union basher), who had the menacing manner and chilly charm of a Chingford (where he was from) undertaker, to head the Department of Employment. Together, they outlawed secondary strikes and strengthened the rights of individuals against closed shops (companies that weren't allowed to employ non-union labour). They also gave employers more clout to sack lousy employees without the unions breathing heavily down their necks, and made it far more likely that those unions would have to dig deep and pay compensation for all the trouble they caused.

Having said all this, however, the economic situation was playing right into Maggie's sweaty palm. With a shrinking market, lower orders, factory closures, mass redundancies, vast reductions of membership and nasty Norm standing over them, the unions were hardly in any position to push their weight around or call any shots. They were (whether you like it or not) never to have the same power again.

Falklands Fury

Meanwhile, miles away from Britain, an event occurred that was to have consequences that no one could ever have foreseen. Way out in the ocean, near to the bottom bit of Argentina, Britain had a tiny, far flung, football-pitch-sized colony called the Falkland Islands. A mere 1800 inbred people lived on this rather gloomy little outcrop with a few inbred grubby sheep.

On 31st March, a group of Argentine scrap-metal dealers landed on one of the islands (South Georgia) and raised the Argentine flag. Cheeky! but not world-shattering. On 2nd April, 12,500 Argentinians invaded without any warning, overwhelming (with no loss of life) the handful of sleepy Royal Marines, who'd picked the short straw and were guarding the islands (see easy but dead boring jobs). It appeared that the cruel military junta who were running Argentina, thought it would be a real laugh to nick back 'their' property before the islanders could have a party to celebrate their 150 years of occupation.

A huge fuss broke out, ending with Britain breaking off diplomatic relations with Argentina (big deal) and the United Nations asking the Argentinians, nicely, to withdraw (even bigger deal).

Maggie Goes Mad
Her that must be obeyed (Grand Führer Thatcher) went potty, seeing the invasion as a direct personal challenge, and with

Can't we find anything smaller to attack?

questionable, to say the least, attempts to find a non-violent solution, including the rejection of US General Haig's peace plan, she prepared a load of warships to be led by the aircraft carriers Hermes and Invincible. They set off at full steam on 8th April on their 8,000 mile journey. Many of us in Britain wondered what all the fuss was about. It certainly didn't seem worth one soldier, sailor or airman even getting a nosebleed over these dreary little sheep-nibbled islands.

All the troops loved it, of course (in the beginning). They at last had a chance to play proper soldiers and shoot their guns *for real*. And they did – much to the joy of the gutter press who descended to the very depths of the cesspit in their so-called news reporting.

As the death toll started climbing, however, world opinion started to look across at Britain and wonder:

a. Weren't we beginning to enjoy all this a little too much? and

b. Wasn't it all a pathetic, sword-brandishing attempt to show that we were still a big tough nation?

Rubbish we told ourselves. All was going fine. The Argies (as the tabloids called them) were dying like flies, all our fab equipment was working a treat and Margaret Thatcher, our brave leader, could deservedly strut around like Churchill and Hitler rolled into one.

Then, on 4th May, our HMS Sheffield was sunk by one of the Argentinian missiles (supplied by our chums the French) and Britain blubbed like a playground bully that had finally been stood up to. Suddenly, against all the odds, the surprisingly brill and brave Argentinian pilots started carving up (and sinking) our boats. Unbelievable cock-ups were caused by our almost totally inept field commanders, who scurried around blaming each other like public school sneaks, and whole battalions of our troops were found to be unfit to even manage an average route march. To cut a long and extremely distasteful story short, however, Britain did gradually start to make corned beef (literally) of the pathetically under-trained, under-equipped (and under-age) Argentinian army. On the 14th July, they surrendered having lost 650 brave young men. We lost 250 of our, equally brave, lads.

The 'war' was won, Margaret Thatcher was a hero, her job was saved, and she had proved once again that no one ever messes with her or the British. Well, that was the theory anyway. More than that, we'd finally managed to beat someone, all by ourselves, without the help of those clever-dick Americans.

History might well disagree, however, as some military experts believe Maggie was damn lucky. If we'd been up against even a half-decent army, or if some of the Commie big boys had joined in, it might well have been a very different story.

Postscript: Only four years later, Argentina beat Britain in the Quarter Finals of the World Cup. Does that, or does it not, say it all!?!?

Meanwhile
January: Oh dear, oh dear. Maggie faced severe criticism at the news that unemployment had reached the all time record of 3 million. Norman Tebbit, unbelievably, blamed the weather.

February: Sir Freddie Laker, who'd brought Britain the cut-price air fare, had to watch in horror as his huge airline took a nosedive and crashed. The recession, rising interest rates, and the decline in the value of the £ against the $ were blamed.
• De Lorean cars, produced in Ireland, backed by £17.5 million of our best British money, also went up the Swannee. John De Lorean, flash ex-boss of General Motors in America, thought he could make a killing with his rather vulgar-looking new sports car. Unfortunately, too many people agreed with me. For years, the US courts tried to pin everything from cocaine dealing to embezzlement on poor John, but to no avail. Interesting to note: if he hadn't gone under, he could have been our last surviving motor manufacturer.

June: *Question.* What's pink and hangs under our London bridges?
Answer. Italian bankers.
On 19th June, Roberto Calvi was found hanging under

348

Blackfriars Bridge. Nobody was quite sure how he got there.

• Lady Diana gave birth to her first heir to the throne. When Daddy was asked what they were going to call the little chap, Charles said rather distractedly 'You'll have to ask my wife, we're having a bit of an argument about that.' The first of many, dare I suggest.

How does one know what they eat?

August: The IRA really blew it public opinion-wise. Not content with simply wiping out soldiers, they blew up a detachment of the Blues and Royals (horse guards), and later the band of the Royal Green Jackets. All-in-all, eight soldiers were killed, but much, much worse, in the eyes of the British public . . . seven horses.

October: Prince (randy) Andrew had to cut short one of his all-expenses-paid holidays in Mustique, a Caribbean island, because the girl he was with was attracting too much attention. Apparently 'actress' Koo Stark had appeared nearly starkers in a bluish movie. Koo!! I think she sounded a lot better than the usual Sloane Rangers he pulled.

September: One of the most distasteful crimes ever seen in Britain was solved. Police found the trousers of Sir Geoffrey Howe, a

Cabinet Minister, stolen from a train while he was asleep. I've heard of pickpockets, but this was ridiculous.

December: 20,000 women held hands to encircle the Greenham Common Nuclear Weapons Base at Greenham Common. The nuclear missiles, about which they were protesting, eventually left in their own good time.

1983

Thatcher Reigns Supreme

All those who *didn't* see Mrs Thatcher as their saviour were gutted at the Tories' resounding victory at the General Election. But it *was* her victory, which ever way you looked at it, and the other parties knew from the start that all their little Davids (e.g. Owen and Steele) could not even touch the Tories' Goliathess.

The shabby Labour Party, led by the crusty (but soft-centred) Michael Foot, was practically wiped out in the South, while the new 'Alliance', this time between Steel's Liberals and the Gang of Four's sadly disappointing new Social Democratic party, only got 23 seats out of a possible 650.

Obviously the recipe for resounding political success in our rather sad little country (which had once bullied the world) was to get it into a war, and then to win that war resoundingly (first making sure the enemy had absolutely no chance of winning). There is no doubt, whatsoever, that 'victory' over the shaky Argentinian junta gave Maggie almost Hitlerian status amongst the vast (and growing) right of the electorate.

'Woy' Jenkins, realising he was flogging a dead ideal with the

Social Democrats, quit in the next few days, along with Labour 'leader' Michael Foot who resigned as PM and went back to his duffle coat and Hampstead supper-table intellectuals (though no one really noticed he'd gone). His place was taken by a jolly, red-haired, freckly 'boyo' from Wales called Neil Kinnock who, vigorous as he was, looked about as likely to be Prime Minister as Basil Brush (sorry, that's foxist).

Meanwhile, suave and handsome Dr Owen took over from Jenkins as head of the SDP and was then not heard of again for ages. He (and the rest of the Gang of Four) had, without any help from others, totally trashed their political careers by failing to come up with the cast-iron policies we'd all been waiting for. David Steel, after yet another broken 'love affair', with David Owen this time, crawled back into his little Liberal basket in Scotland and carried on dreaming.

Young Upwardly Mobile Professionals
We'd seen the birth of Sloane Rangers, punks, Hooray Henrys, hippies etc. etc. but now it was time for a completely new phenomenon. The 'yuppies' (see heading above) were a new mutation, and were beginning to make themselves felt in Britain – especially in the South, and especially in London. Due to Maggie's monetarist policies, credit had become very much the buzz word, and with it came the possibility to live wildly beyond one's means without ever (seemingly) needing to account for it. Suddenly every other car seemed to be a BMW or Porsche; wine and champagne bars spread like socially transmitted diseases; over-priced gymnasiums heaved with sweaty estate agents while house and flat prices went soaring through their roofs and kissing all and sundry on both cheeks became the 'in' thing at every opportunity.

Young people with less qualifications than Daffy Duck began making fortunes in the city – dealing in stocks, futures or simply money – all at a time when manufacturing, oddly enough, was in decline. The yuppies did all the things that in the past only 'old money' had done: attending summer balls and point-to-points, wearing brown trilbies and those awful snot-coloured waxed green

351

I say Emma — fancy a spot of supper this evening?

Sorry Charles, I'm washing my Porsche!

jackets and buying cottages in France (while writing patronising books about them). To these fabulous Thatcher's Children, Maggie and her Chancellor, the profoundly greasy Nigel Lawson, were like gods. At last they'd made it possible to make paper fortunes, to buy whatever you wanted (whether you had the cash or not) without having to get your hands remotely dirty. Okay the chances were that their nerves would be shot away by the time they were thirty, but who cared? There were always plenty more where they came from. If you needed any more proof that the world was going screwy, the winner of 'Mastermind', that torture chamber for brainiacs, in 1983 was a certain Christopher Hughes – a (wait for it) London tube train driver.

Telly With Cornflakes

Another new phenomenon was the introduction of television the moment you opened your eyes. Obscenely jolly presenters, wearing too heavy make-up to cover the circles under their own eyes, fronted programmes, from naff mock living rooms that were about as inane as the newspapers they were replacing. Britain was beginning to suffer from too much news and current affairs. Indeed, you only had to fart in an unusual way and some precocious rookie reporter would be knocking at your front door for an interview.

The world seemed to be changing at an alarming rate. Suddenly, the safety police made you wear seat belts in your own car, which they then proceeded to incapacitate by strapping a horrid yellow clamp on one of its wheels if you were parked in the wrong place. Even if your car wasn't clamped, there was a fair chance the IRA would shove a bomb under it as they did outside Harrods in December 1988. If you did manage to get moving, then it was possible that the police would pull you over, drag you out and then shoot you, as they did only a stone's throw from Harrods, to a young guy called Stephen Waldorf whom they'd mistaken for someone else.

Cowboy Capers
Science fiction came a little closer when that old celluloid cowhand, Ronnie Reagan, announced a futuristic non-offensive missile shield called Star Wars right across the States to keep out the 'Evil Empire' (three guesses who they were?). Needless to say, the Russians did find it offensive, more or less claiming that it simply wasn't fair fighting (quite right). Mind you, they were fine ones to talk about fairness. In September, Russian fighters shot down a Korean airliner 'by accident', killing 269 passengers – and they didn't even say sorry. They did, however, claim that the plane had been spying over Siberia. Nice one, Russia. You often get a

couple of hundred people going on spying holidays over barren wastelands.

Meanwhile

February: Who says civil servants are boring? Denis Nilsen was arrested on 11th February when police discovered two human heads, some flesh and a hand in his back garden in Hornsey, a suburb of London. Later the remains of 14 other bodies (all male) were found in and around the house. Nilsen was later found, strangely enough, to be homosexual. I must admit, it doesn't seem to me a very nice way to treat your boyfriends.

April: Britain's biggest robbery ever occurred when gunmen prised £7 million from a Security Express van.

May: Cliff Richard, the Dorian Grey (or should I say Heathcliff) of the pop world, celebrated 25 years in the business. Anyone else would have had the grace to retire but not our Cliff. Can you imagine him prancing around into his sixties? Good grief!

July: Mrs Victoria Gillick broke down after a High Court Judge refused to rule that it was illegal for a doctor to supply girls of under 16 with contraceptive pills without their mum's and dad's say so. Mrs Gillick didn't appear to believe in contraception herself as she had 10 nippers of her own!

September: The Social Democratic Party leader, David Owen, wasn't that thrilled with his limp little liaison with the Liberals. His party swore they'd have nothing to do with them for at least five years.

October: Smarmy Cecil Parkinson, who looks like everybody's idea of an upmarket lounge lizard, was fired from the Tory cabinet – much to everyone's delight. He'd been caught with his pinstripes well and truly round his ankles when it was discovered he'd just jilted his former secretary who was expecting his baby. As we've all learned, however, lying and cheating never really does you permanent harm in politics. He was later made a peer by his old mate Maggie.

December: Mehmet Ali Agca, the tetchy Turk who'd tried to kill the Pope, met the great man in his prison cell. Pope John was visiting the prison as a Christmas treat and even left a little gift for Mehmet. I bet it wasn't a cake with a file in it.

1984

Big Brother is Watching You

It was kind of spooky to note that, in the year that was the subject of George Orwell's famous book *1984* (written in 1948), 'Big Brother', a kind of world government that he predicted would one day rule our lives, seemed perilously close.

Firstly, Thatcher's Government, heavily breathed on by the Yanks, took the unprecedented step of banning unions at GCHQ, the secret government communications headquarters at Cheltenham, offering each of the employees £1000 to keep their traps shut. The Government said that they'd been forced to do it because the union movement had seen GCHQ as a weak link, as everything they handled was so damned sensitive. The unions could have, therefore, if they'd so desired, blackmailed the Tory Government into higher wage claims.

Secondly, a junior clerk at the Ministry of Defence split to the *Guardian* newspaper about the arrival of American Cruise Missiles at the Greenham Common base, and went swiftly to prison (without passing GO) for her trouble, highlighting the conflict between security and a country's right to know what the hell is going on.

Thirdly, our much boasted about 'special relationship' with America was shown to be the crock of horse-manure that it really was. Everyone over here suspected that instead of being the 'you scratch my back, I'll scratch yours' deal that Maggie and Ronnie were supposed to enjoy, the old Yankee thespian was manipulating her like a glove puppet. The question then became, who was controlling Reagan? Several incidents took place over the next few years that made us wonder whether we, or even those that spoke for us, had any real say over our destiny.

Trouble Down T'Pit

Arthur Scargill, that ferret-like champion (and president) of the moaning miners, saw union strength as the key to the building of a society fit for the working man. Thatcher, the pit-bull champion of the right, saw the unions as the main reason why the economy was rapidly disappearing down the post war plughole (and two fingers to the working man). She'd backed down three times from closing pits owing to little Arthur's threats – but not this time.

The '84 miners' strike, called to see who really had the biggest stick, started on 15th March. All the men-turned-yobbos that weren't underground, travelled the country preventing anyone else doing likewise. What they failed to grasp was that, due to cheap oil from the east, practically free gas and oil from our own North

Sea, smokeless zones in cities and 'nuclear' electricity, the demand for coal was becoming about the same as a drink of water to a drowning man.

On the miners' side – if, as in the past, essential industries had put their tools down, the Government would have found it difficult to send the troops in to keep things going because by 1984 the technology was becoming too sophisticated for soldiers to operate (and that ain't that sophisticated). Also, coal supplies were reckoned to be good for another 300 years, whereas the 'free' oil and gas would probably run out in 30 years or so.

Despite all this, Scargill didn't dare to have a national ballot and put it and himself to the test as he knew damn well he wouldn't get the majority he needed, so he decided to stick with the violence and bullying that had served him so well (and seemed so much more fun).

WIFE, KIDS AND ARTHUR SCARGILL'S EGO TO SUPPORT!

Bad Timing

Anyway, talk about a stupid time to have a fuel strike. The beginning of spring, and the imminent warm weather, is not exactly brilliant if you want to hold a country to ransom for coal, especially if the reserve coal supplies are as high as Scargill's ego.

By May, the nastiness started in earnest. The normal shirt-pulling scraps on the picket lines became much more violent, and then a couple of strikers dropped a huge slab of concrete off a bridge in South Wales. It landed, 'coincidentally', on a passing cab taking some miners to work, so killing the driver. Then Scargill, using a false name (Ferdie Ferret?), shot over to Paris to meet one of the frightful Libyan Leader, Colonel Gaddafi's, right-hand men. He had gone there, it was alleged, to get money and, unbelievably, guns, to fight the good fight. Gaddafi later claimed to have given the cheeky chap £163,000, which Scargill allegedly used to pay off his personal mortgage.

The strike seemed to go on forever, and many of the miners, who hadn't been exactly dying to strike in the first place, went through hardships the like of which hadn't been seen since the 30s. They then, grudgingly, began drifting back to work.

Maggie Digs In

Thatcher, and *her* new puppet American Ian MacGregor, Chairman of the Coal Board, who came only second to Noel Edmonds in subtlety, just sat back on her throne, knowing full well that Scargill's hypnotic (and despotic) hold over his fellow miners simply couldn't last. Anyway, any character assassination could be left to the man himself.

The writing was well on the wall by December when his boys, realising they were backing a loser, began traipsing back underground with their spades between their legs. Thatcher had 'won' another battle and her revolution was now fully secure. The battle with the union (any union) was over for years to come.

Meanwhile

January: Top pop group, at the beginning of the year, was Culture Club, which was led by half-man, half-pantomime dame (and half-wit) Boy George.

February: Borevill – sorry – Torvill and Dean beat the Ruskies to the Olympic Gold Medal for the recently included 'sport' of ice dancing. Hands up for Olympic Flower Arranging – it's just as naff!

April: Fatherly love? I don't think so. Marvin Gaye, one of the fabbest of the old style soul singers, was shot dead by his dad (an ex-church minister) over an argument about insurance. You can bet it wasn't life insurance.

June: Talk about milking the applause. Eric Morecambe, one of our funniest and most loved entertainers, died of a heart attack having taken six curtain calls at the Tewkesbury Theatre. His sad little straight man, Ernie Wise, later implied that Eric had held him back career-wise. Sure Ern, just as Batman held Robin back!

• Another sad departure, that of Sir John Betjeman, the teddy bear like Poet Laureate, occurred this month. His great skill had been to make us review, with affection, all those mundane, tasteless things that we'd always taken for granted.

July: There's a welcome at McDonald's, unless you happen to be waiting at the San Ysidro branch, California. Oliver Huberty (such a jolly name) strode into the restaurant and fired indiscriminately, killing 20 and injuring 16 men, women and children. C'mon Ollie, the Chicken McNuggets weren't *that* bad!!

September: The world expert on all things architectural, Prince Charles, compared the new extension of the National Gallery to 'a monstrous carbuncle on the face of a well-loved friend'. I wonder who got to the mirror first, Princess Di or Mrs Camilla Parker-Bowles?

October: The cowardly IRA hit the bull's-eye when, on 12th October, they blew up the Grand Hotel in Brighton, where the Cabinet was staying while attending the Tory Party Conference. One MP died and more than 30 were injured, including the normally unruffable Norman Tebbit. Maggie was, as usual, unhurt – one of the advantages of being an Iron Lady.

November: There were two female Prime Ministers in the world at the beginning of the month, but by the end Mrs Thatcher was alone. Indira Gandhi, Prime Minister of India, was assassinated by her bodyguards (bad choice, I'd have said) as she walked in the garden of her New Delhi house (well, old New Delhi house). The night before, she'd said to a reporter 'If I die today, every drop of my blood will invigorate the nation.' Seems like her bodyguards took her at her word.

December: Everyone in Britain had watched helplessly as millions of starving Ethiopians perished on our tellys every night. Bob Geldof, him of The Boomtown Rats, shocked our mean politicians by getting off his backside and actually doing something. His single 'Don't They Know It's Christmas', though awful, was recorded with some of the pop greats, provided loads of much-needed money to help the drought-wrecked country. Friends of all people, Grand Empress Thatcher, refused to drop the £500,000 VAT bill due on the record's profits, probably as revenge for being shown up so badly.

1985

The Poorly Pound

There couldn't have been a better time for the Labour Party to launch their strongest attack on Margaret Thatcher as the Tories had left practically an open goal. The economy was as unpredictable as a royal marriage and only those fast-burning city wise guys could really understand (and profit from) what was going down. Unemployment was soaring, manufacturing was plunging, the stock market was booming, but the £ had plummeted so low against the $ that (for the first time ever) they were nearly the same value. This had the nasty side-effect of a Britain rapidly filling with awful department-store dressed American tourists, who were buying up just about everything that wasn't screwed down (let's face it, they'd already had our London Bridge).

Poor Neil Kinnock, however, had turned out to be no match for the magnificent Margaret in Parliament. Instead of witty repartee, he just went redder and louder. Indeed, the last person even to

begin to make her look foolish had been Jim Callaghan who, like Wilson, had disappeared almost without trace.

Loonies

Neil had his own problems, however, dealing with what came to be known as the Loony Left, whose golden boy seemed to be 'Red' Ken Livingstone. When the howl went up on the announcement that the Labour-led Greater London Council was to be scrapped by the Government, Kinnock must have secretly heaved a sigh of relief, as their 'leftie' antics had been getting too much hilarious tabloid coverage. Ken's GLC had supported and financed everything from gay and lesbian groups to peace movements and ethnic tenant associations. Following his lead, many other local governments started employing one another's officers until it all became one huge job for the boys – in other words, a lucrative carve-up by the extreme left.

Livingstone had become the male equivalent of tabloid-sized Samantha Fox (a blond bimbo currently famous for her huge b . . . rain) as he could also always be relied on to fill column inches ridiculing the Royals, admiring the IRA, and mocking monetarism by giving away nigh on £9 billion to the daftest of causes while in power (£250,000 of which was allegedly spent on his farewell party). But by now the looniness had spread. Haringey was giving courses on homosexuality to school kids, comparing Hitler's policies to Thatcher's union reforms, and ordering everyone to drink only Nicaraguan coffee. Lewisham voted £64,000 towards financing complaints against the police, and Hackney gave up its cosy little town-twinning arrangements with France and West Germany in favour of the Soviet Union.

Across the rest of the country the labour left were not only loonified but pretty sinister too. In Liverpool, a group called 'Militant Tendency', who were about as left as you can go before meeting up with the far right, had become almost a branch of the Communists, and were getting a stranglehold on the city council led by John Hamilton and his horribly flash deputy Derek Hatton (who was already receiving £10,000 year for a 17-hour week from another labour council). They were throwing around so much dosh that everyone in Liverpool (provided they were lesbian, black, one-parent or communist) thought every day was Christmas and praised them greatly. It was not only infuriating to Thatcher's Government but jolly embarrassing to Neil Kinnock. In the end, the corruption within 'Militant' became so blatant that the easy-going Kinnock had to pull his Welsh finger out and wage war on them, which pushed his ratings quite high for the first time ever. But the damage was done. The Loony Left had put paid to the Labour Party being taken seriously for years and years to come. Instead of a two-party system, it was now a one-party system and almost a one-woman system. Thatcher was as near as you could get to being a fully paid up dictator.

Gorby Mania

Unbelievably, news came from Russia that the next supreme head of the 'Evil Empire' (USSR) was a rather jolly-looking sort, called Mikhail Gorbachev, who had a birthmark that looked suspiciously like a map of America on his forehead. His wife, Raisa, seemed positively normal and nice, unlike most other Soviet leaders' wives, who had looked like Les Dawson's (God rest his soul) ugly sisters.

Only a few months earlier, Reagan, who'd been the butt of just about every joke in America and Britain, nevertheless romped home with a resounding victory to take a second term as President of the United States of America. A new game was set with Gorby and Ronnie as the two main contestants and the increasingly cocky Mrs Thatcher fully believing that she was the third.

Britain's Hooligans win 41-0

On 29th May, Britain's reputation abroad hit the decks when our own home-grown British football hooligans went on the rampage during the Juventus-Liverpool match, causing a riot which crushed to death 41 and injured 350 Italian and Belgian supporters. Football haters and fans alike were not that displeased when the Football Association banned English teams from playing abroad until further notice.

Music Mania

It's now the middle of the 80s and time to see what's going down on the music scene – man! From America, we had the ear-splitting country rock band ZZ Top, a group consisting of two long white beards with three men attached. Also, they sent us the androgynous (but brilliant) Prince, who looked like just about everything that your mother wouldn't like to meet. Bruce Springsteen, who'd perfected the greasy-truck-driver-with-the-mean-guitar look, was selling more records than anyone else, while the soon-to-be-weird Michael Jackson, for some obscure reason bought ATV Music, whose jewel in its crown was the rights to all the earlier (and better) Beatles songs. He paid £34 million which, one day, could have come in very useful (see page 247).

England's Wham, consisting of the pretty George Micheldopulous (Michael to you) and Andrew Ridgely (who?), became the first group to go to China. They claimed it was a goodwill trip, but I bet the potential un-got-to 200 million record buyers could just conceivably have had something to do with it. Unfortunately the poor Chinese, who for donkey's years had been forced to live on a diet of whiney, screechy patriotic songs,

a. Couldn't make head or tail of their music, and
b. Didn't find the two lads nearly as yummy as the girls back here did.

Wham were sharing the UK charts with the 'Why-am-I-so-gloomy-and-so-rich' Phil Collins, the 'Which-of-us-is-getting-the-most-limelight' Eurythmics, and the 'Does-being-outrageous-really-mean-that-I-can't-have-hair' Elton John.

Meanwhile

January: Sir Clive Sinclair, the computer wizard, who was everyone's idea of a boffin, proved that even geniuses have to have a day off. The silly scientist brought out an electric car, called the C5, which resembled a surgical boot with wheels on. If you want to travel around at 5 m.p.h. looking a total prat, before having your head cleaved from your body by an overtaking milk float, then this, dear readers, was the motor for you. Two months later production was 'suspended'.

February: Terry Waite, resembling R. Hood's huge best mate 'Little John', had the job of doing all the dirty work for the Archbishop of Canterbury. As his 'Special Envoy', Terry had the unenviable task of going round the most dangerous places in the world trying to sweet-talk nasty people into giving him our political hostages back. On 8th Feb., he did manage to get four released from Libya. So far so good!

April: The Government announced plans to ban all alcohol from football stadiums. Now I might be a bit dim, but wouldn't there be a faint danger of them getting totally sloshed *before* the match?

May: Roy Plomley, the immensely stuffy, but rather dear, host of radio's 'Desert Island Discs', that strangely English symbol of 'making it', went to his great island in the sky. I wonder if they put a copy of *The Bible, The Complete Works of Shakespeare*, and

his chosen luxury (a radio?) in his casket with him?

July: Mangy Bob Geldof did it again. His vast Live Aid concert at Wembley, starring the cream of rock music, raised a staggering £40 million to help the hungry Ethiopians. Geldof was, all but, made a saint by the embarrassed Establishment. Mind you, you'd have to be a saint to be married to Paula Yates.

September: Up and up he goes. Jeffrey Archer, darling of those people who only read one book a year (smothered in suntan oil), was made Deputy Chairman of the Tory Party, a decision as unlikely as one of his plots.
• Laura Ashley, queen of safe, twee, suburban decoration and wimpy women's clothing, fell down the stairs to her death. Anyone, however, who thought we'd seen the last of those long flowery frocks and sissy chintzy curtains was sadly disappointed.

October: Just as the AIDS scare was reaching its zenith, the news came that the ultra-smooth film star, Rock Hudson, had just died from it. People were most shocked by the possible implication that this 'rock'-like symbol of machismo had never really fancied all the beautiful women he'd starred with. What a waste!

November: Maggie Thatcher and the Irish Prime Minister, Dr Garret Fitzgerald, signed what was regarded as the monumental Anglo-Irish Agreement. It gave the Irish Republic a proper saying in the running of Northern Ireland. Needless to say, it had as much impact as a rabid mouse in a football stadium.

1986

Westland Wonders

In January, the whole country was given ringside seats to a pitched battle within the Tory Cabinet. It was all over a once rather prestigious, but now sinking, helicopter manufacturer called Westland, who the flamboyant Michael Heseltine (Defence Secretary) wanted to save by selling to a sort of European helicopter consortium (Eurochopper?). His rival in the Government, swarthy Trade and Industry Secretary, Leon Brittan, admitted leaking to the press a government law officer's letter criticising the way Heseltine did his job. Brittan, who loved the Yanks and free enterprise, thought Sikorsky the US helicopter giant should put some of their cash into Westland, and had leaked this letter to make Heseltine look an incompetent twerp, so blowing any chance of a European deal.

Hot-head Heseltine had resigned a couple of days earlier, after charging out of a Cabinet Meeting in a fit of pique, when his boss Maggie had ticked him off by saying that in future all his public utterances should be vetted by her. Many of his Cabinet colleagues thought Heseltine's sudden disappearance meant that he'd been caught short and had gone for another leak but when, hours later, he hadn't returned, their pennies dropped as well! Heseltine was soon to become the darling of the back benchers, being the first person to dare to stand up to her-that-must-be-obeyed.

The whole smutty little affair backfired on Mrs T. when she tried to deny knowing anything about the famous first leak. Everyone, fans or not, then realised that her way of doing things needed severe watching.

Kinnock had yet another open goal when he got up to make his 'let's-trash-Thatcher-and-all-she-stands-for' speech in the Commons, but the ball dribbled to a stop before reaching the goal mouth and Maggie got out of the whole debate virtually unscathed.

All this was much enjoyed from the touchline by old Edward Heath who, never having recovered from being deposed by a 'mere' woman, seemed to have a personal vendetta against poor little Margaret.

Russian Roulette

Anyone who was the tiniest bit bothered about the way we got our nuclear power, shuddered when they heard of the fire at the Chernobyl nuclear power station in the Ukraine region of the USSR. Not without good reason. An American satellite, which just 'happened' to be flying overhead wearing its binoculars, noted that the station had literally blown its top off. A cloud of cancer-causing, tree-withering, milk-curdling horribleness had leaked right over Scandinavia and even threatened Northern Europe. Almost amusingly, the number of American tourists due to 'do' Europe mysteriously dropped, as they obviously thought we were all glowing and buzzing.

I wonder how they'll market radio-active milk?

America Blunders

The United States was getting into a right pickle internationally. There'd been a bit of a ding-dong between US and Libyan jets over the Mediterranean, but when America launched a full scale surprise attack on Libya, setting off from Britain (to save petrol), everyone accused them, and us, of war-mongering (who us? Never). Maggie was also accused of being simply the stool-pigeon of the Americans, having no say in what they did or didn't do.

On top of this, someone spilt the beans and claimed that the cash made by the Yanks from selling arms to Iran (dodgy in the first place) had been used to finance the Contra rebels fighting the leftie government in Nicaragua. The 'Irangate scandal', as it was called, nearly threw Reagan from the saddle. A horribly slick, all-American colonel, Oliver (Ollie) North, took most of the rap (lightly, on the back of the hand) when he admitted doing an 'arms for hostages' deal with the Iranians, using our dear, but somewhat naive, Terry Waite, as an innocent pawn. Reagan was later forced to admit that he knew all about it. By this time, however, the American people, who hadn't forgotten Nixon and rather expected lying and deception in high places let him off with a caution.

Condoms Galore

The Government launched its biggest ever health campaign in November, to try to stop the ravages of the AIDS virus from swamping Britain. Most at risk seemed to be male gays, bisexuals and needle-pricked druggies, but experts confidently expected Acquired Immune Deficiency Syndrome (AIDS) to huff and puff at the rest of us until it blew our defences down. The message was 'stick to one partner, use condoms, and if you have to take drugs, don't share your needles'.

Meanwhile

January: Mrs Thatcher and President Mitterand of France simply couldn't wait to meet each other underground. The Channel Tunnel project, which had started and stopped like a seaside donkey, was finally to go ahead. But when?
• The American Challenger space shuttle went up in smoke – literally – when it blew to pieces seconds after take off. All seven of the crew were tragically blown to kingdom come. Back to the drawing board.

February: One of the dangers of letting your Prime Minister out for a walk by his or herself is that people might really show what they think of them. Olof Palme, PM of Sweden, was strolling home from the movies when a man jumped out of the shadows and shot him dead. I bet our Mrs Thatcher would've frightened any attacker off!

April: Some people choose terrible partners. Poor pregnant Anne-Marie Murphy was stopped by customs as she was about to board a plane to Tel Aviv, and found to be carrying a 10lb bomb in the bottom of her bag. It was timed to go off over London while she and her 360 fellow passengers were ordering their first drinks (Molotov cocktails?). Nezar Hindawi, her Jordanian boyfriend, who'd promised to meet her in Tel Aviv later, was arrested in London, and charged with planting the bomb on the hapless girl. I believe Anne-Marie later called the romance off. Some people are so unforgiving.

• I hope Clint Eastwood said a bit more than he did in his movies when he became Mayor of Carmel, California. He was paid $200 a month. Hardly a fistful of dollars.

May: Super-cricketer Ian Botham was banned from first class cricket for smoking dope. Strangely enough, they didn't seem to mind him being a loud-mouthed yob.

June: Baa baa black sheep, have you any wool? Well Cumbrian lambs might have been all right for that, but you couldn't eat the little bleaters. They'd been contaminated by that horrid Chernobyl cloud.

July: Friend of the Africans (remember the VAT demand (see page 196), Margaret Thatcher, restated her opposition to sanctions against South Africa, because 'it would hurt the blacks most'. Mind you, Maggie, they did have far, far less to lose than your white chums.

August: Drag out those Royal coaches, it's time to wave those rather tattered flags and stir up a bit of patriotism. This time it was for the wedding of the loud, freckly, red-head (sounds like Neil Kinnock) Sarah Ferguson who was getting hitched to Prince Andrew. Had all the guests realised what was going to happen to this love match, they'd have bought their wedding presents sale or return.
• Henry Moore, the sculptor, who put his whole into his holes, died on 14th August. Many reckon he was to sculpture what Picasso was to painting. Others think he was to sculpture what Shakespeare was to plumbing.

October: The long awaited Big Bang, a nickname given to the turning over of the London Stock Exchange to computers on 27th October, turned out to be a damp squib when the whole system went down after an hour. (It was all right later, however, when they'd changed the plug.)

• Jeffrey Archer resigned as Deputy Chairman of the Conservatives when it was alleged that he had tried to finance a prostitute's quickly arranged foreign holiday to avoid a scandal. He said that he had never met the girl, but thought it a good idea to give her money to go away.

November: It was a sad month for movie fans. The great Hollywood heart-throb Archibald Leach died. Archibald Leach? I hear you cry. Sorry, he was slightly better known by his stage name Cary Grant.

December: Just as sadly missed, SuperMac, Harold Macmillan, died aged 92. We all looked wistfully back to a time when you could look up to a Prime Minister as a father figure (but not mother figure!).

1987

Waite-ing in Beirut

Brave Terry Waite, the Archbishop of Canterbury's Special (if a bit too trusting) Envoy was over in war-torn Beirut trying to save foreign hostages held by the extremely nice 'Party of God', whose boss was that extremely nice Ayatollah Khomeini. One day the huge man dismissed his guards, saying that some extremely nice men he'd met were taking him to see the hostages. Many might have thought it was like going into a lion's cage and asking the lions to look the other way, but not our Terry. His shining belief in his fellow man positively glittered as he left with his 'guides'. Needless to say, he disappeared without trace.

Enterprise Goes Under

One of the great tragedies at sea happened on 6th March when the car ferry *Herald of Free Enterprise*, carrying hundreds of passengers, literally up-ended just off the coast of Zeebrugge (Belgium). It was like a nightmare remake of that film *The Poseidon Adventure* with passengers trapped underwater in the gradually sinking hull. Over 200 men, women and children died the most frightful death in the near-freezing water. It turned out that the Dover-bound ferry had suffered the same fate as the one mentioned all those years before off the Irish coast (see page 40): some silly idiot had forgotten to close the huge doors that let the cars and – given half a chance – water in.

Thatcher Goes Walkabout

Meanwhile, Maggie put on her warm underwear and ventured to Moscow to discuss disarmament with new-boy Gorbachev. The Russians, always fond of a dictator, seemed relatively pleased to see her, and some even kissed her on the cheek (the cheek!). In a supermarket she bought, for no explicable reason, a tin of pilchards and a loaf (probably because it was all they had).

Didn't someone else once do something with loaves and fish?

In June, her Iron Ladyship was re-elected for a staggering, history-making third term. All the opposition parties, crushed by the result, either blamed each other or the weather.

Property Madness

One of the reasons for her High and Mightiness's runaway victory was still based on the fact that if you *had* money or property, the Tories made sure you got even more (albeit on paper). House prices were still going through the roof and, if you had a reasonable sized house, especially if it was in the South, you could lounge around, safe in the knowledge that it would be earning you almost as much as if you worked.

To give you some idea of how silly it got, a Mrs Grace Newbold offered £36,000 for a converted shed measuring 5ft 6ins by 11ft in Knightsbridge. If that wasn't bad enough, it was decorated throughout with Laura Ashley wallpaper.

Sex and Nippers

The most amazing chain of events started on 29th June when Dr Marietta Higgs, a local paediatrician (and nosy parker) in Cleveland, announced that hundreds of kids were being 'tampered with' by their mummies and daddies. Over 200 children were promptly whipped away from their homes and put into care. The whole business got so out of hand that parents even became frightened of bathing their children in case they were done for indecency. The stupid woman was later found to be as wrong as all the claims she'd made but the damage, unfortunately, had already been done.

England Gets Windy

On 16th October, a light breeze turned into a wind. Then the wind turned into a bit of a gale. As it increased, TV viewers rang Michael Fish the TV weatherman (the one who dresses like a 70s office boy), to see if it was going to get any worse. He looked at his bit of seaweed and laughingly told them not to worry. That night 110 m.p.h. winds ripped through Southern England causing the worst damage this century. Trees fell like British Test wickets, especially in Sevenoaks (now 'One-oak', after the demise of the other six).

Stocks Hit the Deck

Another worst for the century! And it simply *had* to happen. On 19th October (Black Monday), £50 billion was wiped off the value of publicly quoted companies. It was like a tower of cards tumbling as all the smart city boys scrambled over each other, trying not to lose their shirts (and red braces), let alone their Porsches and smart docklands flats. It was the end of a Thatcher inspired 'bull' market that had seen shares shoot up three and a half times over the previous three years. The sight of grown men weeping as they watched their VDU screens tell them that the game called 'Get Rich Quick' was up, was enough to make even the bravest of onlookers . . . laugh his head off!

This was just the beginning of the next all-too-predictable decline in the nation's fortunes, soon to be labelled the Recession.

Good News

After a year of horrible news, a hint of better things to come happened on 8th December when Ronnie and Gorby (without Her Maggie-sty) signed the first-ever treaty to start sending their nuclear weapons to the breaker's yard. Everyone remarked how well the old cowboy and Comrade Map-head seemed to get on. Reagan could only remember one bit of Russian – 'Doverai no proverai' which meant 'Trust but verify'. Later Gorbachev was to look patronisingly at the poor old yank and mutter witheringly 'You repeat that at every meeting.'

Meanwhile

January: The term 'political correctness' hadn't even been born but poor old Noddy suffered from it anyway. MacDonald's Publishers daftly admitted, after a hammering from whinging nothing-better-to-do critics, that Noddy's world (by Enid Blyton) was ageist, racist and sexist. All the golliwogs instantly got their cards, and Big Ears was severely reprimanded for spending so much time alone in bed with little Noddy.

February: Andy Warhol, the wacky, misunderstood American sleaze-merchant and painter, died during an operation. Warhol who looked, unlike Big Ears, to be everyone's idea of a child molester, was the first person to make us study an everyday object (like a soup can) and give it the same respect as a famous academic painting. His haunting prediction 'in the future everyone will be famous for fifteen minutes' seems almost inevitable given the gutter press's insatiable appetite for every aspect of our personal lives.

Oh Julian lovey! You've eaten the art!

March: The huge British band Frankie Goes To Hollywood did exactly that – and Paris and Rome and Scunthorpe. The extremely camp group went in separate directions (in more ways than one), after having their own fifteen minutes of fame. They were hardly to be seen again.

May: Now there's vandalism and vandalism. British Telecom, in its infinite wisdom, went on an orgy of destruction. They removed a major feature of our national heritage when, to beat the soon-to-be-upon-us conservation laws, they tore down hundreds of our filthy, urine-smelling, never-working, always-occupied, red telephone boxes. They replaced them with always clean, always efficient, but totally soulless plastic booths.

July: Oxford University refused for the second time to give Her Extreme Cleverness Margaret Thatcher the honorary degree she so richly deserved. Funny really they seem to give everyone else one.

September: At least Andy Warhol was honest when he took the art market for a ride. Vincent Van Gogh, who'd sold his stuff for a couple of drinks and a cheese roll, would have laughed his other ear off if he'd been at the Christie's auction when his *Sunflowers* painting (£8.99 at Boots) sold for £24 million.

October: The whole weight of modern American science was put behind a no-holds-barred search for the Loch Ness Monster. After scanning the whole pond with Sonar they came up with nothing. Isn't it weird, the more people *don't* see the damn thing, the more they believe it's there. Beats me!

November: Lester Piggot, the jockey who looks like a Steven Spielberg make-up department's reject, was jailed for three years for failing to pay over £3 million tax.

December: Quote of the year by novelist Martin Amis:
> 'How do we prevent the use of nuclear weapons? By threatening to use nuclear weapons. And we can't get rid of the nuclear weapons *because* of the nuclear weapons.'

1988

War and Peace

1988 was an odd year for the British. While the rest of the world was putting away their slings and arrows of discontent, the tiff in our own back yard (Northern Ireland) seemed to be getting worse. Reagan and Gorbachev, although visually as unlikely chums as Kermit and Miss Piggy, seemed to be getting almost indecently matey and were falling over to sign each other's bits of paper. The long, drawn-out Iran Iraq war, which nobody over here seemed to give a damn about (I wonder why?) was finally running out of steam (and bullets) and the 20 year old 'quiet war', to decide who was going to control Angola and Namibia, also appeared to be grinding to a halt.

In May, the Ruskies left Afghanistan, realising they were pi . . . urinating into the wind. They just couldn't crush the spirit of the people (or the rebels). Even the embryonic rumble between the States and those nice Iranians, resulting in the bombing of Iranian oil platforms and the shooting down of one of their airbuses, came to a shaky peace when both sides realised the whole business was getting out of hand.

Leaders Leave

One major, and one *very* minor, leader resigned. Wrinkly Ronald Reagan (President of the USA), who had recently (and stupidly) let it slip that all his decisions were based on the advice of his spidery wife Nancy's astrologer, left the White House. Then David Steele (leader of anything he could get his hands on), finally got the message after 12 years that the country would rather have the likes of clever-dick Jeffrey Archer or smoothy adulterer Cecil Parkinson in power than him. He'd simply run out of people to try and jump into bed (politically-speaking) with.

More Grub for Africa

If you'd gone out on the streets today (5th Feb) you'd have been sure of a big surprise. No, it wasn't the Teddy Bear's Picnic, it was even more childish. Normally normal people, like bank clerks and policemen, could be observed wearing stick-on red clown noses to celebrate Comic Relief – another wizard wheeze to get money out of the British for African aid.

Impersonating a police officer eh?

Happy Birthday Mandela

Cynical people might have wondered, when yet another huge concert, this time for the birthday of imprisoned Nelson Mandela and the Anti-Apartheid Movement, took place at Wembley, where all this would end, and who and what these concerts were really for? They might conceivably have thought the whole business was yet another world-wide, ego-massaging showcase for ageing rock stars like Midge Ure, Boy George, Paul Young, Joe Cocker, and the Bee Gees (who needed more than a concert to save them) to name but a few. Or they might have thought that it gave an opportunity, in a couple of fame-filled, self-indulgent hours to show how 'right-on' they all were – even the ones that hadn't even heard of old Mandela before.

Actually when you get down to it, who gives a damn? It was all in a good cause.

No Aid for AIDS

It is interesting to note, however, that when the Action Against Aids organisers tried to jump on the bandwagon later in the year, our 'caring' rock stars weren't that interested.

Was AIDS no longer trendy?

Maggie Goes to the Poles

Over in Poland, our own tireless champion of the rights of the working man, Maggie Thatcher, congratulated Lech Walesa and his merry men on their struggles for freedom and union recognition. Many people, back home, wondered if they were hearing right. Surely this couldn't be the same Margaret Thatcher that had crusaded almost single-handedly for years to snap the back of the unions in Britain?

Her timing as usual, was immaculate, as the deepest rumblings ever heard in the modern world were coming from the Soviet Union. Estonia had joined a growing bunch of states ruled by Big Brother to demand that they go it alone. This was like a slap in the face for poor Mr Nice-Guy Mikhail Gorbachev, who wanted to have all the regions run directly from Moscow.

In fact, at the end of the year, he gave the whole world a huge Christmas present when he announced that he was to chop the number of Soviet troops by 500,000. Having said that, however, it wasn't that fab a gesture. For a start, they simply couldn't afford all their soldiers (the Soviet Union was practically bust) and secondly, large as that number might seem, it only represented 10% of the whole army.

Designer Drugs

Not much has been said so far about the huge revolution in the highly profitable illegal drugs industry that had plagued (and stoned) the youth of Britain for years.

When this book began, in the mid 40s, only rather arty people were known to smoke marijuana and, with a few upper-class exceptions, the use of cocaine and heroin was still only really connected with medicine. This was mostly the case until the early

60s when the earthy rhythm and blues cult hit the teenage clubs and pubs. A lot of the early bands came out of art schools, where they'd been puffing away like steam trains for years, but it was the Rolling Stones' drug trial that brought the whole business out into the open.

Acid (LSD)

It was in the hippie period that young people, mostly from the middle classes, started to 'turn on and tune in' in much greater numbers. LSD (D-lysergic acid diethylamide) came from the States (as did most things) and became freely available. LSD was the drug that enabled the participant to fly, swim or make love to anything from an egg whisk to a daffodil, all in the comfort of his or her own psychodelic bean-bag.

Cocaine

The eighties saw us copying (from the dear old States again) the use of smart designer drugs like cocaine, which soon came after the cheese and biscuits at ultra fashionable advertising or media type dinner parties.

Ecstasy

Ecstasy became synonymous with that other 80s phenomenon, the 'rave'. Enterprising whizz kids hired (illegally) ginormous spaces like warehouses or even open fields and then circulated by word of mouth that a vast party would take place on a secret date. Trillions of teenagers would (and still do) jig up and down non-stop to the point of exhaustion, to ear-crunching, repetitive Acid House music, fortified by ecstasy 'tabs' easily available from local dealers. These were the first parties where alcohol consumption was practically non existent (the two don't mix). The jury's still out, however, over the harmful effects of this relatively new drug.

Crack

The last and nastiest of the new drugs crept in from the States where in some cities it was literally reaching plague proportions. 'Crack', a derivative of cocaine was, and is, the perfect drug if you want to kill yourself just that little bit quicker, being almost instantly addictive and, better (or worse) than that . . . cheap.

Meanwhile

March: Prince Charles appeared to be more than piste-off when he and his party skied off-piste in Switzerland, and were caught by an avalanche. Tragically, one of his friends was killed in the accident.

June: Mike Gatting, Captain of the English cricket team, was fired for 'irresponsible' off-field behaviour. People muttered that sadly cricket, the sport of gentlemen, was becoming as populated with yobs as its rather common younger brother, football.

August: Bad year if you happened to be a seal. A horrid mystery disease was sealing the fate of thousands of the poor dears round Britain.

September: The 'speed' attained by black American sprinter Ben Johnson, at the Olympics in the 100 metre final, turned out to have been taken *before* the race. He and eight other athletes were disqualified for taking illegal drugs.

October: The Turin Shroud, one of the Catholic Church's most sacred relics, because it was supposed to hold an imprint of Jesus' head, was found to be a fake. Strangely enough, the old shroud-man looked rather like a cross between Father Christmas and Jimmy Hill (the football guru).

November: There seemed to be a little trouble brewing in sleepy old Yugoslavia. The Serbs, it appeared, were rather anxious to be independent. Oh well, we thought, it would probably blow over.

December: For some time, another woman Tory Politician, Edwina Currie, had been making a bit of a prat of herself with unsolicited foot-in-the-mouth statements. This time, she suggested that most British eggs were infected with the killer disease salmonella; just what you needed to hear as you were about to tuck into your soft boiled egg (with soldiers). Overnight, the egg business was smashed. Chickens throughout the country were clucking annoyed at having been 'laid off'.

Fresh Salman

The year opened with the most extraordinary event. Salman Rushdie, a hugely talented writer (so we've been told), released a book called *The Satanic Verses* which caused more hullabaloo than anything ever published before (including *Noddy in Toyland*). In the book he, according to those very nice Iranians, took the mickey out of Islam, the *Koran* (their bible) and their prophet which, in the great scheme of things, wasn't the brightest move he ever made.

That very nice Ayatollah Khomeini declared to the world that poor Salman, who was only trying to make a £ or two, was now under a permanent sentence of death and offered a million bucks to the first person to kill him. His very nice Moslem supporters then went absolutely crazy, burning the books and threatening anyone who had had anything to do with *The Satanic Verses* (mostly the poor staff at Penguin Books). He then threatened death to England and America, which we all, on both sides of the pond, found a little unreasonable.

Since then, the poor author of the now bestselling book has been in permanent hiding from the few very nice hit squads

Terribly sorry Miss Rushdie. Your cheque to the plastic surgeon seems to have bounced.

chasing around trying to find him. Salman Rushdie has, therefore, lived in literally hundreds of different places and has a permanent bodyguard (paid for by us) to keep a look out for anyone unusual coming to his various front doors offering poisoned apples (like the wicked queen in *Snow White*).

In June the Ayatollah died and all those Iranians forgot about Salman Rushdie (but only for ten minutes).

The Wind of Change
The huge rusty Iron Curtain was amazingly beginning to creak open, and the stench of stale air was gushing out. The Communist world was bursting out of its faded, far too restrictive, worn-out work clothes. The whole brave experiment that Mr Lenin had started in 1917 simply hadn't worked. Young people in Moscow, Peking or Warsaw had given the Communist ideal the big thumbs down and now simply wanted, for better or worse, to put on their Levis and Reeboks, strap on their Walkmen and ease down to the shopping mall for a Big Mac and a large Coke. They were simply fed up to the back teeth of having a Big Brother breathing down their necks telling them what they should do or think. In China, unfortunately, it all happened too soon and hundreds of revolting students were massacred in Tiananmen Square, Peking, on the orders of the wrinkly authorities, who were terrified of democratic elections.

No Wall for Humpty
Perhaps the ugliest and most symbolic manifestation of Communist oppression came tumbling down in November, never to be put back together again. The 28 mile long Berlin Wall, which for so long had kept the German people apart, was pulled apart, brick by bloody brick. The Cold War was over. All that remained to be asked was – now what?

And Back in Britain?
The hugest joke was that, certainly in this country, the very thing that all those poor Eastern bloc persons dreamed of, freedom

through capitalism, was turning out to be just a different tune played on the same flat piano. Unless you were so loaded that the economy didn't really affect you (and there were still quite a few of those left), your average British man in the street was feeling pretty disillusioned. Just about all the aspects of his pre-Thatcher life which gave him security against hard times, be it through the health service, education for his kids, or the social services, were simply falling apart through lack of finance. The house that he'd worked so hard for was now, for practically the first time in history, reducing in value. Worse he might even have been encouraged (thanks to Thatcher and her monetarist policies) to borrow more and more to the point that he now might owe more than it was worth. Crime and violence were reaching new heights, especially among the young, whose prospects of work after school were becoming as likely as winning the World Cup.

On top of all this, Maggie's henchmen were starting to stab each other in the back, as they realised what a dog's breakfast they were making of running the country. While they all squabbled, however, careful observation uncovered a rather funny little grey man with a set lipless grin on his face, lurking in the background, hanging on to the hem of his leader's skirt. No prizes will be given for guessing his name.

Tunnel Vision

The Channel Tunnel, to which we were all indifferent, was now well under way and, as long as the English and French diggers

didn't miss each other – making one, instead of two, tunnels – they could reckon on joining up in a couple of years' time. The problem then became how, and by what route, the punters at this end and 'les punters' at the other, were going to get to the tunnel. The French, typically, got on with the job right away, while we were (and still are now) arguing about whose houses the damn train line was going to run under.

Meanwhile

February: Angels go underground. The latest import from the States were the Guardian Angels, a group of New York vigilantes who, not content with making life difficult for their own subway muggers and rapists, decided to come over and make life a misery for ours.

March: Heavyweight World Champion Mike Tyson, the nearest thing to a pit-bull terrier on human legs, came over and savaged our dear, but ever so slightly slow, Frank Bruno, who had stupidly challenged him. Frank then went back to panto where the worst thing you could be hit by was a custard pie. Behind you Frank!
• Later in the year, as a result of a new fashion among yobs to have dogs that could do their throat-tearing for them, the American pit-bull terrier was banned (and then put down – tee hee!) or, in Tyson's case, sent to prison for rape.

April: Madonna, that ridiculous caricature of the modern woman, was fired by Pepsi Cola who were about to use her for a £5 million promotion, due to pressure from the church. The ad was to show a black Christ weeping tears of blood after being kissed by the singer. Ah well, that's the way it must get some people.

May: A funny little Briton, Jackie Mann, who looked like Biggles' granddad, was abducted in Beirut. That's nothing! Everyone was *still* looking for poor old Terry (it won't be a long) Waite.

1990

Thatcher Wobbles

The dream that was Thatcherism was now turning into a nightmare. For a start, Britain had imported £20.31 billion quid's worth of goods more than she had managed to flog abroad. The mortgage rates had soared to new heights (15.4%), which meant that loads of poor devils who'd borrowed up to the hilt, encouraged by the building societies and Maggie, were now being chucked out of their homes because they couldn't make the repayments. Inflation rose to 10.9%, ambulance drivers were on strike and, not totally Maggie's fault, all our cows went round the bend with the weird 'Mad Cow' disease that made them wag their stupid heads from side to side.

Can humans catch that cow disease?

Maggie was also getting a terrible ragging for her personal pet 'poll tax' which, although representative of her 'if-you-ain't-making-it-tough-luck' politics, was proving to be almost too unfair a stunt for even the Tories to pull. What the poll tax did was to replace the old rates, which were levied according to the size and

July: Ken Dodd, the buck-toothed comedian who resembled a Spitting Image reject, was acquitted of defrauding the Inland Revenue. Shame really, many people were rather looking forward to crazy Ken and all his daft Diddy Men being off the scene for a few years.

September: Crawly Archbishop of Canterbury, Robert Runcie, thought he'd get tons of heaven points, when he offered the Pope Supreme Primacy, in other words an acknowledgement that he was 'top dog' in the religious stakes. The Pope thought it was quite a gas, but loads of Protestants said that our Archbishop had got no right to give away the top job to a blinking Catholic.

October: Hungary became the next country to show two fingers to their Soviet 'masters' when it announced the birth of a new Hungarian Republic. The ruling Communist Party, seeing the way things were going, quickly changed its name to the Socialist Party and promised unheard-of, free elections.
• Two months later, Czechoslovakia followed, digging out and cheering their old hero Dubček who'd been so humiliated 20 years earlier by the Soviets.

November: A brilliant, fabulous, never-to-be-forgotten, Red Letter Day (23rd) for all those people that didn't think that Maggie was quite as marvellous as *she* did. Sir Anthony Meyer (nicknamed 'Sir Nobody'), a mere backbencher, shocked the press when he became the first Tory ever to stand up and say he could do the job a darned sight better than his boss.

December: Wow! What a year. It ended with the execution of the appalling Rumanian dictator Nicolae Ceauşescu and his Mrs on Christmas Day (that'll be one they don't forget). Out with them went the whole of the Communist Party in favour of the brand new National Salvation Front. The Commies were now tumbling like ninepins.

value of the property you lived in, with a flat rate simply geared to the individual inhabitant. To put things a little clearer, every *individual* had to pay poll tax but the amount she or he paid varied from area to area. It meant that the Duke of Westminster, who probably has more money than Michael Jackson, the Queen and me put together, could end up paying the same as an old age pensioner living in Hackney. Pretty fair eh! The extremely well off, of course, thought it was fab, but those in the middle and right at the bottom were not so sure.

Wimpy Labour

Now, your chance, Labour! If an opposition party couldn't capitalise on all this garbage, then they really should have packed their bags and gone home. Labour couldn't, and didn't!

Neil Kinnock proved he had the killer instinct of a damp sheep by totally failing to hit Maggie where it hurt most (deep in the ego) and his ramshackle flock of what often seemed like refugees from a church hall debating society, were light years away from anything that could conceivably be considered a future government (unless it was of Toytown). One of the only guys with any fire in his belly was a no-nonsense, say-what-you-think, damn-the-consequences MP called Dennis Skinner, nicknamed the Beast of Bolsover. He reminded us of some of those long-lost, old style, cloth-capped, committed socialists who used to put ideals before their obsession with personal advancement. Had there been a few more like the Beast, things might have been a lot different.

Thatcher Beaten

This discontent came to a head when Sir Geoffrey Howe (him of the silly hair), who'd resigned from Maggie's Bratpack a week earlier, realising that nobody else, especially from the other side, was going to put paid to her, suddenly turned on his mistress and savaged her like an untrained fox hound. When others in the anti-Thatcher Tory camp smelt blood they all began tearing at her until she could no longer stand (as leader).

The new Prime Minister, can you believe, was that funny little background-grey man, with the voice and presence of Mr Bean's dim brother – John Major. About the only thing remotely interesting about him was the fact that his dad had been a circus acrobat, a really useful background for someone with the top job in politics. Everyone thought he'd also be torn to pieces by the opposition but, continuing the circus analogy, it turned out to be like putting a novice lion tamer into a cage of . . . bunny rabbits.

Thatcher was gone. Whether we liked her or not (answers on a postcard), in ten years she'd become as famous as any Prime Minister in history. She'd dragged us out of one recession and, after de-nationalising many of our major industries and smashing the unions, had left us in a worse one. Small businessmen, who'd followed her like the Israelites followed Moses into the Red Sea, were abandoned like drowning kittens.

Maggie had been a passionate nationalist, showing an *unhealthy* disrespect for foreigners, and blamed the likes of mega-European Nigel Lawson for wrecking her dreams of being Empress of 'Great

Britain the Great' again. Most of all, many believed she'd become the champion of all those nice people who live in nice houses (well out of the inner cities) who reckoned that if people weren't successful, it was their own bloody fault.

On a different level, she had taken on almost queen-like status and indeed many royal reporters have since said that our Queen, who apparently couldn't bear the grocer's upstart daughter (and disagreed with her on most things) saw her Royal self vying with Maggie for top woman status amongst her loyal (ish) subjects.

But to those of us, however, who were sick of being patronised in that oily, you-know-it's-all-for-your-own-good voice, designed to make us feel like retarded children, it was goodbye and good riddance. Now we had this new, enigmatic, strong, brave and handsome leader to make things better again. Superman? No, John Major.

Yippee! It's War Again
In August Iraq, led by the kindly-looking but murderous Saddam Hussein, rolled over into poor little oil-rich Kuwait and took the country by storm because, it was claimed, they had nicked £2.4 billion quids' worth of their oil. Those selfless protectors of the world (and their own huge oil interests), the United States, hardly drew breath, before dispatching the largest force ever seen into Saudi Arabia to stop Saddam going any further. Anything-but-stupid Hussein speed up the peace treaty with those very nice Iranians (what's a million lives amongst friends?) and prepared to fight the mighty but (to all Iraqis) evil West.

Sides soon started to be taken and before long the Palestinians joined the Iraqis. Britain simply couldn't wait to send troops alongside of 'our best mates' the Yanks, and even France sided with us, sending another 4000 men to Saudi. The UN surprised us all by giving the Allies permission to go in and liberate Kuwait, and then President Bush surprised us all (even more) by offering to pow-wow with Hussein before going in with guns blazing. The world chess board was now set up, all that was needed was for someone to make the first move.

391

Meanwhile

February: Good news. Nelson Mandela was freed at last from prison in Cape Town. Bad news, he was met by Winnie his Mrs who'd been up to all sorts of mischief while he'd been inside. As we all know, Nelson Mandela went on to witness the end of apartheid, the first free elections and his own inauguration as president.

March: A couple of weeks after the mind-numbing vote of the Central Committee of the Soviet Communist Party to abandon the Commie's guaranteed monopoly on power, thousands of Soviet citizens, the bit well and truly between their teeth, hit the streets demanding more and more reforms. The West looked on dumbfounded.

April: British customs officials seized loads of lengths of, what were labelled, petroleum piping bound for Iraq. Big deal I expect you think. It turned out that if you were able to put all the bits together, they would form something strangely resembling a huge gun, capable of firing gigantic nuclear shells hundreds of miles. Somebody, somewhere had a lot of explaining to do (and still has!).

Anyone seen Jack?

May: Just to prove that Mad Cow Disease (see page 224) couldn't be passed on to us, Agriculture Minister John Gummer, who strangely resembled a mad human, made his daughter eat a £1.60 hamburger (along with himself). Little Cordelia seemed fine, but was reported to make occasional, strange moo-ing noises whilst waving her little head about.

June: The Government unveiled its proposed 'hard ecu', which was apparently the first step towards a single European currency. Over the next few years, the poor British public were to be subjected to a deluge of unutterably boring reporting on the subject, involving something called the Maastricht Treaty. If you want to know more, you'll have to buy another book, as I can't understand a word of it. Maggie, you might have guessed, was totally against losing our £, but no one really listened to her as she was well on the skids by now.

July: A horrid new tabloid phenomenon in the form of a rather witless footballer, called Paul Gascoigne, became a regular feature of the gruesome, gutter press. Geordie 'Gazza' (as he was stylishly nicknamed) came to almost film-star status after blubbing his eyes out in the middle of a World Cup game on telly. Pathetic!

August: Irish Brian Keenan, one of the Beirut hostages, was freed, looking absolutely awful, after 1,597 days in captivity. First question he was asked was whether he'd seen our Terry (Waite) lately?

September: Yet another war with France. This time over, can you believe? Juvenile sheep! French farmers were getting their pantalons in a twist over the amount of British lambs being sold over there. Over 400 of the little dears were torched after being hijacked in France. Luckily, although it was poor compensation for them, they were dead already. The fires were reportedly put out with industrial quantities of mint sauce.

October: For the first time since the war, Germany became one big powerful country again, when East and West joined up. From now on all the rest of the world had to look out for was funny men with little black moustaches.

December: We all thought it would never happen. English and French tunnellers celebrated, with champagne on their side and plain water on ours (which says it all), when they finally met in the middle.

Quote of the Year: 'It's a funny old world' – Margaret Thatcher (ex-Prime Minister).

1991

Instant War
Well, he wouldn't listen would he? Saddam Hussein continued to taunt the mighty Americans (and little us) until Bush (and then Major) had had enough. On 17th January Baghdad didn't know what had hit it when operation Desert Storm was launched. The brilliant 'invisible' American Stealth Bomber avoided Iraq's radar, tiptoed up to the city and sent one of its 'smart' bombers literally through the Baghdad streets like a flying carpet, ignoring all speed limits and traffic lights, until it reached the telecommunications centre which it blew to pieces.

Faced with 700,000 Americans and backup forces from another 30 countries, the mighty Iraqi army seemed somewhat weedified and after a month during which 97,000 air attacks pounded Iraq, killing 50,000 and wounding another 100,000 soldiers (let alone civilians), a saddened Saddam ran away. Kuwait was now free and America could light its big cigar again. Its oil interests were safe.

Masterful Major
Britain lost only sixteen soldiers, nine of which were killed by mistake by the gun happy Yanks. At home, the British man-in-the-armchair soldier seemed rather disappointed that this smashing TV war (which was never going to affect him) was over. Little John Major couldn't believe his luck at having been on the right side of a war in an otherwise underwhelming year. Unfortunately poor John didn't get the same adulation that 'super-hero' Maggie had received for her pet war. Judging by his almost continuous robotic grin, however, Major seemed to rather like being Prime Minister and didn't notice that most of his 'subjects' thought him a bit of a wally.

Maastricht Moves On
Wally or not, at the end of the year Major finally signed the highly controversial (and deeply boring) Maastricht Treaty, setting 1999 as the date for a single currency throughout Europe, and extending the powers of both the European Commission and European Parliament. Needless to say, Major claimed it as a victory for Britain, while the Opposition said he'd condemned us to the 'slow-lane' in a two-tier Europe. Any slower and we'd be in the lay-by I'd have thought.

The Party's Over
The events in Russia were turning into a music-hall farce. The hardline Communists had finally had enough of President of all the Soviet Republics, Gorbachev's, reforms and overthrew him in a real Mikhail Mousevich coup, putting him under house arrest at his country residence. His former rival, caricature Russian and extreme reformer Boris Yeltsin, the new President of Russia, now rallied to his call for help. Yeltsin had also been held under a sort of house arrest while all this to-ing and fro-ing and coup-ing was going on but he now returned to Moscow, where he stood on a

tank (the sort with a gun) outside the Russian Parliament and demanded the return of his old enemy Gorbachev, calling himself the champion of democracy.

The coup fell to bits and Gorbachev returned to Moscow in triumph. Unfortunately Yeltsin had smelt the faint but heady aroma of absolute power and realised that if he played his cards right (by making Gorby look stupid) he could get to be top man himself. Yeltsin then shocked the western world by actually suspending the Russian Communist Party.

Here in Britain, we couldn't believe what we were hearing. After years of pussy-footing around the huge Russian bear for fear of what he might do if we made him cross, the decrepit old beast suddenly keeled over. The Soviet Union was disintegrating before our very eyes.

In December, Gorbachev resigned as the first (and last) President of the whole of the Soviet Union, having presided over probably the most amazing seven years of Soviet history. Unfortunately, all his power had come from the Communist Party and when it was disbanded it had simply cleared the path for bolshy Boris. As Gorbachev spoke, the red flag was lowered for ever over the Kremlin. Just to put the boot in, Yeltsin later accused 'his new chum' Gorbachev of bringing the Soviet Union to dictatorship. The Russians had finally perfected the knife-in-the-back school of politics.

The Bouncing Czech

In the middle of the night of 5th November, one of the major figures in British business and public life, Robert Maxwell, mysteriously plopped off his fab yacht parked somewhere off the Canary Islands. The exuberant, outspoken, rags to riches tycoon had become a household name by owning a string of businesses and publications headed by the *Daily Mirror*.

His immensely fat naked body was mistaken for a whale (great white) when spotted floating nearby, but nobody had a clue whether he'd simply gone for a midnight dip or had tried to do himself in.

It eventually emerged that Maxwell had been swindling his own newspaper's pension fund holders to the tune of £400 million. This plunder had been used to stave off creditors trying to get some of the £1.5 billion he owed. Suddenly, like rats leaving a sinking yacht, all his erstwhile crawly friends said that they'd always hated him. The whole Maxwell story and the mystery of his death soon became open house for every comedian and satirical magazine.

Gullible's Travels

Only the hardest of us could fail to have glistening eyes at the news that the brave, but somewhat gullible, Terry Waite, who by this time must have run well out of travellers cheques, had been released. His jaunt up the road to meet some English hostages in Beirut had lasted five years, most of which he'd spent chained to a wall in a windowless cell (I bet they don't mention that in the travel brochures!). By the time he got back, the Archbish. that he'd been doing all the Special Envoying for, had actually retired and had to be dragged out of mothballs himself. I would have thought the now *Lord* Runcie, should have taken his back wages (plus overtime) to meet him, to make up for sending him on such a daft and dangerous mission.

Waite, released with American Tom Sutherland, was the last of the British hostages to leave Lebanon.

Yugoslavia in Trouble

Sleepy Yugoslavia seemed to be getting itself into all sorts of bother while the rest of the world looked on helplessly. The trouble was that Yugoslavia was really a holding name for six republics: Slovenia, Croatia, Serbia, Bosnia Hercegovina, Montenegro and Macedonia, all of which had a deep distrust and even hatred of one another, owing to their different racial and religious origins. If this weren't bad enough, it had long been the case that throughout Yugoslavia the townspeople had no time for the countryfolk and vice versa.

Only a leader with the power of Marshal Tito had been able to keep all these factions apart and paper over the cracks in the hugely divided country. Tito, who had always managed to keep his communist regime free from Russian dominatin, had run, what almost had to be, a police state until his death in 1980.

In 1991, all the states outside Serbia and Montenegro declared themselves independent as they were well fed up with growing Serbian domination. The top Serb, the warmongering Slobodan Milosevic, hoping to be boss of the whole lot, wouldn't have it and declared their actions illegal. The blood started to flow when he sent the Yugoslavian army (largely Serbian) to sort the Croats out. Terms like 'ethnic cleansing' were used as Serbian soldiers started throwing Croatians out of their homes in order that they could be occupied by them and theirs. But this was just the beginning.

Meanwhile

January: In an inspired piece of clairvoyancy, John Major announced that on no account would the poll tax ever be abolished.
• Why do the British always get everything wrong? 10,000 NHS beds were made ready for the injured in the Gulf War. As it happened, however, the injured could have had loads of beds –

each. Great isn't it! The only sure way to get an NHS bed these days is to go and get shot up thousands of miles away, in a war that's got nothing to do with you in the first place.

February: A rude, crude, sexist (but jolly funny) magazine called *Viz*, pitched to appeal to a readership with a mental capacity of a dim dormouse, became the publishing success of the decade. Strangely enough, retailers, who would normally shy away from such degrading material (acting as our moral guardians), seemed to stock it without a whimper. I don't suppose that could have anything to do with the loot they were making.

March: The poll tax that John (why-does-everyone-have-a-go-at-me?) Major said would be with us for ever . . . suddenly wasn't. It had taken the Government this long to think up an even unfairer way of grabbing our money – the community tax.

April: London Zoo let it be known that they might have to close due to lack of funding. Loads of animals were seen lurking around Job Centres trying to get work in circuses.

May: A Mars a day helps you work, rest and . . . zoom into orbit with a rocket strapped to your backside. Helen Sharman, who had worked in the famous chocolate factory, became Britain's very first woman to go into orbit. She beat 13,000 rivals to fly with the Russian Soyez TM-12 spacecraft.

June: Five homosexual couples were married in Trafalgar Square at a huge Gay Rights demo. Poor Nelson must have blushed when he saw what was going on and remembered asking Hardy to kiss him!

August: *Terminator 2: Judgement Day* had its premier in London. It featured a half-man, half-robot character played by the half-man, half-gristle Arnold Schwarzenegger – a former Mr Universe. If his brain's half as developed as his body he might even make President of America? Let's face it, Ronnie did.

September: Women were finally allowed into the all-male inner sanctum of The Magic Circle, the professional body for conjurors and illusionists. Their membership multiplied with alarming speed (one of the advantages of being sawn in half every five minutes).

October: Another woman with that magic touch (and who many would have willingly volunteered to saw in half) was Maggie Thatcher. Having brought us to a major (and Major) recession, she ended up writing about how she did it, flogging the sad tale for £2.5 million. And they say there's justice!

November: How odd, that at a time when church attendance was receding like Paul Daniel's hairline, the most popular boys' names were Matthew, James, Joshua, Joseph and Luke. Names like Rebecca, Hannah and Rachel well outscored previous royal favourites like Elizabeth, Margaret, Diana and Anne. Oddly enough nobody wanted to call their kid Fergie!

December: The Queen, on her Christmas broadcast, hinted she'd no intention of abdicating. Purely coincidentally, a new telly was ordered on Boxing Day for Highgrove, Prince Charles's house. I understand his was mysteriously smashed.

Quote of the Year: 'The great, the jewel and the mother of battles has begun.' Saddam Hussein

1992

Annus Horribilis

On 23rd November 1992, our gracious Queen Elizabeth (God save her), at a banquet to celebrate 40 years on the throne, told us all that she'd had an *annus horribilis* (Latin for bad bottom?). She certainly wasn't kidding, and as most of us royal watchers realised, she wasn't really just talking about the last year, but a complete decade. A decade that had seen the whole standing of the 'Firm' (Royal Family) tumble at such a rate that one might be forgiven for wondering whether they'd found some sort of public *bad*-relations company to get them out of the whole blooming monarchy business.

Personality Plus

Many people believe that the rot started when the younger members of the Windsors, a rather boring family, of rather average intelligence (bang goes my knighthood!), discovered the media and in particular telly. Many of us then began to lose interest in them because, in their individual crusades for publicity, they let us know how uninteresting they actually were. By demystifying themselves to such an extent, they almost begged the question: what are we actually for?

Most of us lesser mortals would, secretly, be happier to see our Kings, Queens and their offspring wearing their crowns and robes every day, wafting about being royal. The last thing we need is to see them slithering down to our level either by choice or by accident. Certainly these staggeringly banal shows like 'It's a Royal Knockout', or even those quirkily funny 'at home with the Queen' documentaries, have done their elite image no good whatsoever.

Prince Charles

Prince Charles was (and is) causing more concern than most. He is known to think himself a bit of an intellectual (because all those toadying mates have told him so) but in fact often seems to be out to prove the old saying that a little knowledge is a dangerous thing. His speech at the GATT agricultural talks in November 1992, for example, when he went completely against Her Majesty's Government's line, left everyone (including the Government) wondering how much damage he might do when (or if) he got the 'big job'. Or there was the time he pitched up in a flash plane, on a bleak, windswept Hebridean island, to make a TV documentary with sleek Selina Scott, only to criticise the natives for leaving their picturesque, but freezing, turf-roofed hovels in favour of snug windproof bungalows.

I say Selina - could you ask their opinion on modern architecture?

Till Death Us Do Part

One of the very few functions left for the Royal Family was to set us poor weak and immoral subjects a good example. In March, however, the Queen's favourite, Andrew, split with the fearful fun-girl Fergie, leaving her in their gross £5 million 'ranch' (nicknamed Southfork) that we'd all so kindly built them. Two months later, she was photographed in the South of France, topless (not that pretty a sight) having her freckly toes sucked (even less pretty a sight) by her Texan 'financial advisor'.

In June, Princess Anne finally got shot of her horsy, Hooray Henry husband Mark Phillips and was soon observed canoodling with some other man in uniform.

Then, surprise, surprise, in December Charles and Di announced their long-awaited separation amidst a plethora of self-leaked rumours about their naughty connections. The country, amazed by the ending of their 'fairy-tale' romance, was initially divided between those who felt sorry for the poor princess with the shy, 'who me?' smile, and those who didn't.

When it came right down to it, what experts were now pondering was, what would happen if dippy Diana, in a fit of royal pique, decided to take her sons and heirs (to the throne) to live abroad? They feared it could well represent the end of the Firm – and even the end of the monarchy.

But How Much Did They Cost?

The horribly ungrateful British also chose 1992 to get a magnifying glass focused on the income of the Royals. Apart from all the millions we were giving HRH to buy her groceries, she actually enjoyed one of the most valuable art collections in the world, was custodian of Buck House, Balmoral, Windsor Castle and Sandringham, and owned two studs full of the very best racehorses (they don't come cheap!) and bucketfuls of priceless jewels. On top of this she had all the Royal parks, the State coaches and horses, a few stretched Rollers, her own Royal ship and even her own train (which was always on time). And on top of *all* that lot, when she went on her international walkabouts, the astronomical bills for her, her family, their staff, her ladies in waiting, equerries and miscellaneous hangers-on (not including the corgis), were sent to the Foreign Office and eventually on to us.

Even though we British were limping through the hardest of hard times, the Royals, in their infinite humility, never hesitated in flaunting their wealth and fab lifestyles. In fact, it was only when the pressure of recession-made resentment got to boiling point, that the Queen 'suggested' she paid tax like the rest of us, even though, with the help of the best accountants in the world, she would, no doubt, 'write off' most of it.

Major Makes It Again

Top of the lacklustre charts, John Major and his tedious Tory team shocked us all by winning another General Election. It wasn't so much a question of how the battle was won but, rather, how it was lost. Neil Kinnock finally realised that if he couldn't beat the weedy Major, he'd never beat anyone, and Paddy Ashdown, leader of the Liberal Democrats, also acknowledged that he'd failed to make any impact whatsoever on what had been a totally disillusioned electorate.

By July, Labour had a new leader in John Smith, a slightly intense Scot, who looked more like your average local building society manager than a future PM. The poor chap had in front of him the most enormous task of reviving a party, not only broken by defeat, but bereft of Tory-conquering ideas.

Mining the Pits

For once, a protest march actually did some positive good. John Major and his gang had to bottle out of government plans to terminate 31 coal pits (and 30,000 miners), when thousands of the desperate diggers and across-the-board consumers took to the London streets on 21st October. The government realised that, although they had no intention of changing their plans, they'd have to be a bit more sneaky about it.

Bosnia Boils Over

What had seemed to the British like another armchair war, in a country that was never going to mean more to us than a few cheap Yugoslavian holidays, suddenly took on an horrific new aspect, when news came of Serbian 'death camps' in Bosnia and the rape of some 40,000 Muslim women and children. Echoes of Nazi Germany sent shivers down the spines of all that could remember the last war when terms like 'ethnic cleansing' were used freely. What had seemed like a relatively simple feud had, almost overnight, developed into the most complex collision of the Serbs and the Croats, the Croats and the Moslems and the Moslems and the Serbs. By the end of 1992, over 1.5 million people had lost their homes. The bottled-up hatred going back hundreds of years was finally uncorked. This conflict certainly wasn't going to be another short sharp scrap like the Gulf War, despite the efforts of David (now Lord) Owen who, with Cyrus Vance (from the States) had been given the job of trying to sort out the mess.

Meanwhile

January: Alison Halford, Britain's most senior policewoman, was fired for being caught romping starkers in a swimming pool with a male officer (perhaps they were looking for his truncheon).

February: Fine, upstanding, military man of integrity Paddy Ashdown, leader of the Liberal Democrats, joined the long list of senior politicians caught cheating on their wives. No worries Paddy, everyone (in the House of Commons) does it these days.

March: Prince Charles now turned out to be the world authority on – wait for it – cheese, when he addressed a meeting in France. He was ranting on about EEC 'bacterially correct' manufacturing methods.

April: You either liked him or not. Benny Hill, the extremely vulgar and sexist comedian, who was one of our more embarrassing exports to the States, died. Feminists did not attend the funeral.

May: Oh dear, now the cold war was over, and the Ruskies were our mates, poor MI5 were left with empty desks and nobody to spy on. They therefore turned their attention to the IRA.

Tell me Bond, what have you done about pensions?

June: 'Names' – rich people who'd been milking huge profits from investing in Lloyds Insurance underwriting syndicates – suddenly faced debts of over £2 billion. It must be admitted that many people cried crocodile tears at seeing all these fat cats getting stitched up. Let's face it lads and ladies, you win some, you lose some.

July: Just as the recession was reaching dizzy heights, MPs, always sensitive to their public's plight, gave themselves a 40% expenses rise. They'd obviously been taking a leaf out of the Queen's book.

August: In case you're wondering how things were getting on in Northern Ireland, they had just celebrated their 3000th victim. And what was being done about these horrendous troubles – zilch!

September: Another MP intent on following royal lines, the Heritage Secretary, Kermit look-alike David (Minister for Fun) Mellor was caught with his socks (amongst other things) down, when a newspaper reported his affair with a young (short-sighted?)

actress. He too was having his toes sucked, though there wasn't a woman in the land who would have traded places. He later resigned over his friendship with a Palestine Liberation Organisation official's daughter, Mona Bauwens, who traded self-publicity for a free holiday for him and his long-suffering family.

November: Clean-cut, though not (allegedly) clean-living, Bill Clinton, from Little Rock Arkansas, became the new President of the USA at 46. More importantly, Hillary Clinton became First Lady.
• Just to round off 1992 nicely for the Queen, Windsor, her favourite castle, caught fire and was severely damaged. The poor dear was seen wandering through the charred wreckage in headscarf and wellies, probably wondering what she'd done wrong to deserve such a year (and whether we, her long-suffering subjects, were going to make her pay the castle menders).

1993

Open Sesame

The year opened with our meanie Queenie, who'd just been let off paying massive inheritance tax, still losing sleep over whether we were going to ask her to put her hand in her own voluminous pocket to pay the amount needed to patch up her charred and uninsured castle. She then came up with a brainwave. Why not open a teeny-weeny bit of Buck House to the public and charge the punters £8 a head to look round it? This, needless to say, appealed to the tight-fisted Firm as it meant that they could make their subjects pay twice for 'their' palace (the first payment being through taxes). It was a bit like the Government Ltd (extremely) selling us back our own nationalised industries by privatising them.

You wouldn't have been exactly killed in the rush, however, and the whole thing turned out to be a bit of a financial flop, which again must have made the poor dear wonder if she was losing her grip.

Major in Major Trouble

Poor old John Major was by now having his own *annus horribilis*, with just about everyone in Parliament (and the press, and the telly, and the radio, and the pubs, and the . . . well, everyone!) slagging him off. Despite telling us reassuringly, in that voice borrowed off an adenoidal Croydon train spotter, that the recession was now over we, the Great British, saw absolutely no evidence of it. Unemployment amongst the young, even if they'd decided upon going to university instead of joy riding and/or drug dealing, was the worst that could ever be remembered. Even those East End barrow boys had been forced out of their jobs in the Stock Exchange and were having to use their Porsches (now not worth much more than a few pounds of carrots) to deliver a few pounds of carrots to the street markets where they'd originally come from. Most of all, you didn't need to be the Governor of the Bank of England to work out that, through taxation, the rich were

Lovely cauliflowers! Two for 50p

most certainly getting richer, while us mere mortals were most certainly not.

Norman Lamont, the Chancellor of the Exchequer (the one that looked like the villain in a Charlie Chaplin movie) took the rap for the hopeless mismanagement of the economy by the Tory Government. Major, realising that he was just as responsible as his friend and supporter, called Lamont in, and promptly . . . fired him. Lamont was replaced by the greasy Kenneth Clarke, who turned out to be a dodgy choice when he later admitted to being poised to grab the premiership should Major receive his own personal knife in the back.

The Tory majority had now dropped to 20 and John Major could at last claim, in all humility, to be the most unpopular Prime Minister since records began, even though he, for the life of him, couldn't understand why.

It was a time when, just as we were realising what a sad bunch our Royals were, Tory ministers were getting caught out left, right and centre owing to their fingers (and toes) being found in just about everywhere they shouldn't be. Again it was open season for the opposition parties to shoot them down like tin ducks in a rifle range, but where were they? John Smith, who'd shown so much promise when he became leader of the Labour Party, didn't even seem to have a boot to put *in*, and as for Paddy Ashdown, he'd simply taken on the role of dear old David Steel, ranting and raving with the same charisma and effect as an angry budgie.

Chinks in Ireland

Little chinks of light began to shine under the bloody Northern Irish door. After just about the worst atrocity ever – the bombing of a perfectly run-of-the-mill shopping street in Warrington – disgust for the IRA finally seemed to reach them, and through various means they let it be known that they were willing to talk if the British Government were too. It was, however, remarked that one of the stumbling blocks might be that, if the violence did cease in the province, there'd be a lot of fiery paddies queuing up at the Job Centre looking on the 'Murderers Required' notice board.

No Light in Yugoslavia

Despite the valiant efforts of Owen and Vance on behalf of the European Community and the United Nations (which had actually made the situation worse) the civil war continued to spiral downwards. The 6000 United Nations troops were busting their guts to get food to the starving people in Bosnia-Hercogovina (where most of the fighting was now concentrated) but were often like piggy in the middle, being fired on from all sides.

Politicians from other parts of Europe, and indeed the world, still resisted involving the lives of their own troops, in a battle which had nothing to do with them (and, unlike Kuwait, had no oil!). So much for the grand statements of the EC and the UN who had promised to protect all European countries. When it got right down to it, they seemed to have absolutely no foreign policy whatsoever regarding poor old war-torn Yugoslavia.

Video Nasties

Continuing on the aggression theme, violent video films and even those mindless video games went on trial when two little lads were brought to book for the most disgusting murder probably ever seen. Toddler James Bulger had been dragged away from a shopping mall (usually a pleasant experience) and savagely bludgeoned to death by two kids only a handful of years older than himself. Men, women and children gasped in horror as the story emerged. The very media that caught them, video, (in the form of a concealed camera) was later accused of inciting these mini-monsters to do this savage crime.

Smacko-Jacko

The year ended with the most extraordinary allegations against the perfectly ordinary, run-of-the-mill multi-millionaire, Michael Jackson, who liked to play with his chimpanzee in his own deserted funfair, or perform in his spooky private theatre surrounded by sick, bedridden kids. It was claimed that the black-eyed, ashen-faced, twitchy singer, with the talking voice of a sub-normal three year old, had had many children to stay in his weird 'ranch' for anything but the purest of reasons.

Meanwhile

It was business as usual:
The world continued to destroy its eco-system . . . Serbs, Croats and Muslims continued to wreck Yugoslavia . . . John Major and his Tory playmates continued to wreck our economy . . . Labour continued to do nothing about it . . . British Rail continued to get privatised . . . the Channel Tunnel continued *not* to open . . . unemployment continued to rise . . . the rich continued to get richer (unless a Lloyd's name) . . . the poor continued to get poorer . . . the Queen continued to get unhappier . . . Princess Di continued to bleat . . . the police continued to get more corrupt . . . Nigel Mansell continued to get more boring . . . Kasparov continued to beat Nigel Short . . . Nigel Kennedy continued to get more pretentious . . . Margaret Thatcher simply continued in the background . . . my favourite comedian, Les Dawson . . . didn't!

Bibliography

C.W. Airne, *The Story of Prehistoric and Roman Britain,* Thomas Hope & Sankey-Hudson Ltd.

Guy Arnold, *Book of Dates: A Chronology of World History,* Kingfisher/Grisewood & Dempsey, 1983

Roy Burrell, *The Oxford Children's History, Vol I,* Oxford University Press, 1983

F.E. Halliday, *A Concise History of England,* Thames & Hudson, 1964

J.A. Hammerton (ed.), *Harmsworth's Universal Encyclopedia,* The Amalgamated Press Ltd.

M.C. Scott Moncrieff, *Kings and Queens of England,* Blandford Press, 1966

Kenneth O. Morgan (ed.), *Oxford Illustrated History of Britain,* Oxford University Press, 1984

Odhams Press, *The British Encyclopedia,* 1933

Peter & Mary Speed, *The Oxford Children's History Vol. II,* Oxford University Press, 1983

The Reader's Digest Assoc. Ltd., *The Last Two Million Years,* 1973

The Reader's Digest Assoc. Ltd., *Strange Series/Amazing Facts,* 1975

R.J. Unstead, *Looking At History,* A & C Black Ltd., 1955

David Walleninsky, Irving Wallace, Amy Wallace, Sylvia Wallace, *The Book of Lists, Vol. I,* 1977. *Vol. II,* 1980

New from John Farman

Jesus the Teenage Years

An affectionate, funny and informative look at the teenage years of the most famous person of all time – Jesus.

* Who were his mates?
* How did he do at school?
* What was life really like in the early years (AD)?
* What made him so special?

A whole period of Jesus's life remains a mystery. But now, best-selling author, John Farman, attempts to tell what it might have been like. *Jesus the Teenage Years* dips into the formative years of the son of God; years during which he probably grew up practising good deeds, learning about life, dealing with haircuts, adolescent spots, girls and the scriptures while preparing himself for the most important and valuable mission of all.

This book is seriously funny. John Farman's version of our hero's teenage exploits will not only amaze and amuse you, but tell you lots of factual information about biblical times and introduce you to some of the great biblical tales. Jesus's diary may not be exactly true, but will certainly make you wonder what the lad from Nazareth was really like.

£9·99

ISBN 0370 323319

The Very Bloody History of Britain

'The Very Bloody History of Britain takes the mystery out of history and puts back all the blood, guts and gore. According to author John Farman – our forefathers (and foremothers) were the most blood-thirsty, disreputable, malodorous bunch of hooligans you could ever hope not to meet in a dark alley. Starting with the cavemen, John edits out all the boring bits of history, telling only the best stories . . . At the end, you still won't be able to recite the 19th Century Corn Laws parrot-fashion, but you may have accidentally learnt something like how civilization began.' *Bookcase*

The Very Bloody History of Britain 1945 to now

'A brilliant combination of fact and humour makes this an excellent addition to Farman's wacky and popular alternative history series. Taking up where *The Very Bloody History* left off, this volume tells you everything you need to know about postwar rationing, the Swinging Sixties and the Thatcher years – and all the bits in between. Illustrated throughout with cartoons, it is an easy way to get to grips with the past.' Julia Eccleshare *The Bookseller*